FIGHTING FOR
A LIVING WAGE

FIGHTING FOR A LIVING WAGE

STEPHANIE LUCE

ILR PRESS an imprint of

CORNELL UNIVERSITY PRESS

ITHACA AND LONDON

First published 2004 by Cornell University Press
First printing, Cornell Paperbacks, 2004

Printed in the United States of America

Library of Congress Cataloging-in-Publication Data
Luce, Stephanie.
  Fighting for a living wage / Stephanie Luce.
    p. cm.
  Includes bibliographical references and index.
  ISBN 0-8014-4287-7 (cloth : alk. paper)—ISBN 0-8014-8947-4 (pbk. : alk. paper)
    1. Living wage movement—United States.   2. Minimum wage—United States.
3. Wages—Law and legislation—United States.   4. Cost and standard of living—
United States.   5. Income—United States.   6. Poverty—United States.
7. Family policy—United States.   I. Title.
  HD4975.L83 2004
  331.2'3–dc22   2004010726

Cornell University Press strives to use environmentally responsible suppliers and materials to the fullest extent possible in the publishing of its books. Such materials include vegetable-based, low-VOC inks and acid-free papers that are recycled, totally chlorine-free, or partly composed of nonwood fibers. For further information, visit our website at www.cornellpress.cornell.edu.

Cloth printing   10 9 8 7 6 5 4 3 2 1

CONTENTS

TABLES

ACKNOWLEDGMENTS

It is difficult to know where to begin with acknowledgments for a book that has been the focus of my work for the past seven years. I began researching living wage ordinances in 1996 when I was asked by Robert Pollin to join a team of researchers at the University of California-Riverside in studying the potential impact of the proposed Los Angeles living wage ordinance. I continued that work in my doctoral dissertation with help from my advisors and committee, particularly Erik Olin Wright, Joel Rogers, and Harry Brighouse. But most important, I've maintained an interest and desire to do this work because of the thousands of people who continue to push forward the living wage movement. Even after all these years I still find this topic exciting and feel lucky to have been a part of it.

I cannot thank all of the people that I have met or talked to here, but special thanks goes to Jen Kern. She has expanded my thinking on the living wage movement and organizing since we first met over the phone in 1997. Her insights and friendship have been some of the benefits I've gained through doing this work. In addition, I've spoken frequently to the following people about living wage campaigns and research: Jared Bernstein, Chauna Brocht, Howard Greenwich, Ken Jacobs, Sara Mersha, Stephanie Monroe, Gyula Nagy, Bruce Nissen, Bob Pollin, David Reynolds, Michael Reich, Christine Silvia, and Paul Sonn. In addition to the people listed above, the following researchers shared their work on living wages with me: Alan Derickson, Andrew Elmore, Don Grant, Oren Levin-Waldman, Ric McIntyre, Paul Osterman, Chris Tilly, and Mary Nell Trautner.

There are too many living wage activists to list—I've met and talked to scores of people across the country. But some on whom I relied for information about campaigns include Marty Bennett, Sandy Brown, Bryan Cassagne, Lisa Clauson, Mary Jo Connolly, Kirsten Cross, Nancy deProsse, Monica Halas, John Halle, Amy Hanauer, Matthew Jerzyk, John Magnesi, Sara Mersha, Barney Oursler, Nari Rhee, Ben Speight, and Linda Wambaugh.

I must also thank my colleagues at the University of Massachusetts-Amherst Labor Center who have provided me with a truly supportive working environment over the past several years, and the past year in particular: Beth Berry, Harris Freeman, Tom Juravich, Dale Melcher, and Eve Weinbaum. In addition, the following Labor Center students have provided valuable research assistance on this project: Aldo Ala, Michael Burns, Ethan Fineout, Dean Frutiger, Ariana Ghasedi, Doug Kandt, Mark Nelson, and Rachael Running. The Political Economy Research Institute provided me with funding for research assistance for part of this work.

When it came time to write this book, Mark Brenner, Dan Clawson, Bruce Nissen, and Eve Weinbaum were especially helpful in figuring out a plan for organizing the manuscript and getting it published. Paula Chakravartty was a truly supportive friend, providing intellectual and emotional encouragement throughout. Mark Brenner and Dan Clawson read the manuscript numerous times and gave exceptionally useful feedback. I owe a large debt to Mara Dodge, Monica Halas, Ken Jacobs, Jen Kern, Bruce Nissen, Paul Sonn, and an anonymous reviewer who gave thorough comments on previous drafts that have substantially improved the end result. Others who have read parts of my work that have gone into this book and given helpful feedback include Gianpaolo Baiocchi, Eileen Boris, Paula Chakravartty, David Cohen, David Fairris, Leon Fink, Jim Green, Ron Hayduk, Michael Reich, Ben Shepard, and Jane Slaughter. I am grateful for the opportunity to attend numerous conferences and workshops where I have been able to speak about my work and receive helpful criticism. Many thanks to Fran Benson of Cornell/ILR Press, who has been helpful from the very start and a pleasure to work with. Thanks also to Lida Lewis for editorial assistance.

It is of course family, friends, and comrades who have provided me with a supportive environment to finish this project. I could not list them all without risk of inadvertently leaving someone out, but I feel sure they know who they are. I am grateful for my nieces and nephews who keep me laughing. The opportunity to be there for the birth of my god-daughter Aisha Chakravartty Baiocchi came just at the right time, when I needed a new perspective and energy to finish the book.

Finally, I thank Mark Brenner. Without him, this book most surely would not have come to fruition. He gave me the wonderful gift of spending six months in Abidjan, Côte d'Ivoire, and it was there where my ideas for this book first developed, in our conversations walking through the streets of Blokosso. Mark has most vigorously supported this project even when I was ready to abandon it, and it seems as if he has read the words in this book even more times than I have. His own work on living wages inspires me to work more carefully; his feedback on my work pushes me to work harder. Most important, his love and comradeship create a home for me.

ACRONYMS

ACORN	Association of Community Organizations for Reform Now
AFL-CIO	American Federation of Labor-Congress of Industrial Organizations
AFSCME	American Federation of State, County, and Municipal Employees
BCA	Bureau of Contract Administration (Los Angeles, California)
BUILD	Baltimoreans United in Leadership Development
CLC	Central Labor Council
CLUE	Clergy and Laity United for Economic Justice (Los Angeles, California)
CWA	Communication Workers of America
DARE	Direct Action for Rights and Equality (Providence, Rhode Island)
EPA	Environmental Protection Agency
FLSA	Fair Labor Standards Act
HERE	Hotel Employees and Restaurant Employees International Union
IAF	Industrial Areas Foundation
LAANE	Los Angeles Alliance for a New Economy
OSHA	Occupational Safety and Health Act
RFP	Request for Proposals
SAAEJ	Southern Arizona Alliance for Economic Justice (Tucson, Arizona)
SEIU	Service Employees International Union
SSC	Solidarity Sponsoring Committee (Baltimore, Maryland)
TWSC	Tenants' and Workers' Support Committee (Alexandria, Virginia)

FIGHTING FOR
A LIVING WAGE

1

THE POLITICS OF
IMPLEMENTATION

What's So Bad about a Living Wage? Paying above the Minimum Seems to Do
More Good than Harm
                    Steven V. Brull, *Business Week*, September 4, 2000

In August 1997, Boston city councilors voted 12–1 to pass a living
wage ordinance. The Boston Jobs and Living Wages Campaign, led by the
community group Association of Community Organizations for Reform
Now (ACORN) in coalition with the Greater Boston Labor Council and the
Massachusetts State Federation of Labor was thrilled to see their year-long
campaign end in victory. Riding on the momentum of previous victories
in Baltimore, Milwaukee, New York, and Los Angeles, the Boston ordinance looked to be the strongest and broadest ordinance to date. The law
would require any firm receiving more than $100,000 in city contracts or
subsidies to pay their workers $7.49 per hour. Even Mayor Thomas Menino
seemed proud of the law, stating: "In these prosperous times for our city,
our state and our nation, it is incumbent upon us to ensure that the rising
tide does in fact raise all boats, not just the yachts."[1]

The law was set to go into effect on July 1, 1998. By spring of that year,
it became clear that implementing the ordinance was not going to be easy.
Immediately after the law was passed, a coalition of business groups
talked about suing the city if the ordinance wasn't amended. By April
1998, city council president James Kelly asked the council to reconsider
certain provisions of the living wage ordinance. By May, Mayor Menino
appointed a Living Wage Citizen Advisory Committee and assigned them
the task of clarifying the ordinance.

As the July 1 implementation deadline approached, the debate over the content of the ordinance intensified. Business leaders objected to several provisions in the law, including those that would require them to publicly disclose payroll records. Opponents claimed that the law would create unnecessary paperwork and have an overall negative impact on the city's economy. Sam Tyler, head of a local employer-funded research organization, called on the city to delay implementation for a year until differences could be resolved. In the end, implementation was delayed and the mayor eventually proposed a new, much narrower ordinance, which would cover many fewer workers. The new version was approved unanimously by the city council in September 1998.

The council then passed off the ordinance to the city to begin the process of implementation. The Economic Development and Industrial Corporation, a division of the Boston city government, was assigned to oversee regulation writing, identify covered contracts, and inform other city staff about the new requirements. These regulations, written in part by the city but in large part by living wage advocates from Greater Boston Legal Services, were completed in March 2000, at which time the city began to fully enforce the ordinance. Despite the enthusiasm of the coalition, city council, and mayor, it took almost three years to hammer out the details before Boston workers began to receive living wage increases.

The experience of Boston is not unique. The living wage movement, started in Baltimore, Maryland, in 1994, has been quite successful. By the end of 2003, more than one hundred ordinances were on the books in cities and counties across the country. But while laws are often passed with much fanfare, many of them go on to languish in the depths of City Hall, waiting to be enforced.

Clearly, living wage laws are not unique in this respect. In fact, a host of municipal ordinances are routinely ignored long after passage. Indeed, it is somewhat surprising that despite these failures, policy implementation, as compared to the passage of laws, has received relatively little attention from researchers. To understand how legislation is crafted and adopted scholars have explored the role of money, social movements, shifting political alliances, lobbying, and the nature of the state. Far less consideration is given to the challenges of enforcing policy on a day-to-day basis after enactment. But as Kerry Miciotto, Baltimore living wage organizer notes, "It takes one kind of power to get a law passed. Getting it enforced takes a whole other kind of power."[2]

How Do Laws Get Enforced?

The idea for this book came from my work with living wage campaigns around the country. I first got involved in living wage research in 1996, working with economist Robert Pollin on a study assessing the potential economic impact of a living wage proposal in the city of Los Angeles. During many months of extensive research on what *might* happen if the law was passed, we began to contact city staff and living wage activists in other cities where laws had already been enacted. We wanted to get a sense of how the ordinances had impacted the local economies and city budgets. What I found surprised me. In some cities I could not even locate a staff person who was in charge of implementing the law. In most cases, neither the city staff nor living wage advocates could tell me how many workers, if any, were receiving raises.

At this point, the living wage movement was still relatively new, and I chalked up these findings to this inexperience, believing that cities needed more time for full implementation. But over the next several years, as I continued studying living wage laws, these concerns resurfaced. Outcomes vary greatly from city to city, but in at least some cases almost no workers were receiving the wage increases mandated by law. Other cities have had much greater success monitoring employers, processing complaints from workers not receiving the living wages, and training city staff to implement the law. Yet in only a few cases have cities imposed meaningful penalties on employers found in noncompliance, or closed loopholes in the laws that allow employers to escape coverage.

Even after several years, activists in some cities such as Baltimore and Los Angeles were still struggling with their city administrations over the issue of enforcement. As the living wage movement grew, and it became clear that the problem of implementation would not disappear, I began trying to understand the conditions under which policy implementation was more likely to occur.

Implementing the Living Wage

This book examines the factors that influence policy implementation. Implementation has been on the agenda of policy scholars for at least the last three decades, since political scientists in the 1970s began to examine why a number of the ambitious "Great Society" programs adopted in the 1960s and early 1970s were never fully implemented.[3] Observers were alarmed that policies passed by elected representatives were not carried out and wrote forcefully about the implications of this neglect for democracy.

For some, the implementation failures were used as ammunition against government programs in general.[4] Policies, they argued, always come with more bureaucracy, and government bureaucrats are never effective. But what if it is not the public sector work force that is to blame for implementation failure but contextual conditions, such as the state of the economy or behind-the-scenes politics among legislators? What if the problem is that government employees have too little and not too much power? Or that there are too few, and not too many, administrators? What if bureaucrats are never given the resources and tools needed to do their job?

Most early scholars realized that understanding implementation failure was more complicated than simply blaming the bureaucracy and that serious research was needed to determine the factors that explained policy outcomes. Since then, implementation research has blossomed with scores of case studies involving federal, state, and local policies, and numerous attempts to synthesize these empirical findings into general theory. This scholarship has effectively pointed to factors that are likely to lead to poor implementation, such as policy ambiguity, lack of communication between different levels of government, incompatible objectives between stakeholders, and failure to commit resources to policy administration.[5] But what factors explain successful implementation?

Much of the early work on implementation can be divided into two groups. First are the "top-down" models that have focused on the role of the policymakers and the actual legislation, claiming that implementation will be more successful when legislators are clear about their policy goals, policies are written to reflect these goals, and there is little conflict among agencies over the implementation process.[6] In contrast, "bottom-up" models acknowledge that implementation is influenced by the actions of legislators and content of the policy but claim that the laws are translated into outcomes at the local level. While top-down models emphasize the importance of legislators and statute writers, the bottom-up model assumes that real implementation is carried out by "street-level bureaucrats"—the public sector workers who carry out policy on a day-to-day basis.[7]

The "top-down" researchers (and others before them) claimed that democratic process is challenged when administrators are given too much discretion.[8] Administrators are not accountable to the electorate, and so it should be the elected representatives who make the decisions regarding implementation. "Bottom-up" researchers argued that this perspective is unrealistic and ignores the fact that administrators are an integral part of policy formation and implementation.[9] Like it or not, public servants are the ones who interact with those affected by a given policy, and they are the ones who ultimately shape policy outcomes.

While it is useful to distinguish between the role of legislators and administrators, the bulk of this research misses one crucial aspect of policy implementation: the role of the community. In recent years, increasing attention has been given to civil society and nongovernmental organizations, and their role in governance. There are different definitions of what constitutes civil society, and different terms used to describe the various organizational forms that exist within it. But the idea generally refers to that which is neither government nor family—something in between the two.

A number of scholars have called for a larger role for civil society in the process of governance: viewing it alternatively as a mechanism to improve the provision of public goods; as an important check on the power of elected officials; and as a general corrective for various government failures. For example, Robert Putnam's work on Italy asserts that with greater social capital, including institutions and organizations that promote trust between citizens, governments are more efficient.[10] Archon Fung and Erik Olin Wright make similar claims, arguing that "empowered participatory governance" models can lead to creative problem-solving, greater accountability, and more responsive public administration.[11] While participation of civil society in governance may be desirable for its own sake, as many have argued, it is important to test the hypothesis that public participation leads to better governance. This includes not only participation in agenda-setting and policy formulation but the administration of programs and implementation of laws once they are adopted.

Another crucial aspect of implementation that is ignored by many scholars is the political content of the policy—in particular, the interests that are served by different types of legislation. While all policy implementation may suffer from some bureaucratic error, the chances of failure are greater for policies that contradict the interests of the dominant class. In our current political economy, this means that policies that regulate markets are less likely to be implemented than those that are supported by business leaders. Indeed, one of the major shifts in public policy over the last generation has been the complete integration of the drive for profit into the priorities of the state, manifested most clearly in the pursuit of a friendly business climate by every level of government. This focus on probusiness policy means that governments may be lax about, or even ignore or resist enforcement, of proworker legislation. As the case of living wage implementation demonstrates, getting proworker laws enforced means challenging that status quo and attempting to build a new logic of economic development prioritizing human needs over the quest for profit.

It is in part because laws designed to enhance workers' rights will face resistance that I argue for a role for civil society in the implementation and monitoring of policy, including living wage ordinances. To my mind, including civil society in policy administration is important for two reasons. First, the traditional agents of policy implementation—legislators and administrators—are often conflicted about pursuing rigorous implementation, since many policies at the local, state, and even federal level are passed *against* their wishes. These are laws that citizens win through protest, rallies, media attention, constant appeals, and long campaigns. Legislators are persuaded through public pressure or fear of losing votes to adopt measures they would not have otherwise supported. Likewise, administrators may be asked to implement policies they don't agree with in principle, or that they object to simply because it means more work for them (often with no extra time or compensation in return). A related constraint stems from the fact that both elected officials and city administrators may hope to move from public to private sector employment at some point down the road. In these cases, doing a good job enforcing proworker laws may limit future career options.[12]

How do we understand implementation in such instances, when the impetus for a policy comes not from the top (legislators), or the bottom (administrators), but from outside the government entirely—from the community? Political scientists generally refer to community members and organizations as "interest groups" or "lobbyists."[13] While they are not ignored entirely in the implementation research, community groups are rarely the central focus.[14] Yet policy implementation must be understood not only from the perspective of legislators and administrators but also that of the citizens and organizations that support or oppose a particular policy. Activists fight hard to ensure policy passage, and they (or those they represent) are often the ones who have the most to gain from effective enforcement. If it is true that implementation is less likely when laws run counter to the ideologies and interests of lawmakers or top government officials, then what can advocates do to ensure that implementation occurs?

A second reason to incorporate civil society in the process of policy implementation is that community participation can enhance state capacity, both directly and indirectly. For example, community members can use outside pressure to force government officials to allocate more resources or hire new staff, indirectly bolstering existing capacity. Community members can also enhance capacity directly by bringing time, resources, technical expertise, or person-hours to the implementation effort. Even in the best of cases, where cities have an adequate number of staff and a reasonable budget, community members can still enhance enforcement efforts, as they are frequently in a better position than government officials to get sensitive or timely information on compliance. And in the worst case, when cities do not have or choose not to allocate the resources necessary for implementation, outside actors can in some instances substitute for the city. Living wage ordinances provide a clear illustration of how community involvement can enhance state capacity in the ways just described. For example, while city staff can periodically visit worksites or audit payroll records, workers themselves have the best knowledge of whether employers are paying mandated wages. Incorporating covered workers into the implementation process is likely to produce better information and stronger compliance than relying solely on city staff. Nongovernmental organizations such as unions or churches, because of their more constant contact with affected workers and their families, are also more likely to have complete and up-to-date information on wage compliance than city staff. Through these direct and indirect means, civil society can help improve the chances of successful policy implementation.

The Importance of Implementation

The United States is often considered as an outlier among industrialized nations. It's the only country lacking national health care, the one with the highest incarceration and infant mortality rates, and one of only a few with the death penalty. Yet, despite its relatively inaccessible healthcare system and punitive approach to criminal justice, there are a host of progressive state and federal policies in place. In fact, a number of U.S. organizations have become quite skilled at getting legislation passed, and they do so with some frequency. But the battle over policy clearly doesn't end when a law is enacted, and many opponents of progressive legislation have learned that it is sometimes easier to let a law pass and subvert it at the stage of implementation than to oppose it outright. There are numerous examples.

Wages and Hours Laws

Federal law mandates that workers who work more than forty hours per week are entitled to time and a half pay. Federal and state laws also set a minimum wage for most workers. Yet employers frequently violate these laws. For example, in 1996 the U.S. Department of Labor estimated that up to 50 percent of the nation's twenty-two thousand garment manufacturers frequently violate minimum wage laws, and two-thirds violate overtime laws.[15] It isn't only small-scale "sweatshops" in the garment industry that break these laws but also prominent employers such as Wal-Mart. Indeed, the nation's largest retailer is notorious for requiring employees to "clock out" at the end of their shift or at their lunch break but continue working. In 2002, a Portland, Oregon, jury found Wal-Mart guilty of violating wage and hour laws in eighteen stores across the state from 1994 to 1999, and thirty-nine class action cases in thirty other states are pending.[16]

Health and Safety Laws

Although the Occupational Safety and Health Act (OSHA) provides workers with a reasonable list of protections, corporations routinely violate the law. Moreover, corporate lobbyists have been successful in their efforts to drain funding away from the agency that implements OSHA, in addition to weakening penalties for noncompliance. There are thousands of OSHA violations each year, and while some violations result from employers' ignorance of their legal obligations, many do not. The pattern of systematic noncompliance is easy to understand when we discover the fact that even when violations are detected and fines assessed, the average penalty for serious violations amounted to only $977 per company in 2002.[17] With penalties this low, it is often in the employer's financial interest to risk violating the law. Even though OSHA legislation was designed to guarantee workers the right to safe working conditions, more than thirty years later there are still close 6 million people injured on the job every year.

Environmental Regulations

OSHA violators are often found to be violators of related environmental policies as well. For example, the *New York Times* reported on the criminal investigation of the Alabama-based company, McWane Inc. Following the death of an employee in 1995, investigators discovered the company had been charged with more than 400 safety violations and 450 environmental violations in only a few short years. The iron foundry had been labeled a "high priority violator" by the Environmental Protection Agency (EPA) for burning tires and for its failure to keep inspections records, maintain wastewater treatment facilities, and obtain necessary permits.[18] McWane is not an anomaly. Each year thousands of companies violate every one of the country's environmental laws. For example, out of 21,847 EPA inspections in fiscal year 1999, 18 percent uncovered punishable violations.[19] This means that almost one out of every five EPA inspections finds a violation of federal environmental law. Rather than developing more environmentally sensitive operations, U.S. corporations have worked to limit the scope of the nation's environmental laws. For example, in the case of the Clean Air Act of 1990, not only did corporations play a large role in pressuring the legislature to water down the bill before it was passed, they also lobbied the EPA to write regulations further weakening its impact.[20] Through direct and indirect pressure in the implementation phase, business leaders were able to alter the Clean Air Act, making penalties harder to enforce and exemptions easier to obtain.

Union Organizing

The National Labor Relations Act of 1935, along with other federal and state laws, gives workers the right to form unions and engage in collective bargaining. Yet research shows that employers frequently violate these labor laws, engaging in a range of tactics designed to intimidate and discourage workers from unionizing. According to the AFL-CIO, 25 percent of employers illegally fire at least one worker in a union drive, and over half threaten to call the Immigration and Naturalization Service when faced with an organizing drive that includes undocumented workers.[21] Employers also frequently force employees to attend one-on-one anti-union meetings, discipline union activists, and threaten to close the plant if the union wins an election. For example, the Union of Needletrades, Industrial, and Textile Employees (UNITE) has filed more than a hundred unfair labor practice charges against Cintas Corporation, the national laundry and uniform rental company. Workers from across the country have told the National Labor Relations Board (NLRB) that Cintas has fought their efforts to unionize with a range of tactics, including "hiring security guards to patrol the plants' parking lots, instructing supervisors to follow workers into the restroom to ensure they won't talk about the union, one-on-one interrogations of prounion workers, illegal threats to close facilities, and hints immigrant workers would lose their jobs." In another case, four thousand workers at the Smithfield Foods packing plant in Tar Heel, North Carolina, attempted to form a union and faced major obstacles. When they came in to work on the morning of the union election, they found a line of county police in riot gear. A fight broke out after the vote count was announced, sending one worker to the hospital. The NLRB eventually found Smithfield guilty of conspiring with police to start the violence.[22]

These are just a few examples of ambitious laws that have been passed and then poorly implemented in the United States. They offer a clear illustration of just how difficult it is to put in place legislation that runs counter to dominant interests, as well as the many ways in which existing laws can be subverted by corporations. Although this book focuses on the challenges involved in living wage implementation, the lessons are more general. Several of the conclusions I draw from the living wage experience apply with equal force to any situation where advocates have succeeded in adopting laws that challenge the status quo and are now struggling to ensure they are carried out.

Data Sources

This book relies on data I collected through a host of living wage-related research. I began studying living wage ordinances and campaigns in 1996. Since that time, along with my University of Massachusetts colleagues Robert Pollin and Mark Brenner, I have conducted economic analyses of proposed or enacted living wage ordinances in Los Angeles and Santa Monica, California; New Orleans, Louisiana; Boston, Massachusetts; and Hartford and New Haven, Connecticut.[23] I've also completed approximately a hundred phone, in-person, and e-mail interviews with city staff, community organizers, city council members, journalists, union and labor council leaders, clergy members, and various living wage proponents and opponents across the United States.

As a researcher, I have been asked to participate in a number of living wage campaigns. I have provided formal testimony to city councils in half a dozen cities and have informally provided technical assistance and data to living wage activists and journalists in dozens of additional cities. This role has allowed me access to a wealth of additional material beyond the ordinances themselves, including internal campaign documents; city records; city council transcripts and reports; and internal city memos such as fiscal notes and mandated implementation reports. I have also collected similar records, including reports and newsletters, from living wage proponents and opponents. In addition, I have drawn from the web pages of city governments and groups active in the living wage movement. All of this has provided me with the vast array of data used throughout this book.

In addition to formal interviews, I have had hundreds of conversations with individuals active in the living wage movement across the country. Throughout the book, where possible, I note when material comes from an interview. But I do not always cite information that came from general conversation, or from recurring discussions held over the past seven years. In particular, I communicated with Jen Kern of ACORN's Living Wage Resource Center at least weekly through much of this period. In addition, I have attended dozens of conferences, strategy meetings, and research roundtables where I received useful information and feedback. These interactions helped shape my thinking on the issues raised in this book but cannot always be attributed to a particular source.

Finally, the book also relies on newspaper and magazine articles about living wage campaigns and ordinances. While media coverage of the campaigns was initially limited, its scope has picked up considerably. There are still cities that have little to no media coverage, but in other places, reporting is extensive. Media articles used for the book are listed in the bibliography.

As I argue throughout the book, the living wage movement provides an ideal opportunity to study implementation. First, the ordinances are relatively simple. Unlike many policies that have vague goals, such as the attainment of "community empowerment" or even "poverty reduction," living wage ordinances have very specific mandates, with minimal ambiguity. This means that the implementation process is more straightforward and easier to analyze than in many other cases.

Second, living wage laws offer a chance to study the implementation of a purely local policy. To date most implementation research has examined federal policy or the application of federal policy at the local level. Because implementation in these cases typically involves cooperation across different agencies within the federal government, or coordination between the federal government and various state and local governments, it is more difficult to isolate the factors involved in successful implementation. The living wage ordinances examined here were enacted by the same local governments responsible for their implementation, allowing us to isolate several factors that may affect implementation.

Third, the ordinances are passing relatively quickly, in a wide range of municipalities around the country. This offers a rare opportunity to compare ordinances from different cities, passed in roughly the same time period. Of course, no policy is passed in a vacuum. Each successive living wage campaign builds off of the previous campaigns. However, the larger macroeconomic conditions that may affect the implementation of the ordinances, such as the state of the national economy and the prevailing ideology about local economic policy, were remarkably similar for most of the cities examined in this book, providing an excellent basis for comparison.

Overview of the Book

In this book, I argue that living wage ordinances are most likely to be enforced when citizens are involved in the process. In particular, those individuals whose wages will rise with the passage of living wage laws have the greatest incentive to ensure strong implementation. Their involvement, or the involvement of organizations working on their behalf, can dramatically improve living wage implementation. By contrast, I argue that policymakers or local administrators are not, for the most part, the ones who have an interest in seeing that living wage ordinances are enforced. In fact, the goals of the living wage movement run counter to the economic development strategies pursued by most U.S. cities in recent decades. For these reasons, this book is written for living wage advocates who are not policymakers. They are the ones who have the most to gain by effective implementation. However, I believe the implications of this work go far beyond the living wage movement and are of value to anyone attempting to enact and enforce a wide range of policies, from curbside recycling to job training programs. As indicated above, policy implementation is an issue that should be a concern for lobbyists and political organizations of all kinds but especially for those promoting legislation that goes against the interests of city leaders or the corporations behind them.

In what ways can community advocates influence policy outcomes? In the chapters that follow, I examine this central question through case studies of various cities that have passed living wage ordinances. Chapter 2 lays out the economic and political context behind the living wage movement. I show that by the 1990s federal and state minimum wage policies, in combination with state and local economic development programs, had created the conditions ripe for a living wage movement. After decades of declining real wages and urban development strategies built on no-strings-attached business subsidies, activists were eager to change course. By promoting a policy which confronted the issue of working poverty, living wage activists found that they could simultaneously build campaigns that were winnable, that delivered real benefits to their constituents, and that challenged the standard economic development discourse championing business climates over people's needs.

Chapter 3 goes through the details of the ordinances and campaigns, which can vary greatly from city to city. Here, I discuss the actors behind the living wage movement as well as their goals for the campaigns. I also discuss the specific components of the various ordinances. In chapter 4 I review four specific campaigns, to show what a living wage campaign looks like. This includes three cases where ordinances have passed, and one where the campaign is ongoing.

In chapters 5 and 6, I explore the factors leading to successful implementation. In chapter 5 I discuss various ways to measure implementation outcomes, and profile variations in implementation across different cities. I lay out criteria for measuring and evaluating successful implementation. Chapter 6 looks more carefully at the possible explanations for implementation failure. In particular, I summarize key findings from the existing research on policy implementation and assess their usefulness in understanding living wage outcomes. In the end, I argue that the clarity of the policy and its goals, the level of conflict between various stakeholders, and the capacity of governments and civil society organizations to enforce the laws are the principle factors that determine implementation outcomes.

What can living wage advocates do when city officials do a poor job implementing the ordinance or refuse altogether? Chapter 7 offers examples of campaigns that have effectively pressured the city from the outside to improve enforcement and monitoring. Their tactics include talking directly to covered workers, helping workers file noncompliance complaints, holding rallies and events to pressure the city, and raising public attention around compliance issues. In some cities, activists have gone beyond using external channels to improve implementation, and have secured formal or semiformal roles in the enforcement process. In chapter 8 I discuss these cases, and provide an overview of the strengths and weaknesses of various models. In chapter 9 I analyze the factors necessary for nonstate actors to influence the implementation process, arguing that a combination of inside and outside strategies is the best way to improve implementation. I show how this model has been used by other nonstate organizations in other policy arenas.

In chapter 10, I discuss other outcomes that result from living wage campaigns. In particular, I look at cases where living wage campaigns help achieve related goals, such as organizing workers into unions, building other worker organizations, or passing additional legislation. I conclude in chapter 11 with a discussion of the implications for policy-making and implementation. To what extent can these results be generalized to other types of policies? Are alternative structures of policy implementation desirable? Are they possible? Is there a role for civil society in the enforcement and monitoring of laws and regulations, and if so, what does that look like?

2

SETTING THE STAGE

The Political and Economic Context

A living wage, as opposed to a minimum wage, would place more money in the hands of the consumers (workers), allowing for an increase in spending. The economy's success lies in the ability of products to be purchased. If workers are paid a living wage, around $13 an hour, all would benefit, from the top to the bottom. . . . Faith and labor can work together to pressure our government officials and businesses to put people before profit.

Joshua Crandall, "Leadership with a Vision," *AFSC Iowa Program News*, 2001

To understand the current political climate in which wage campaigns have been conducted, one must first situate cities and counties in the historical context of U.S. federal and municipal policy. The living wage movement has emerged as a response to the failure of Congress to keep the minimum wage apace with inflation. It also arose in the context of a very specific urban agenda. As federal social programs have dried up since the 1980s, money available for cities has dwindled. Facing budget shortfalls and a declining industrial base, city governments across the country intensified efforts to attract new, and retain existing, businesses. They developed a host of lures, from the industrial revenue bond to the enterprise zone and tax abatements. Meanwhile, city administrators have also worked to downsize their budgets, laying off staff and privatizing services.

In short, urban policy has focused on what social scientists Clavel and Kleniewski call mainstream rather than progressive strategies for economic development.[1] In part, these kinds of policies have become the mainstream because they appeared to offer a survival strategy for cities facing dwindling federal revenues during the past several decades. These mainstream policies included efforts to attract new businesses to provide jobs for local residents and generate a greater local tax base. They also incorporated measures to stretch revenues by cutting expenditures—primarily, through layoffs and outsourcing.

I argue that this "survival strategy" coupled with the declining minimum wage created the conditions for the living wage movement. Ironically, that same strategy made city governments resist implementation of living wage ordinances. If your main strategy for economic growth depends on creating a "friendly business climate" to attract new development, and your strategy for cost cutting depends on outsourcing service provisions to the lowest bidder, it is against your interest as a city manager to enforce the living wage. City managers think they can't provide a friendly business climate when they enact regulations on businesses. They believe they can't save their city money unless they require contractors to provide city services at the lowest possible price.

This chapter discusses the economic and political context of the living wage movement, starting with the history of the federal minimum wage and its relation to poverty, and then analyzes trends in municipal economic development policy.

Minimum Wage and Working Poverty

The first living wage movement in the United States began in the late nineteenth century, as workers in industrializing countries saw that they would not be able to stop the growth of wage labor. If workers could not abolish the system of wage labor, they would at least fight to make sure that employers paid workers their "full fruits of labor."[2] A living wage was understood to mean "a family wage,"—an amount necessary for a male worker to support a wife and children at home.[3] Despite the gendered connotations of the family wage, many women were among the leaders of the early fight for a living wage. They pushed for minimum wages, limited by the courts to women and children, as the first step toward a living wage even though some workers and reformers equated the minimum wage with a women's wage, adequate only for subsistence. The first state minimum wages were passed between 1912 and 1923, but by the 1930s, because of new court rulings and shifts in the strategy of women reformers and the labor movement, states and eventually the federal government passed minimum wages for all workers, male and female.[4]

The federal law, ratified in 1938, was called the Fair Labor Standards Act (FLSA). Despite its broader coverage, it still included major coverage exemptions, such as domestic and agricultural workers. These exemptions particularly affected African American workers who were disproportionately represented in the exempted industries. The FLSA established a federal minimum wage of twenty-five cents an hour, to be raised to forty cents by 1945. The law did not establish a formula for determining the wage level, and the wage was not indexed to inflation. This meant that future revisions were left up to congressional action. Over the years, Congress revised the FLSA several times, broadening coverage to retail establishments (1961), hospitals, nursing homes, schools and colleges, and laundries (1966), as well as domestic, and state and local government workers (1974). Today the minimum wage covers four specific categories: (1) firms that have at least two employees and that do at least $500,000 per year in business; (2) "hospitals, businesses providing medical or nursing care for residents, schools and preschools, and government agencies"; (3) individuals not covered in the first two categories but whose work regularly involves them in interstate commerce (e.g., they produce goods that will cross state lines); and (4) domestic workers.[5]

Several states have set state minimum wage rates higher than the federal level at different times since the passage of the FLSA. As of late 2003, twelve states—mostly in the West and Northeast—and the District of Columbia had rates higher than the federal standard, ranging from $5.50 in Illinois to $7.16 in Washington. Only Washington and Oregon have a minimum wage that is indexed to inflation. Seven states, all in the South, have no state minimum wage. Two states have state rates lower than the federal; however, this affects only those workers not covered by the federal minimum wage.

The value of the minimum wage and the types of workers covered have always been hotly contested. Despite unwavering public support for regular increases to the federal minimum wage, employer lobbyists, particularly from low-wage industries like restaurants and hotels, have been vociferous opponents.[6] Although the real value of the minimum wage (the value adjusted for inflation) rose consistently from 1938 to 1968, the trend has been reversed ever since. By the end of the 1980s, under a more conservative political climate, the real value of the minimum wage was $4.50 per hour (in 1999 dollars), the lowest it had been since 1955.[7]

This decline has had serious consequences. Although there is debate about the best way to measure poverty, even with existing federal measures, it is clear that poverty among people holding jobs began to increase in the 1980s. According to analyst Catherine Chilman, the number of "working poor" began to increase in the 1970s and rose sharply after the drastic welfare cuts implemented by the Reagan administration in 1981.[8] This resulted in a 28 percent increase in the number or working poor from

1978 to 1987. In 1989, the Bureau of Labor Statistics (BLS) published its first report on the topic. BLS analysts Bruce Klein and Philip Rones found that one-third of all poor people in the United States could be classified as the working poor. Although many of them were in poverty because they could not find enough hours of work, fully two-thirds of the working poor worked full-time but were in poverty because of low wages. Despite economic growth in the latter part of the decade, the number of working poor stayed relatively constant, at approximately 6.3 million workers. With the recession that hit in 1990, the number started to rise again.[9]

By the early 1990s the working poor had become a national concern. A search of news media database Lexis-Nexis from 1989 to 1995 shows 987 instances of the term in 1989 and a jump to 4,642 instances by 1995.[10] With growing numbers of families feeling the pressure of declining real wages, attention turned to policies to address this problem. Although Clinton gave lip-service to raising the minimum wage during his 1992 presidential campaign, he gave little notice to the issue after he came into office. According to his memoir *Locked in the Cabinet*, Robert Reich, Clinton's secretary of labor, urged the president to increase the wage for several years before 1995, when Clinton finally gave tepid support to a ninety-cent increase.[11] Following the Republican party's 1994 congressional sweep, there were few vocal advocates in Congress for raising the minimum wage. By this time, almost a third of the wage-earning work force was earning below $7.50 per hour.

In addition to declining real wages, many Americans faced other forms of economic insecurity. Although unemployment rates were not high in the 1990s, many people were working harder as forced overtime increased, work weeks grew longer, and some were forced to take multiple jobs to keep up.[12]

The federal government's failure to raise the minimum wage was not the only problem facing low-wage workers. As real wages for most workers fell, local governments were undergoing their own changes, resulting in further negative consequences for these same workers.

Municipal Economic Development

Following World War II, many older cities began to suffer economic distress. Faced with aging public infrastructure and outdated plants and equipment, businesses searched for new sites in the suburbs or newer cities. After a postwar effort by the labor movement to unionize southern states failed, U.S. corporations left northern cities for the low-wage South.[13] Residents, following jobs and looking to buy homes, also moved out of the cities. As a result, city tax revenues declined dramatically. Soon, inner cities were facing increasing poverty and deteriorating surroundings. As most cities did not have the financial resources to address revitalization on a serious scale, the federal government stepped in to begin the process. The first national program to attempt to revitalize cities, the "Urban Renewal" program, was created in 1949 by the Truman administration as part of a solution to the postwar housing shortage.[14] However, Urban Renewal seemed to hurt city residents more than it helped, as a "loophole" in the law allowed cities to use powers of eminent domain to tear down low-value inner-city residences in order to build highways and large commercial developments to replace them.[15] Although some housing was built under the program, a tremendous amount was demolished. By 1966, "10,700 acres of the total 27,000 acquired by renewal agencies had been shifted from residential to nonresidential uses."[16]

In the 1960s and 1970s, the federal government created a host of social programs to address urban poverty and deteriorating inner cities. The Community Action Program, created as part of the War on Poverty in 1964, was soon followed by the Model Cities program. Neither was very successful in improving city economies.[17] They were eventually replaced in the 1970s by the Economic Development Administration, the Community Development Block Grant, and the Urban Development Action Grant programs. These programs provided funding to local areas to generate community economic development projects aimed at creating jobs and alleviating poverty. From the start, the federal programs were designed to give funding and assistance to cities to rebuild themselves in their own way. While this allowed for flexibility and local control, it did not provide a coherent national industrial policy that would help coordinate efforts between regions. Rather, cities and states began to compete with one another for funds and for competitive positions in domestic markets.

In the 1980s, the Reagan and Bush administrations severely reduced federal funds for urban redevelopment programs. For example, in 1981, Reagan cut $7 billion in aid to cities by drastically slashing the budgets of most development projects. In 1987, Urban Development Action Grant programs were cut altogether. As local development agencies looked for more funds, they turned to private business to build "public-private partnerships" for urban redevelopment. According to development researcher Judith Kossy, local economic developers "became 'entrepreneurs' in negotiating deals and structuring projects."[18]

The result of this "privatization" of municipal development policy was a further prioritizing of business over citizen needs. Urban dwellers suffered doubly as large businesses that once provided the core of urban employment have closed their doors and relocated to southern and other ex-urban production sites, as well as to other countries. As conditions in the cities worsened, wealthier white residents, followed by many working-class whites and, more recently, blacks, left for the suburbs. This flight left a declining tax base and contributed to fewer city services and further urban decay. By 1996, almost 20 percent of residents in cities were living in poverty.[19]

Mainstream Strategies for Economic Development

In response to these economic concerns and the reduction in aid from federal sources in the 1970s and 1980s, many cities and states created their own development programs and intensified their efforts at competing for funds in the 1980s and 1990s. Since federal and state funds were less available, cities were forced to rely more on private business for funds, which, in turn, meant that they were more dependent on these businesses. The goals of urban development shifted away from poverty reduction and toward building public-private ventures to expand regional markets and create a business-friendly environment.[20]

While southern states had been marketing themselves to northern firms since the Civil War, the North and Midwest, faced with economic decline and a shrinking of federal assistance, began to heavily compete in the 1970s and 1980s.[21] The number of local and state agencies involved in economic development increased dramatically, and private companies began commissioning studies to rank state business climates. City governments searched desperately for strategies to revitalize their economies. Economic development became a top priority for many local leaders. For most, the response was to develop policies to attract capital, reduce the size of the municipal government, and operate the city itself "like a business." The effort to downsize government was twofold. First, there was a financial crisis in many cities that resulted in cutting programs. Second, those creating the business climate rankings considered big city budgets as a negative, creating an indirect pressure on cities to privatize.

Paul Peterson's *City Limits* was one of the early influential works on local economic policy and the race for cities to make themselves attractive to business. Peterson describes how the constraints placed on cities by the high mobility of capital (the ability of business to move freely) forced them to compete to attract and retain private firms in order to create and maintain jobs, wealth, and tax revenues. The need to cater to business led to the creation of a multitude of policies designed to lower the costs of production for individual firms. Peterson asserts that while "cities constantly seek to upgrade their economic standing," they don't have the range of policy alternatives or regulatory powers available to them that national governments do. The only option, then, to attract business is to establish a favorable business climate and make themselves more attractive to business interests.[22] These policies could also be termed profit-led strategies, since profit becomes the critical "bottom-line" in development decisions. They include lowering taxes on capital and on profits, reducing costs of investment by providing low-cost public services and infrastructure, offering low cost or free land to potential investors, relaxing business regulations, and keeping wages low by discouraging unionization.[23]

In addition to creating internal economic development departments, city administrators pursued the creation of public-private ventures that would aggressively market the region. Political scientist Eve Weinbaum writes about Tennessee Resource Valley (TRV), an example of a public-private venture created to attract business to a fifteen-county region in eastern Tennessee. TRV goes to great lengths in its effort to market itself, including providing laptop computers with interactive CD-ROM drives. According to Weinbaum,

> These individual computers are shipped out, free of charge, to prospective businesses considering relocating. The CD-ROMs contain TRV's digitized advertisements about the region, and the potential client can click on full-color video spreads on a number of subjects. Besides conveying the necessary information, the high-tech format is intended to persuade clients that the area is fully equipped for the electronic age. Along with print ads, frequent trade show appearances, and recruitment visits, these computers put TRV's budget into the millions of dollars.[24]

Clearly, competition between cities and regions has become a big business in itself, creating the need for a host of public, private, and joint economic development agencies. By 1990, there were between fifteen thousand and eighteen thousand similar public and private organizations in the United States promoting local economic development, whereas only a handful had existed a few decades earlier.[25]

The line between public and public-private agencies is fuzzy, in part because of the close working relationships between similar organizations in a particular region. For example, when Richard Riordan was mayor of Los Angeles in the 1990s he created the Los Angeles Business Team, a government entity with an initial budget of $5 million, to help promote Los Angeles and assist businesses in taking advantage of public subsidies. The Business Team works with a host of other city agencies, including the Committee for Economic Development, Los Angeles Office of International Trade, Minority Business Opportunity Committee, Los Angeles Community Development Department, and the Los Angeles Community Development Bank. Los Angeles is also home to public-private organizations such as Genesis LA, which oversees a multimillion dollar capital fund intended to revitalize the inner city. Private organizations that deal with economic development include the Los Angeles County Economic Development Corporation, South Los Angeles Economic Alliance, Valley Economic Development Center, Los Angeles Chamber of Commerce, and others. Because all of these organizations work together in efforts to attract business to the region, it's hard to differentiate between public and private.

These organizations have access to hundreds of programs to assist businesses wishing to relocate or expand. Urban planning professor Laura Reese groups forty-two policy tools available to most city leaders and economic development officials into four major categories: marketing, financial, land and property-management, and governance and infrastructure.[26] Marketing tools include creating city departments to market the region, employing liaisons that work with firms considering leaving or moving to the area, and establishing links to solicit foreign businesses and develop export markets. Financial tools consist of tax abatements, subsidized and guaranteed loans, grants, tax increment financing, bonds, shared equity in projects, and in-kind services. Land and property-management tools comprise land acquisition and clearing, land support such as water and sewer services, and industrial property management. Finally, governance and infrastructure tools include reducing environmental regulation, streamlining building inspection, zoning variances and building and/or improvement of roads, parking, and airports.

In practice, city governments (as well as counties and states) have used these tools to provide millions of dollars in incentives to private businesses, ranging from tax breaks, low-interest loans, direct grants, job training, and managerial expertise in location decisions.[27] One scholar estimates that by the mid-1990s, economic development programs were costing cities and states $48.8 billion per year.[28] In hard economic times, the easiest road to job creation appears to be wooing companies (and therefore jobs) away from one region into your own.

What is the impact of these subsidies on development? A number of states have admitted that they do not collect data on their economic development programs and have no way to verify whether promises to create jobs are met. For example, due to poor record-keeping and the failure of the California Trade and Commerce Agency to meet its mandated responsibilities, the state had no way to measure whether the $53 million given in state tax incentives between 1988 and 1992 stimulated business development or job growth. As one sign of the problem, the California State Auditor produced a report in 1995 titled, "The Effectiveness of the Employment and Economic Incentive and Enterprise Zone Programs Cannot Be Determined."

Other public agencies have noted the negative outcomes of the tax break giveaway strategy, including the Federal Reserve Bank of Minneapolis. In a 1995 report titled, "Congress Should End the War among the States," Federal Reserve vice presidents Melvin Burstein and Arthur Rolnick argued that the practice of luring business with incentives hurts the national economy. In addition, in the long run, the costs associated with the subsidies usually outweigh the benefits to the state: "While states spend billions of dollars to retain and attract businesses, they struggle to provide such public goods as schools and libraries, police and fire protection, and the roads, bridges and parks that are critical to the success of any community. Surely, something is wrong with this picture."[29]

In 2002, the Massachusetts State Senate Post Audit and Oversight Bureau released an analysis of that state's economic development incentive program. The program was started in 1994 to encourage business relocation, retention, and job creation. Although Massachusetts' law mandates that the state review the program every two years, the state failed to collect data or monitor compliance during the program's first eight years. During that time, while businesses received $43 million in state tax breaks under the program and an unknown amount in local waivers, no one in the administration could verify that the program had an impact on the economically distressed areas it was meant to help. In fact, the Oversight Bureau found that many of the tax breaks were given to businesses outside of the targeted zones, including projects in legislator's home districts. When officials in Fall River, a city with one of the highest poverty rates in the state, looked at firms within their borders, they discovered that ten companies were receiving tax breaks without creating new jobs. One company, Main Street Textiles, had promised in 1999 to retain 613 jobs and create 537 new ones in exchange for participation in a tax waiver program. Three years later, the company had reduced its work force by 64, yet received waivers of $590,000 in city taxes and $1.5 million in state taxes for 2002 alone. Mayor Ed Lambert went to the state and attempted to decertify the companies. The state refused, claiming that ending the deal would make Massachusetts look anti-business. In the end, Lambert was able to renegotiate the city's agreement with Main Street Textiles and some of the other firms, though the state maintained and even extended their arrangements with the companies.[30]

Data on the impact of economic development programs increasingly shows that the mainstream strategy is not effective for economic growth or job creation. According to Peters and Fisher, experts on state enterprise zones, "while a few early studies did find enterprise zones to be effective, most of the evidence suggests that zones have almost no influence on local growth."[31] Looking at seventy-five zones across the United States in the period from 1990 to 1998, they find that on average, each job that a state or local government can lure to the region through a zone tax break results in about $18,000 in revenue over a twenty-year period. On the other hand, for each unnecessary zone incentive package (meaning, the plant would have been built without the incentives), the government loses about $6,600. Peters and Fisher find that there are far more jobs that are receiving incentives unnecessarily, resulting in an overall negative revenue. They conclude overall that the net "total state-local revenue loss of $59,000 for every new job induced by incentives."[32]

There are many examples of states and cities providing large giveaways through enterprise zone tax breaks as well as other incentives in the race to attract new business. The nonprofit research organization Good Jobs First tracks many of these deals and calculates the cost per job: the total subsidy divided by the number of jobs created by the new development. For example, a report by Good Jobs First on economic development deals in Washington, D.C., shows that the first three projects approved under a new Tax-Increment Financing program resulted in a $75 million subsidy for Gallery Place, $46 million for the Mandarin Hotel, and $6.9 million for the Spy Museum.[33] Dividing these subsidies by new jobs created shows a cost of $80,000 per job for Gallery Place, $92,000 per job at the Mandarin Hotel, and $49,460 per job at the Spy Museum. Note that this doesn't guarantee that the new jobs will pay a living wage, provide benefits, or provide job security.

Neighboring Baltimore has not fared much better. Good Jobs First reports that since the late 1970s, the city has spent more than $2 billion in building and maintaining its tourist industry. Yet Baltimore continues to suffer economic hardship, and three-quarters of its nonmanagerial tourist work force earn less than poverty level wages.[34] The city, state, and federal governments heavily subsidized the construction of the Baltimore Orioles' baseball stadium, Camden Yards. Estimates by the Brookings Institute show that the stadium results in a net loss of $11 million per year to state taxpayers.

Perhaps the most appalling examples of city giveaways come from those municipalities that came up with large sums for corporate tax breaks and subsidies, only to see the subsidized business create no jobs or leave the area after a short period. New York City has experienced this on several occasions, notably with its Chase Manhattan subsidy.[35] In 1988, New York gave the bank $235 million in subsidies in a twenty-two-year agreement to stay in the city and not relocate across the river to Jersey City. Since then, the company has cut thousands of jobs, including 5,720 in 1995 and 2,200 in 1998. In 1999 Chase announced that it was moving another 3,500 jobs out of New York to other states. Then in 2000, Chase blatantly violated the intent of the original agreement when it accepted $100 million in subsidies to move thousands more employees to Jersey City. Clearly, there were no mechanisms for New York to force Chase to live up to their promise to stay in the city.

Despite case after case of cities losing out on economic development deals that result in few or no jobs, or only low-wage no-benefit jobs, city managers continue to pursue a strategy of low-cost competition with other regions. In addition to providing subsidies, other tactics for creating a friendly business climate include downsizing the public sector work force and contracting out public services. As Archon Fung and Erik Olin Wright argue, the space for downsizing and contracting out was created in part because of the failures of the state. When governments failed to enforce the laws and implement policies passed in the 1960s and 1970s (such as adequately funding urban redevelopment programs), it opened the space for the right to reduce the power and role of the state through "deregulation, privatization, reductions of social services, and curtailments of state spending."[36]

Downsizing. In addition to using tax incentives to lure companies, city administrators have also tried to make their cities attractive by creating an image of a city without business regulation or an expensive or troublesome work force. In the 1980s, mayors began downsizing public government to reduce payrolls, attacking public sector unions, and privatizing city services (selling off and/or contracting out) to lower city budgets and provide lucrative contracts to the private sector.[37] Examples suggest some of the story of the 1980s. In Toledo, Ohio, "government streamlining" resulted in 40 percent of the city's work force being laid off between 1979 and 1982. Newark, New Jersey, reduced its work force from ten thousand to four thousand in the 1980s. After federal budget cuts hit city budgets in the early 1980s, Phoenix had its first city layoffs in more than twenty-five years.[38]

Government data suggests that the civil service downsizing trends of the 1980s may have been reversed in the 1990s. In fact, owing to basic population growth, the BLS cites local and state governments on the list of top-ten largest growth industries for the decade. However, a closer look at the data in most places shows that employment growth has been primarily in law enforcement and public education, whereas jobs in administration and other services have been cut, outsourced, or placed on hiring freeze.[39] BLS employment projections for 1998 to 2008 predict local government employment increases (excluding education) in all occupations to average 12 percent to maintain pace with population growth and service needs. However, this includes a 44 percent increase in corrections officers, 34 percent in police and sheriffs, and only a 0.8 percent increase in cleaning and building services, janitors, and food service workers. For other service occupations, the BLS predicts significantly fewer jobs, including some often contracted out or filled with temporary workers: bookkeeping clerks, data entry, secretaries, and file clerks.[40]

Outsourcing.   Elliot Sclar argues that the "urge to privatize" has grown sharply since the early 1980s, as part of an ideological shift toward a weaker state and a freer market.[41] While there is little empirical research on contracting trends, the data that do exist show that contracting out services increased sharply in the late 1980s and early 1990s. A private research organization, the Mercer Group, surveyed large cities in 1996 and found that between 1987 and 1995 cities substantially increased the amount of services contracted out. For example, in 1987, these cities contracted out 52 percent of their janitorial services. By 1995, the figure was 70 percent.

The Mercer Group study found that other services were affected as well. Street maintenance contracting rose from 19 to 38 percent; solid waste collection from 30 to 50 percent; and data processing operations from 16 to 31 percent.[42] Reports from the National League of Cities show that the pace of contracting out slowed somewhat in the latter 1990s as cities reported greater financial health, but in the year 2000, 28 percent of cities still reported that they were contracting out new services as a strategy to cut costs.[43]

Whether contracting out results in savings is not clear. According to Sclar, some cases show that fiscal savings promised by this strategy have not been realized, either due to corruption, mismanagement, added costs of contract oversight, or other factors.[44] Indeed, in a 2003 survey of municipalities, 22 percent of city managers reported that within the past five years, their local government had brought back in-house services they had previously contracted out, because of poor quality, problems with monitoring, or insufficient cost savings.[45] But in other cases, municipalities find that contracting out is a cheaper option than performing the service in-house. Often, however, this is not because of greater efficiency attained by managerial expertise but because contractors pay less in wages and/or benefits, or restructure work arrangements. For example, a study of eight services in the Los Angeles area found that many contractors paid wages similar to those paid municipal employees but that the private contractors hired fewer workers to do the same job, relied more on part-time workers, terminated employees more frequently, and used more expensive machines.[46] Janitors earning about $12 per hour in the 1970s were earning less than $5 per hour by the early 1990s.[47]

In either case, the end result was the same. As municipal managers pursued a strategy of labor deregulation in the hopes of creating a friendly business climate, workers suffered because of weakened public sector unions and a reduction in the number of high-wage, stable jobs. Unable to win a higher federal minimum wage due to political resistance, and lacking power in municipal wage bargaining due to threats of privatization, activists turned to their local governments to pass living wage ordinances.

Progressive Strategies for Economic Development

Municipal employees who were losing jobs or experiencing wage reductions, along with community activists and unions (among others) who had general criticisms of mainstream strategies, began to search for a "new development paradigm" for economic growth and job creation in the 1980s and 1990s.[48] As mounting evidence showed the failures of mainstream strategies, critics looked for other ways to address issues such as wage inequality, poverty, and urban decay.[49] Pierre Clavel and Nancy Kleniewski call these "progressive policies." They "are based on a different set of assumptions about the relationship between capital and communities" than mainstream strategies, in that they "are expected to harness, shape, and encourage the private sector in the pursuit of social goals defined by the community as a whole."[50] Edward Goetz adapts this definition and states that these progressive policies emphasize expanded public regulation of private property, promotion of alternatives to the private market, greater public intervention in the development process through public ownership and industrial and community planning, identification of specific community-based or other politically defined groups to which to channel the benefits of development, and increased participation of citizens and community-based groups.[51]

Some analysts claim that these progressive strategies are simply a renewed attempt at building the welfare state by bringing "big government" into development decisions. However, the progressive policies referred to here differ from the "traditional liberal solution" of spending more money for social services and creating new governmental agencies to combat the problems of poverty. Rather, they are attempts to change the economic and political structures that produce inequality in the first place. Moreover, in contrast to traditional liberal solutions, such progressive policies rely heavily on extra-governmental institutions such as neighborhood associations, unions, and community groups.[52]

These kinds of policies include projects such as local enforcement of the Community Reinvestment Act to require community-based lending and reliance on community development corporations to pursue such things as affordable housing construction. Recent legislative efforts have also focused on placing various restrictions on private firms who hold contracts with cities or states. These efforts include plant closings legislation and corporate accountability laws, which place restrictions on companies that receive public money to expand or relocate. Worker Retention Ordinances provide job security for employees. For example, in Washington, D.C., if a building owner switches to a new subcontractor for the provision of janitorial services, the new subcontractor must maintain the existing work force. Other progressive policies include raising wages through increasing state and federal wage standards or through prevailing wage legislation, promoting single-payer health care, and providing job training.[53]

Living wage ordinances are another example of a progressive strategy. The actors behind the campaigns seek to revitalize economic conditions from the perspective of working people. They challenge mainstream policymakers' assumption that placing restrictions on the receipt of public money will hurt the economy in the long-run. According to Twin Cities New Party member Mary Jo Maynes, "Living wage policies are part of a larger effort to rebuild our urban communities and create sustainable regional economies."[54] Indeed, in many cases, the main goal of the campaigns is to challenge existing ideas of how local governments are run and how economic development occurs.

The idea of using the purchasing power of the government as a means to enact economic change is not new. Of course, the power of government as buyer is the focus of Keynesian thought. But beyond this, labor advocates have used public sector purchasing as a source of leverage over private sector contractors. For example, Congress passed an act in 1892 setting an eight-hour workday for all mechanics and laborers employed directly by the federal government or by contractors and subcontractors. This was amended in 1912 to cover all employees on any government contract.[55] In 1936, Congress passed the Walsh-Healey Public Contracts Act, mandating employers holding federal contracts worth ten thousand dollars or more to pay their employees the prevailing wage for work in the industry. In addition, Walsh-Healey set an eight-hour workday, forty-hour work week, strengthened health and safety requirements, and prohibited the use of child and convict labor on contracts. Although there were several motivations for the act, one main one was to hold the government up as a model employer, with the hope of raising labor market standards for all workplaces. According to economist Edward Denison, another motive behind the act came when the Supreme Court struck down the National Industrial Recovery Act of 1933 (part of Franklin D. Roosevelt's first "New Deal"), invalidating government control over private sector wages and hours.[56] The Walsh-Healey Act was another attempt to establish (much more narrow) wage and hour standards. It set the stage for the 1938 Fair Labor Standards Act.

When labor advocates have been blocked politically or legislatively from passing more wide-ranging policy covering the private sector, they have often turned to public sector policy as a place where progressive policy inroads can be won and can set the stage for broader change in the future.

Living Wages and City Administrators

How do city managers react to progressive strategies as an alternative to mainstream ones? The living wage movement shows how difficult it is for most mayors to transition away from their standard approach to economic development. For the most part, they see a living wage ordinance as contrary to their goals. Speaking of the Toledo ordinance, former mayor Carty Finkbeiner said that he "swallowed hard" to accept it. "Our job was to bring in jobs, not drive away jobs," said Finkbeiner.[57] The *Pittsburgh Post-Gazette* reports a similar story: "Publicly, the Murphy administration has been largely silent on the ordinance, except to say that the bill could drive away business, especially in neighborhoods."[58] Other mayors have been active opponents of the initiatives. Cleveland mayor Michael R. White sent out a mailing with a letter expressing concern about creating "an expensive taxpayer-supported bureaucracy" and said the city may lose jobs to other cities that have "relatively uncomplicated regulations."[59] Los Angeles mayor Richard Riordan, Chicago mayor Richard Daley, and St. Paul mayor Norm Coleman deserve special mention, as outspoken opponents of the living wage proposals in their cities. Coleman referred to living wage supporters as "Marxists" guilty of "social engineering," and claimed the ordinance would bring economic devastation to the city.[60] All three deployed key staff members to work on defeating the ordinances. These examples show the degree to which city administrators have defined their role as city leader as one of fostering conditions conducive to economic growth, and the degree to which they have equated growth with friendly business climate.

Conclusion

Despite examples of new kinds of progressive policies and a plethora of evidence about the drawbacks of mainstream strategies, city officials have been slow to abandon the status quo approach to economic development. Although it is difficult to obtain adequate data to evaluate the impact of these strategies on job growth and community revitalization, the information that does exist suggests that the strategies are not paying off. Providing large tax abatements and subsidies may help entice new businesses to the area, but the costs per job often fail to outweigh the benefits.

Living wage ordinances are an example of a progressive strategy developed to counter the trend in mainstream economic development and urban politics. The ordinances vary in their provisions and the organizations supporting them have numerous goals for their campaigns, but a common theme is promoting policies that help low-wage workers rather than owners of capital. In the next chapter, we will see how the living wage movement developed in the 1990s, as a response to the trends discussed here.

3

OVERVIEW OF THE MOVEMENT

Few would have predicted, on a cold Baltimore day in December 1994, that the seeds of a national grassroots movement were being sown. That day, after a substantial battle, a powerful labor-community coalition brought to fruition its campaign for a local living wage law, as the city of Baltimore passed a law requiring that firms with city service contracts pay their workers a living wage.

Jen Kern, "Working for a Living Wage," *Multinational Monitor*, 2001

Living wage ordinances take many different forms, particularly after debate and negotiation in city councils. In general, however, most of the ordinances follow a basic guideline of requiring firms that receive public money from a municipality or state to pay their employees a wage significantly above federal or state wage floors. The idea is not a new one: similar laws that require federal, state, or local contractors to pay a prevailing wage have existed in the United States for most of the past century (including Davis-Bacon laws and the Federal Service Contract Act). Rather than require the prevailing local market wage by industry, living wage ordinances set a wage floor for all jobs covered by the law. Commonly, the living wage is set at or above the federal poverty guidelines for a family of four (in 2002, this was approximately $8.70 per hour; in 2003, approximately $8.85 per hour).

Following the first modern living wage victory in Baltimore,[1] more than a hundred city councils and county boards around the country passed similar ordinances in various forms by late 2003.[2] A list of these places suggests that there is no discernible pattern in adoption of ordinances. They have been passed in large metropolises, such as New York, Los Angeles, Chicago, San Francisco, and Boston, as well as in small ones: Ferndale, Michigan; Hudson County, New Jersey; Eau Claire County, Wisconsin; Fairfax, California. There are heavier concentrations in the

Northeast, Midwest, and West, but ordinances have also passed in southern cities such as Durham, North Carolina; San Antonio, Texas; Louisville, Kentucky; Broward County, Florida; and Richmond, Virginia. Traditionally liberal university towns like Madison, Wisconsin; Ann Arbor, Michigan; and Berkeley, California have ordinances, as do areas not known for being on the forefront of local policy: Cumberland County, New Jersey; Des Moines, Iowa; and San Fernando, California.

A full list of cities and counties can be found in appendix A, table A.1. The number of cities and counties with ordinances is slightly lower than the number of successful campaigns, for two reasons. First, in a few cities, multiple campaigns have been waged. For example, the City of New York passed a fairly narrow ordinance in 1996. In 2002, a new living wage coalition emerged to get the city to pass a much more comprehensive ordinance. These count as two separate successful campaigns; however, they apply only to one city. Second, a handful of ordinances have been repealed since passage. Again, these count in a list of living wage ordinances adopted but do not count in a list of existing ordinances. Table A.1 lists 101 cities and counties that have passed one or more living wage ordinances as of December 2003. Approximately 41 million people live in cities or counties covered by living wage ordinances.

As the movement experienced success, the living wage concept spread to new arenas. In July 2000, the city of Santa Monica, California, passed an ordinance that would apply to large private businesses in that city's downtown tourist district. This meant that thousands of hotel, restaurant, and retail workers would have seen their wages go up to approximately $10.50 an hour plus benefits. However, a business coalition opposing the living wage was able to get an initiative onto the ballot in November 2002 to rescind the ordinance. The Chamber of Commerce and its allies— principally large nonunion hotels—spent millions of dollars on the effort. They employed a variety of tricks, including disseminating deceptive "Democratic voter guides" and "pro-choice voter guides" advocating a vote against the living wage.[3] After a hotly contested race, the ordinance was defeated 50.98 to 49.02 percent.

New Orleans also came close to expanding the living wage concept. In 1996, living wage supporters led by ACORN gathered more than fifty thousand signatures to put an initiative on the ballot that would establish a citywide minimum wage one dollar above the federal minimum.[4] Although the wage increase was not large, it would cover tens of thousands of workers and their families. When polling figures showed the measure had widespread support, hotel and restaurant lobbyists went to the state legislature and got them to pass a state law outlawing local wage ordinances. Although Louisiana was a "home rule state," meaning that municipalities had legal rights to set their own laws, the state legislature declared that they would overturn home rule in this case, as a city minimum wage, it was argued, would cause undue economic hardship for the state.

Living wage advocates fought back in court and eventually won the right to get the initiative back on the ballot. In February 2002, 63 percent of voters approved the measure. Opponents returned to the courts, stating that the 1996 state law prohibited the city from implementing its new measure. The district court ruled in favor of keeping the ordinance, but the state supreme court eventually ruled against the living wage ordinance in September 2002. It is unlikely that living wage proponents in New Orleans will give up their fight, as they already are considering other possibilities for raising wages in their city and state.

In 2003, two new cities adopted citywide living wage laws. In February, the Santa Fe, New Mexico, City Council passed an ordinance requiring all firms with twenty-five or more employees within city borders to pay a wage of $8.50 per hour starting in 2004, to go up in increments to $10.50 by 2008, and then be indexed for inflation. In November, voters in San Francisco approved a ballot measure to establish an $8.50 per hour minimum wage (indexed for inflation) for almost all employees in the city. The Santa Fe ordinance is facing legal challenge, although much of the opposition's case was thrown out in late 2003.

Other developments are occurring on college campuses. Student groups at a few schools, such as the University of Virginia and Swarthmore, have been fighting for living wages for several years now. The topic received international attention in the spring of 2002 when students at higher-profile Harvard University undertook a three week sit-in to demand that the administration begin paying all workers and subcontracted employees a minimum of $10.25 per hour. Although the students did not win their exact demand, Harvard agreed to form a committee to look into the issue and develop recommendations for addressing the situation. Eventually, while rejecting the principle of a living wage, Harvard president Lawrence Summers adopted a number of the students' demands, including a one-time wage increase to between $10.83 and $11.30 per hour for all low-wage workers. Summers also agreed to wage parity between workers hired directly by Harvard and outsourced workers, meaning that the university could not use outsourcing or the threat of it as a way to undercut wages.

Even more important, the case caught the attention of students across the nation. The Student Labor Action Project, an offshoot of Jobs with Justice, is working with the United Students against Sweatshops (USAS), Association of Community Organizations for Reform Now (ACORN), and the American Federation of Labor–Congress of Industrial Organizations (AFL-CIO) to coordinate campaigns and provide support for campus living wage struggles. Versions of living wage ordinances are already in effect at Wesleyan, Johns Hopkins, Harvard, and Stanford universities. Other universities that have won some partial gains for workers through living wage campaigns include Cornell, Valdosta State (Georgia), William and Mary, Princeton, the University of Connecticut, and the University of Tennessee.[5]

The Organizations Involved

Living wage coalitions are varied and diverse. Though campaigns have sprung up from all quarters and represent the grassroots efforts of hundreds of disconnected organizations and individuals, there are a handful of groups that have been leaders in the movement. One grassroots, low-income community organization especially active in the movement is ACORN. After ACORN, it is difficult to pinpoint any one national organization heavily involved in the movement, but Jobs with Justice, a national organization of labor-community coalitions; and the Industrial Areas Foundation (IAF), a network of neighborhood congregation-based groups founded by community organizer Saul Alinsky, have also been involved. The New Party, a national political party, had been active in some of the earlier campaigns but is now almost defunct as a national organization. One of its spin-off chapters, the Working Families party in New York and Connecticut, continues to be active in living wage campaigns. The Green party has increased its involvement in the movement in recent years.

The labor unions that are most involved are the Service Employees International Union (SEIU), the American Federation of State, County, and Municipal Employees (AFSCME), and the Hotel Employees and Restaurant Employees Union (HERE), but dozens of other unions have played a role in particular campaigns. The AFL-CIO endorsed the living wage idea as part of their "America Needs a Raise" campaign in 1997 and sponsored national conferences for activists to share information about their efforts. In many areas, the state labor federations and local AFL-CIO labor councils are heavily involved and have even begun to initiate some of the campaigns themselves.

In addition, a number of religious organizations have been active in living wage campaigns. In addition the IAF, other national groups include the American Friends Service Committee, a service organization founded by the Religious Society of Friends (Quakers), and Direct Action and Resource Training Center (DART). They also include particular churches and pastors, as well as local interdenominational organizations such as Elm City Congregations Organized, which was a leading force in the New Haven living wage victory. In the 1990s, General Conventions of the Episcopal church, the United Church of Christ, and the Methodist church passed resolutions in support of the living wage movement and calling on churches to pay their own employees a living wage. The living wage movement also received endorsements from groups ranging from the Jewish Council for Public Affairs to the National Interfaith Committee for Worker Justice.

Finally, local affiliates of groups such as Legal Services, the Gray Panthers, the National Organization for Women, the National Lawyer's Guild, the Rainbow Coalition, and Senior Action have been active in various campaigns. Other groups active in some campaigns include Coalitions for the Homeless, Human Services Coalition, student-labor organizations, and environmental groups.

Goals of the Campaigns

Given the number and diversity of organizations participating, it is not surprising that their reasons for getting involved vary. As concern over corporate subsidies rises, some view living wage campaigns as a way to place limitations on public money given to business. Others, such as members of AFSCME, see these reforms as a way to discourage the outsourcing of government jobs. Since the public sector was one of the only areas where unions saw growth in the 1970s and early 1980s, this attack on public sector employment was particularly painful for organized labor. Furthermore, the transition to privatized city services dramatically reduced the quality of these jobs: "These were good, middle-class jobs for non-educated and disproportionately minority persons," says Jared Bernstein of the Economic Policy Institute.[6] "And as these jobs have been contracted out to the private sector, their rates of pay have fallen." Some view legislation that discourages such outsourcing as a way to restore the availability of good public jobs in cities and to rebuild the public sector unions.

Other labor activists hope the living wage can be a tool for organizing workers in those nonunion service jobs once performed by public employees. For example, many city contracts now go to low-wage workers to clean city buildings. Organizing these workers to fight for a living wage can be a first step toward organizing them into a union. Chris Owens of the AFL-CIO remarks in an article in *Dollars & Sense*: "Living wage campaigns are important both for raising the wage floor of the most vulnerable workers and for providing a new model of labor/community collaboration that extends organized labor's relations with non-unionized workers."[7] In fact, connecting with these workers is one reason why service sector unions such as SEIU and HERE are leading the campaigns for a living wage in many cities. According to Dennis Houlihan, researcher for the public sector union AFSCME, "A lot of unions are looking at these like Davis-Bacon [prevailing wage] laws— legislation to help with organizing. . . . The unions want legal representation for these workers in the end."[8] Prevailing wage laws have helped unions organize construction workers by "taking wages out of competition." When nonunion contractors are required to pay the same wage as unionized contractors, they must compete for jobs on quality rather than on wages. Houlihan's quote suggests that unions are not only interested in getting higher wages for workers covered by the living wage but union contracts.

Community groups have been involved in the campaigns as an attempt to address the extreme poverty and economic inequality faced by their constituents. As Chris Tilly writes in an analysis of the living wage movement, a number of community organizations had spent time in the 1980s "tying requirements—particularly job creation and access to jobs for disadvantaged populations—to city subsidies, development tax breaks, or city contracts."[9] However, those organizations soon realized that even when they were successful in getting jobs for their constituents, those jobs often paid low wages. Many supporters from these groups have become increasingly convinced that a more effective means of addressing poverty and other social problems is through the creation of jobs that pay family-sustaining wages. For ACORN, the living wage concept provided a new twist on the corporate accountability campaigns of the 1980s. According to Jen Kern of Living Wage Resource Center, ACORN saw in the living wage movement a chance to build coalitions, particularly with unions, while pursuing a winnable, popular goal.

Kern also argues that it wasn't just that ACORN wanted to follow-up on the campaigns of the 1980s but that living wage campaigns offered the organization a chance to fill their larger self-interest. As a mass-based organization, ACORN always looks to represent more people and to demonstrate power. The living wage movement allowed ACORN to go into the community and talk to people, and every signature on a petition or postcard was a new name and address to be contacted. It was a clear fit with the needs of current and potential members.

The living wage movement also has been a natural fit for many faith-based groups. As Episcopalian minister Dick Gillett writes, the living wage movement is about more than just wages, as the term itself has a moral connotation.[10] Gillett and others have argued that the premise of the living wage idea—"that all God's children should have enough to eat and be treated justly"—can be found in the Bible and other major religious documents. Father William Maestri, arguing in favor of the New Orleans living wage ordinance, writes that Pope Leo XIII called for the right for a living and family wage in 1891, in the "Rerum Novarum."[11] In fact, many of the early living wage advocates in the United States around the late 1800s and early 1900s were Catholic priests. For a variety of religious organizations, the call for a living wage is about morality as well as economics.

Beyond the moral argument, it is important to recognize that faith-based groups are community institutions. As such, churches have an interest in making their communities self-sustaining. A living wage for residents could mean more stability and more resources for workers *and* the church. For example, when workers are working two or three jobs, they have less time to commit to church activities. When church members earn low wages, they have less available for tithing.

Another goal of living wage activists has been to change the entire framework used to analyze and discuss economic policy. The New Party, which was heavily involved in starting and running some of the early campaigns, saw living wage ordinances as only one step in a long series of much-needed reforms to change the way in which economic policy is made in the United States. In their view, most political decisions, including those regarding community economic development, are made by those with the most money, rather than by those directly affected by the policy. In the case of municipal policy, this often results in benefits flowing to wealthy firms, in the form of city contracts and public subsidies. Living wage legislation is one attempt to place restrictions on the receipt of public money. Promoting it is a way to argue that cities should not subsidize poverty wage jobs. According to past New Party chair Joel Rogers, "These campaigns raise simple, powerful questions about economic governance in our country."[12]

Finally, labor unions and community groups such as ACORN view the living wage movement as an opportunity to build progressive coalitions among groups that have not worked together closely, or at all, in some time. The labor movement has experienced a long-term decline in membership and political strength in the past several decades. Despite this decline, unions, for a number of reasons, have failed to reach out to possible allies to fight for common causes. First, some U.S. unions have a legacy of exclusionary, racist, and sexist practices. This strained or even severed the ties between many unions and community groups, leaving both sides suspicious of one another.[13] However, it was not only suspicion that kept labor unions from working in coalition with other unions or community groups. For the past several decades, many unions—especially in the private sector—did not pursue new organizing in their own workplaces or industries, let alone broader social movement organizing.[14] In some cases, this was the result of a corrupt or bureaucratic leadership, but in other cases, it was due to inertia or failure to understand the benefits of membership growth. Regardless of the reasons, the late 1970s and 1980s witnessed a dramatic decrease in new organizing, the number of work stoppages, and the presence of labor in local and national political activity.

Labor's weaknesses were not only internal: unions have also faced serious challenges to their strength from reorganization of the workplace, economic recession, weak labor laws, and increasing ideological attacks by governments and employers. The AFL-CIO has brought attention to the increase in attacks on unions in recent years, as more firms hired union-busting law firms, more employers engaged in illegal anti-union activities, and the National Labor Relations Board frequently failed to enforce labor law. Such a political climate intensified the retreat of labor. It became more difficult for unions to develop and sustain political allies. Many in the labor movement realized the need to rebuild and create new alliances, and the living wage movement seemed to offer an opportunity to do that, given its appeal to community and religious organizations.

Of course, the weak ties between labor, faith-based groups, and community organizations were not only the fault of unions. In many cases the latter ignored the need to organize workers and did little to connect with low-income workers' organizations. The end result was weak alliances between organizations that might otherwise have worked together. The living wage movement has offered a useful bridge across old differences and provided an opportunity for effective new alliances.

Resources

Different groups bring different resources to living wage coalitions. In smaller cities, campaigns have been waged with all-volunteer labor, private and in-kind donations. In larger cities, more resources are generally needed to conduct the kind of outreach needed for a strong campaign. In a few cases, labor unions and community groups have been able to donate staff time and office space to the campaigns. For example, the Detroit area labor council provided the campaign with office space and funds to produce 300,000 pieces of literature. The South Central Federation of Labor in Wisconsin and a local political party teamed up to provide a staff person and resources for the Madison and Dane county living wage campaigns. In any campaign that ACORN leads, ACORN head organizers serve as de facto campaign managers, using ACORN offices, phones, and staff time to support the campaign.

Coalitions have also raised grants from foundations to pay for staff and materials. Organizations such as the Unitarian Universalist Veatch Program, Public Welfare Foundation, and Discount Foundation have all supported living wage coalitions. The San Francisco–based Tides Foundation established a living wage initiative in 2000 and has been a major donor for dozens of campaigns. Larger campaigns, such as those in Los Angeles and Santa Monica have received sizable grants in the tens of thousands of dollars from various foundations, which have enabled them to hire organizers, produce educational materials, and conduct research. Smaller coalitions that don't have access to labor union or community group staff time or resources have had to be more resourceful. For example, the Richmond, Virginia, living wage coalition received a two-thousand-dollar grant from the Resist Foundation. They used that to pay an organizer one hundred dollars per week for six months to do part-time outreach to temporary workers hired by the city to get them involved in the living wage campaign.

Finally, several organizations provide technical support to living wage campaigns for little to no cost. These include the Brennan Center for Justice at New York University, which provides legal assistance;

the Political Economy Research Institute at the University of Massachusetts-Amherst, Economic Policy Institute, and the Institute for Labor and Employment at the University of California-Berkeley, which provide research assistance; and the ACORN Living Wage Resource Center, which offers a wide range of campaign advice. (For a full range of resources and contact information see appendix B.)

Details of the Ordinances

Due to the range of goals behind living wage campaigns, it is not surprising that the ordinances themselves differ in content and scope. Coalitions dominated by unions have fought to include language that helps labor organizing. Some community groups have favored provisions promoting access to jobs, such as requirements for local hiring. Below, I review the dimensions of ordinances, explaining what they usually cover, and where they often differ.

While all of the laws require a subsection of employers in a locality to pay their employees a wage rate higher than the current federal or state minimum, there is substantial variation in the campaigns waged to pass them and in the details of the laws. The campaigns and ordinances differ along a number of dimensions, such as:

- the political method of pursuing them (legislative ordinances versus ballot initiatives);
- political jurisdiction of the proposed law (city council, county board, school board, or university);
- the wage and benefit levels;
- the firms and workers that will be covered by (or exempted from) the ordinance;
- the process of implementing and monitoring the ordinance;
- the enforcement process and penalties for noncompliance.

Ballot Initiatives versus Legislative Campaigns

Most of the living wage campaigns that apply to firms receiving public contracts or subsidies have been run as legislative campaigns (see table 3.1). Most minimum wage campaigns have been run as ballot initiatives. Ballot initiatives, which require proponents to collect a certain number of

Table 3.1. Successful and failed living wage campaigns (as of December 2003)

Type of campaign	Passed	Failed
City council ordinance	73[a]	10[b]
County board ordinance	22	4
Ballot measure	6[c]	6[d]
Adopted by other bodies:		
School board	3	0
University	4	NA[e]
Library board	1	0
Hospital	1	0
Transportation board	1	0
Road commission	1	0

Source: Data compiled by the author.

[a] Four of the city council ordinances have since been repealed by council vote: Hempstead, NY; Omaha, NE; Hazel Park, MI; and Pittsburgh, PA. Another, the Santa Monica, CA, ordinance, was repealed by ballot initiative. (There were two separate ballot measures in Santa Monica, CA, related to the living wage. The first, Proposition KK, was an effort to pass a narrow ordinance that would prohibit the city council from passing a broader ordinance. That was defeated in 2000. The second, Proposition JJ, was to repeal the ordinance passed by the council. Proposition JJ passed in November 2002.) The Monroe County, MI, ordinance was repealed by county board vote.

[b] Defeated ordinances: Albuquerque, NM; Alleghany County, NY; Ann Arbor, MI (by veto); Camden, NJ (by veto); Charlotte, NC (by veto); Chicago, IL; Kalamazoo, MI; Knoxville, TN; Letcher County, KY; Montgomery County, MD; Nashville, TN; Rockland County, MD (by veto); Santa Rosa, CA; Syracuse, NY; and Ventura, CA. Note that in Ann Arbor, Chicago, and Montgomery County, a later version of ordinance was eventually passed.

[c] One of these, the St. Louis ordinance, was struck down in court in 2001; another, in New Orleans, was struck down in 2002. A new version of the St. Louis ordinance was then passed by the city council in 2002.

[d] In Denver, Missoula, Minneapolis, and St. Paul, later versions of ordinances were passed by city councils.

[e] It is difficult to track failed campaigns. While it is easy to track ordinances that are outwardly voted down, more campus campaigns lose because they simply die out over time. For this reason, I was not able to measure which campus campaigns have actually been defeated.

signatures in order to place measures before the voters, are not allowed in all states and cities. Legislative campaigns are aimed at passing ordinances through elected officials on city councils, county boards, school boards, or state legislatures.

The major advantage to a legislative campaign is that it can be much cheaper than a ballot initiative because it does not involve the resources required for signature gathering or expensive advertising for voter education and turnout. Ballot initiative campaigns have been massively out-spent, as business interests have poured in millions of dollars to defeat the wage increases through direct-mail campaigns and other advertising. The National Restaurant Association has been the largest funder of the opposition groups, but large multinational corporations such as McDonalds, Philip Morris, and Texaco, as well as smaller businesses, have contributed as well. For example, in 1996 opponents of the statewide minimum wage increase in Missouri spent $1.9 million, while proponents spent $180,000.[15] Proponents of the St. Paul living wage ballot initiative were also outspent ten to one.[16]

With much greater funding, the opposition is able to reach voters through television and radio advertising as well as through individual mailings to homes. Bob Burtman writes in the *Houston Press* that the coalition opposing the Houston living wage initiative (which would have raised the citywide minimum wage to $6.50 an hour) put out a "barrage of ads and mailings from the Save Jobs for Houston Committee" with the message that the ordinance would lead to:

> Cops and firefighters yanked off the streets. Higher taxes. Thousands of jobs lost. Soaring prices for such essentials as food and prescription drugs. The wholesale destruction of small businesses. Streets riddled with pot-holes. Swollen welfare rolls.[17]

This type of literature delivered to thousands of homes in the city is difficult to combat without major funding. However, the difference in funding is not as important in legislative campaigns, where community members and campaign supporters at least have access to elected officials and equal time at council hearings.

Another advantage of city council–based legislative campaigns is that the outcome can be easier to predict than with ballot initiatives. Proponents can target those council members who are opposed or are wavering on the vote and answer their concerns directly before the measure comes up for a vote. By the time a city council votes on an issue, a well-organized campaign usually knows what the outcome will be.

However, there are some drawbacks to legislative campaigns. One is that the legislative process introduces a problem of open-endedness. While ballot initiatives have set dates and deadlines, legislative calendars are forever changing, and are sensitive to lobbying and election cycles. This has led to speeding up and slowing down of the campaigns, depending on the council's schedule and on efforts from proponents and opponents who persuade members to rush or stall the process. An ordinance can get held up in committee indefinitely and never be brought to a council vote.

A second drawback is that the legislative process can put the negotiating of the ordinance into the hands of the council and out of the hands of those running the campaigns and the activists supporting them. Most ordinances undergo substantial revision over time as "inside" council members try to craft the ordinances into something more likely to pass. For example, the Milwaukee city ordinance went through nine revisions before it was finally passed. As the negotiation occurs, the strength of the ordinance is whittled down—something that would not happen to a ballot initiative.

Finally, ordinances passed by ballot initiative may be harder to overturn. Whereas a city council ordinance can be vetoed or simply repealed by a majority vote of the council, ordinances passed by "the will of the people" generally can only be altered by supermajority vote, state legislation, or legal challenge.

Political Jurisdiction

Most living wage campaigns have been targeted at the city or county level, though some have been aimed at school boards, states (e.g., statewide minimum wage campaigns), and universities. There are even living wage ordinances that apply to a transportation board (San Diego), road commission (Washtenaw County), hospital (San Antonio), and library (Little Rock) (see appendix A, table A.2). While state-level minimum wage campaigns cover more workers, they are harder to win, since more money is required and state legislators are not as responsive as local legislators to community members. For example, it is usually much easier for proponents to get low-wage workers, who would be affected by the wage increase, to city council hearings than to state legislature hearings. It is also easier for community groups and unions to do intensive door-to-door canvassing to turn out the voters on the city level. This is in part due to resources but also because many community groups, religious organizations, and labor unions have only a local base and not a statewide or multidistrict presence.

It is of note that although a number of efforts have been made, no state has yet passed a statewide living wage ordinance that would apply to state workers and/or service contractors. The closest case came in

California in 2003. The state legislature passed a statewide living wage law that would have provided ten dollars with or twelve dollars without health benefits to state employees and employees of state service contractors, but Governor Gray Davis vetoed it just before the vote to recall him.

Coverage of the Ordinances

The coverage of the ordinances (firms and workers) is perhaps the dimension along which there is the greatest variance. Minimum wage campaigns attempt to raise the wage floor for all workers in a given jurisdiction.[18] While all states have the authority to raise minimum wages, cities and counties are sometimes restricted from doing this by state law. In fact, due to the success of the living wage movement, business leaders have pushed states to adopt laws prohibiting municipal wage policies. As of the end of 2003, nine states have passed such laws in response to local living wage organizing, and others are looking to do so.

Unlike minimum wage laws, traditional living wage ordinances target workers whose jobs can be traced to public dollars. These coverage categories have included (1) workers employed by city service contractors; (2) employees of firms receiving economic development subsidies; (3) subcontractors of the above two categories; (4) employees of firms holding city leases; and (5) direct public employees. These categories will be described in detail below. I also describe geographic or location-based ordinances and discuss some of the common exemptions in living wage ordinances.

Contracts. Living wage ordinances typically cover only city service contracts and not contracts for the purchases of goods, such as supplies or equipment.[19] The ordinances rarely cover all service contracts let by a city. Usually, there is some form of dollar value cutoff (such as five thousand dollars per year in city contracts in Milwaukee and twenty-five thousand dollars per year in Los Angeles). Others exempt small businesses (such as those with fewer than five employees in Ypsilanti, Michigan), while others apply the provisions only to selected types of contracts. The Jersey City ordinance applies only to contracts for clerical, food service, janitorial, and unarmed security services. In almost all cases, the ordinance covers only those workers doing work on the city contract itself, and not all workers employed in the firm. As table 3.2 shows, 91 percent of all ordinances cover service contract employees.

Table 3.2. Number of living wage ordinances with selected coverage (as of December 2002)

Ordinances that cover:	Number	% of total
Service contractors	86	91
Subcontractors	44	46
Economic assistance	39	41
Direct employees	23	24
Concessionaires, lessees, or tenants	13	13
Total ordinances	95	100

Source: Data compiled by the author.
Note: This includes ordinances passed and still on the books through December 2002. The table does not include university living wage ordinances.

Financial Assistance Recipients. In addition to city service contracts, ordinances often cover recipients of financial assistance for economic development. This includes tax breaks, subsidized loans, tax increment financing, subsidized bonds, and other types of public subsidies given to firms for business location, expansion, or retention. The coverage generally includes only those employees working on the subsidized site, not all employees of the firm. Most ordinances that include subsidy recipients have a fairly high threshold. For example, St. Paul's ordinance applies only to those firms receiving $100,000 or more in assistance. As of the end of 2003, 41 percent of all ordinances covered employees in this category.

Subcontractors. In addition to the foregoing categories, 46 percent of all ordinances explicitly cover subcontractors of service contractors, economic development assistance recipients, or both. The laws only apply to those subcontractors doing work on the contract or subsidized site.

City or County Employees. In many locations, public sector workers are already unionized and receive wages above the living wage. However, the increasing use of part-time and temporary workers by city governments has lowered the wages of city employees and made it necessary to include direct city employee coverage in living wage ordinances. A growing number of ordinances—now 24 percent—have done so.

City Leases and Concessionaires. A minority of ordinances (13 percent) apply to businesses that hold leases, or operate concessions on city property. This can include such things as retail and food vendors in city-owned airports or sports arenas. It also includes restaurants or hotels operating at city-owned ports. For example, the Los Angeles city ordinance covers concessionaires in Los Angeles International Airport. The Berkeley ordinance applies to the restaurants and hotels leasing land at the city marina.

Location-based Coverage.   A newer form of ordinance is based on firm location, rather than connections to public money, as mentioned at the start of this chapter. As of late 2003, five such ordinances have passed, although two (New Orleans and Santa Monica) have subsequently been repealed. Proponents are looking to expand these kinds of campaigns in the future, as they have the potential to cover many more workers.

Exemptions.   More than half the ordinances have three or more exemptions on the types of contracts or employees covered, although these exemptions vary widely. Common exemptions include part-time or seasonal workers, interns or students in job training programs, persons with disabilities working in special employment programs, and construction workers (since they are usually covered by prevailing wage laws). Many ordinances do not apply to managerial or supervisory employees and a number exempt professional services, such as engineering or legal services. In Alexandria, Virginia, some city landscaping services are done by contractors who employ workers from the city jail. The ordinance specifically exempts incarcerated workers from the living wage.

Nonprofits.   Some living wage laws exempt nonprofits altogether. In others, only those nonprofits that do not have highly paid CEOs are exempt, such as ones where the CEO earns no more than eight times as much as the lowest paid employee. More and more municipalities are attempting to cover nonprofit employers, as living wage activists have come to realize how many low-wage human service workers work for city and county contractors. States usually funnel money for childcare and home care work through counties rather than cities, so the nonprofit coverage issue is most relevant at the county level.

Wage and Benefit Level

The ordinances also differ in the wage and benefit level that firms are required to pay. According to John Howley, national research director of SEIU, the wage level is usually chosen by what the campaign thinks is the highest possible wage they can use and still win: "You must be careful in designing the provisions, down to the exact dollar amount that you select, because that will become the focus of the whole campaign. You can design an initiative to provoke sympathy from voters or it can be designed so that it doesn't do that, and that people think it is unrealistic."[20] Earlier ordinances required employers to pay wages which were equal to or greater than the U.S. poverty income guidelines for a family of four. The hourly wage required in 2003 for a full-time year-round worker to reach the poverty line for a family of four (two adults and two children), with only one wage earner, was approximately $8.85 an hour.[21] Of course, this amount will change yearly, as the federal poverty line is adjusted for inflation.

Many experts have critiqued the method used by the federal government for determining poverty levels. In particular, critics point out that federal poverty thresholds are not adjusted by region or family size, and that they use unrealistic assumptions about the proportion of household budgets going to food. In a study commissioned by the U.S. government, scholars concluded that more accurate subsistence thresholds should be somewhere between 125 and 150 percent of the current poverty levels.[22]

Living wage proponents also know that federal poverty levels are not high enough to support most workers, and that in reality, poverty line wages are not really living wages. A number of organizations such as the Economic Policy Institute and Wider Opportunities for Women have attempted to develop more realistic measures of the income necessary to meet a family's basic needs.[23] As more and more campaigns succeeded and the movement gained power, organizers began to push for higher wage levels. It is not the case that each successive ordinance passed is more encompassing than the last; however, there is an unmistakable upward trend. For example, the ordinance passed in Fairfax, California, in 2002 set a minimum living wage of $13 an hour with or $14.75 without health benefits. In addition, ordinances are being drafted with more benefits, such as health care and paid days off. Table 3.3 shows that with the exception of 1995, the average nominal and real value of living wage levels won has increased each year since 1994, until a slight fall in 2002.

Most of the ordinances contain provisions for phasing in the law. Usually, the new wage is only required for new contracts and firms with existing contracts are not required to adhere to the living wage until their current contract expires. Several of the ordinances introduce the wage increases gradually. For example, the Baltimore rate started at $6.10 per hour in fiscal year 1996 and increased each year until it reached $7.70 an hour in fiscal year 1999. Other ordinances require that the living

Table 3.3. Average wage won in living wage ordinances, by year[a]

Year	Number of ordinances	Nominal average wage	Real wage (in 2002 $)
1994	1	$6.10	$7.45
1995	2	$8.03	$9.54
1996	7	$7.18	$8.28
1997	8	$7.98	$9.00
1998	8	$8.96	$9.95
1999	15	$9.18	$9.97
2000	15	$9.50	$9.99
2001	24	$10.37	$10.60
2002	17	$10.46	$10.46

Source: Author's calculations from living wage ordinances.
[a] Based on wage won in first year of ordinance implementation and on the wage level without health benefits in cases where multiple wage levels are included.

wage be indexed so it will be adjusted upward automatically each year according to the cost of living.

Additional Provisions

As more and more living wage ordinances are passed, supporters have attempted to add additional provisions onto the laws. For example, as table 3.4 shows, 66 percent of ordinances now include health benefits. Another 63 percent index the wage rate. Another common provision is "anti-retaliation" language—this prevents employers from firing or disciplining employees who speak publicly about living wages, or who file complaints of noncompliance. This is found in just over one-third of all ordinances.

The Boston and New Haven ordinances are two examples of laws that require covered employers to make a good faith effort to hire through community hiring halls. This gives local residents first priority for new jobs created through economic development subsidies. This is found in 11 percent of living wage ordinances. The San Jose, California, and Hartford, Connecticut, ordinances include a "labor peace" clause, which gives the council the power to deny contracts or subsidies to employers who have a history of bad labor relations. This is a kind of labor language found in 25 percent of ordinances. Other kinds of labor language include clauses such as one found in the Minneapolis ordinance. When awarding eco-

Table 3.4. Number of living wage ordinances with
selected provisions

Ordinances that cover:	Number	%
Health benefits	63	66
Wage indexing	60	63
Anti-retaliation	34	36
Labor language[a]	24	25
Paid days off	16	17
Jobs/community hiring halls	10	11
Unpaid days off	9	9
Worker retention	7	7
Pension	1	1
Total ordinances	95	100

Source: Author's analysis of living wage ordinances.
Note: This includes ordinances passed through December 2002.
Cities for which copies of the ordinance could not be obtained are
not included. The table also does not include university living wage
ordinances.
[a] Labor language includes such provisions as labor peace agreements,
preference for employers who sign neutrality agreements, and prohibi-
tions on using public money for union-busting activity.

nomic subsidies or contracts, the city of Minneapolis gives preference to
those employers who are neutral in union organizing drives.

Living wage proponents have also fought for public disclosure of information on funding for economic development, as it is often difficult to
obtain. The Boston ordinance mandates that employers submit reports
not only on wage levels but also on their hiring and training plans. The
Santa Clara County law requires subsidy recipients to publicly disclose
the number of jobs created, the wages and benefits paid, and any other
public monies being sought by the company.

Monitoring and Penalties

As with the other elements of the ordinances, provisions for implementation, monitoring, and enforcement differ greatly. Implementation can
(but does not necessarily) involve designating a specific department or
office to oversee the process, writing regulations for the ordinance after
enactment, reviewing contracts and subsidy agreements to determine
which firms are covered, training city staff about the requirements of the
ordinance, developing materials to notify employers and employees
about the living wage, and ensuring living wage language is put in all
request for proposals in new contracts or subsidy agreements.

A crucial part of the implementation process is monitoring. In the best cases, monitoring involves city staff answering questions and investigating complaints from workers (or third parties, where the ordinance allows it) about noncompliance, collecting and examining employer payroll records, visiting worksites to verify that employers have posted required notices about the ordinance and that employees are receiving the correct wage.

Should an employer be suspected of noncompliance, the city should have a procedure established to investigate that claim, allowing both parties to present their side. This is part of the enforcement process. In some cities the procedure is elaborate and allows for several levels of appeal. Penalties vary but typically include the city withholding payments to the contractor, terminating or suspending of the contract, denying the contractor the right to bid on future contracts for a specified period (one year after the first violation, three years after a second), and ordering payment of back wages to employees. Stronger ordinances require employers to pay penalties to the city or county as well, such as a fine of fifty dollars per employee per day of noncompliance (e.g. Baltimore), or five hundred dollars per employee per week (e.g. Miami-Dade and Oakland). Some include granting an aggrieved worker "private right of action," which specifically allows the worker—or a representative of the worker (such as a union)—to sue the employer in court in order to obtain back wages and payment of attorney fees.

Table 3.5 shows the number of ordinances that have specific language for different monitoring and enforcement provisions. The most common language is the right of the city to suspend the contract or subsidy of an employer found to be in noncompliance. Still, only 70 percent of ordinances spell out the city's right to do this. In just over half (56 percent) of ordinances, cities may prohibit employers found to be in noncompliance with the ordinance from bidding on contracts in the future (usually for three years).

The least common implementation provisions include the following: Just over one out of five ordinances requires employers to submit additional data to the city, such as the race and gender composition of their work force. Roughly one-quarter require employers to submit payroll records on a regular basis, and the same percentage require contractors to sign a form agreeing to pay the living wage as a condition of being considered for a contract or subsidy.

Table 3.5 suggests that many living wage ordinances have fairly weak language on monitoring and enforcement. However, this table does not highlight the changes in ordinance language over time. As the movement

Table 3.5. Number of living wage ordinances with monitoring and enforcement provisions

	Number	%
Employers in noncompliance may lose their contract	61	70
Employers in noncompliance prohibited from bidding in future	49	56
Must post notice or poster to notify employees of living wage	42	48
Employers in noncompliance subject to fines	37	43
Employers in noncompliance must pay back-wages	37	43
Employee/unions have private right of action (ability to sue employer)	36	41
Must make payroll records available to city on demand	35	40
Ordinance designates particular department to oversee enforcement	32	37
Employer must sign agreement to pay living wage to get contract	23	26
City can withhold contract payment in order to pay living wage to workers	23	26
Must submit payroll records on a regular basis	22	25
Must submit additional information on employees[a]	19	22

Source: Author's analysis of living wage ordinances.
Note: This includes ordinances passed through December 2002. Cities for which copies of the ordinance could not be obtained are not included. The table also does not include university living wage ordinances.
[a] Such as race and gender of employees.

grew and campaigns shared information with each other, the incidence of certain provisions has increased. For example, although only 18 percent of ordinances passed before 2000 required employers to submit payroll data on a regular basis, 31 percent of those passed since have included this requirement.

As mentioned earlier, living wage campaigns look different in every city. But over time, the national resources available to the movement have grown and improved. In particular, the National Living Wage Resource Center (ACORN) and the Brennan Center for Justice (at the New York University School of Law) have provided guidance to living wage campaigns in drafting their ordinances. Paul Sonn, attorney at the Brennan Center and advisor to living wage campaigns across the country, has worked with other lawyers and Jen Kern of ACORN to develop model enforcement language. Now, campaigns can adopt best practice enforcement provisions from other ordinances.

Interestingly, there are two areas of enforcement language that have become less prevalent over time. First, fewer ordinances now require employers to provide additional data, such as race and gender, for their contracted work force. Twenty-nine percent of ordinances passed through 1999 required this, compared to only 16 percent for ordinances passed in 2000 or later. Similarly, language granting cities the right to withhold payment of contracts in order to pay employees of contractors in non-compliance dropped from 45 to 12 percent over that time period.

We will see later that having strong language is not enough to guarantee effective enforcement and monitoring. However, the statutory provisions of an ordinance can provide a solid foundation for implementation struggles. This includes procedures for educating workers about their rights, investigating noncompliance, penalties for employers who violate the law, remedies to workers, protection for employees who file complaints, and institutional roles for living wage advocates in the monitoring process.

Who Has Benefited?

It is difficult to measure the number of workers who have benefited from living wage campaigns. For reasons detailed in later chapters many cities do not keep accurate records of the number of employers covered by living wage laws, let alone the number of workers they employ, or the percentage of those who had been paid below the living wage level. Complicating matters is the fact that some ordinances take awhile to be fully implemented, as they are phased in as contracts come up for renewal. As we will see, enforcement is weak in some cities, leaving workers who are eligible for a living wage pay increase without one. Finally, we have no measure of the number of workers indirectly benefiting from the campaigns. This includes workers who receive "ripple effect" wage increases (workers who were already paid the living wage level or higher but who receive a raise when lower wage workers are bumped up to the living wage). This also includes workers who receive pay increases through unionization efforts indirectly connected to living wage campaigns.

Despite the challenges of measuring coverage, estimates of workers directly covered by the laws ranges from 100,000 to 250,000 workers as of late 2002. While this is a small fraction of the total low-wage work force, the number is not insignificant. As we shall see in the next section, the raise can make a significant impact on workers' lives. Also of interest is the total dollar value of living wages. Again, as discussed earlier in this chapter, it is difficult to measure this amount. But let us take a simple exercise to show the potential of this movement. Let us assume 250,000 workers are benefiting from a living wage ordinance, and those workers average a $2 per hour wage increase for 1,500 hours of work per year (many low-wage workers cannot find full-time work, so this is based on 30 hours of work for 50 weeks a year). This results in a total of $750,000,000 per year in wage increases—three-quarters of a billion dollars in money redistributed from firms, city governments, and consumers into the paychecks of low-wage workers, at an average of $3,000 per year per worker. Of course, this increase in income would not translate into a $3,000 net gain, as workers would need to pay taxes and may lose out on eligibility for selected public services.[24] However, this crude exercise shows the potential redistributive power of the living wage movement, even when coverage is relatively low.

Who Are the Workers?

The technical language of the final ordinance and even the details of the campaign obscure the real story of the workers affected. Some critics also discount the impact of the ordinances because they do not cover large numbers of workers. However, for those workers who are covered, the wage increase can make a significant difference. For example, the Alexandria living wage ordinance has already had an impact on a few hundred workers. One of those workers is Makonnen Habtemeriam, a sixty-eight-year-old immigrant who had been a schoolteacher in Ethiopia before immigrating to the United States but now works full-time in a city-owned parking garage.[25] For Habtemeriam, the living wage meant a raise from $7.16 to $10.21 per hour by 2001, which was an additional $122 per week before taxes. Although this was not enough to make Habtemerian wealthy, this brought him above the federal poverty line, increasing his gross income from $14,893 to $21,237 per year. One of the main benefits was the impact on his family. He was able to spend more time with his wife and two daughters. "It makes it much easier to meet my obligations," said Habtemerian. "My daughters need school supplies, and they are getting very expensive." He added, "Now I'm only working one job, and the main thing is I get to have time with my wife and my children. Sometimes I go to the theater or a concert. These things give some meaning to life."[26]

Another person to benefit was Habtemerian's co-worker, Mussie Habetezion, a twenty-eight-year-old from Eritrea. Habetezion's dream was to attend college, but he was struggling just to survive on low-wage jobs. For several years, Habetezion had been working three jobs: at the parking garage, at a 7-Eleven convenience store, and at a CVS pharmacy. Most days, he would work sixteen hours, doing a full eight hours at the garage and then another eight-hour shift at the 7-11 or CVS. The living wage ordinance had a big impact on his life: with the extra money, he was able to quit his third job, buy a computer, and enroll in a computer class.

The impact of the ordinances is not limited to Alexandria. In Westchester, New York, Working Families party member Debra Smith works at a nursing home and as a homecare worker. She explained why she got involved in the living wage campaign: "I'm not doing this for the money—I enjoy my job. I enjoy making people feel good," she said. "But I have to make enough to buy my kids a coat for the winter." Smith starting working in homecare in 1984, for approximately $2.50 an hour. But by the late 1990s, the minimum wage had only gone up to $5.15 per hour. Meanwhile, the cost of living—particularly housing—had skyrocketed. Rent for a studio in Debra's neighborhood was up to $900 per month— about $15 *more* than the total monthly income for a full-time worker at minimum wage. When someone knocked on her door to tell her about the campaign to organize homecare workers into a union she knew she had to be involved. Through the union campaign, she was drawn into the Westchester County living wage campaign. Debra's wages went up to $10 per hour (indexed to rise with inflation) plus health benefits. She now has a union contract and some job security. After the living wage was passed, a picture of Debra with one of her clients was in the newspaper. When her supervisor reprimanded her for neglecting her duties to have the photo taken, Debra let her supervisor know that her client was well-taken care of and did not mind having the photo taken. She also told her supervisor that she could not be reprimanded: the ordinance gave Debra the right to be an outspoken advocate for the living wage, on or off the job.

Conclusion

This chapter provides an overview of the current living wage movement, giving some of the details that characterize the campaigns. When the movement began in the early 1990s, it was easy to describe a typical living wage law. As time passed and the movement became more successful, that became harder to do. Living wage supporters pushed the limits of what kinds of campaigns they ran, and what leverage they would use to fight for a living wage. By the end of 2003, almost ten years into the movement, the term *living wage* is ubiquitous, and "living wage campaign" is used for a variety of efforts, from ordinances applying to city-service contractors, to university policies, to citywide minimum wage laws.

The movement is expanding because there is a need: the federal government has been reluctant to raise the minimum wage and millions of workers continue to earn poverty level wages. But perhaps more important, the movement continues because there are a broad range of organizations that have a strategic interest in pursuing this kind of campaign. For community and student organizations, a living wage campaign can help build membership. For labor unions, it can help create a climate more favorable to union organizing. And for these groups and others, the campaigns can build new coalitions between groups that have not worked together before. This is attractive at a time when progressive politics have been on the defensive, and organizations feel they are stronger when working in groups. This may be particularly so given a perception that "the opposition"—those that oppose redistributional policies—have themselves been successful in building coalitions. While the number of workers directly affected by the ordinances is modest, the opportunity to build coalitions to fight a broader political agenda is quite valuable.

4

A CLOSER LOOK AT LIVING WAGE CAMPAIGNS

Living wage campaigns are the most interesting (and under-reported) grass roots enterprise to emerge since the civil rights movement.

Robert Kuttner, "The 'Living Wage' Movement,"
The Washington Post, August 20, 1997

It takes a huge ego to imagine that you are smarter than the marketplace.

"A Bad Idea" (editorial), *Florida Times-Union*, November 16, 2001

Most academic research on policy implementation starts with a policy after it's enacted. But both the nature of the campaign and the choices made during it influence implementation. This is especially true for those policies that run counter to the interests of city managers, or for cases where city leaders have little to no motivation to implement on their own. It is important, therefore, to understand living wage implementation as an extension of living wage campaigns. But just what does a living wage campaign look like? In this chapter we'll look at successful campaigns in Boston, Massachusetts; Tucson, Arizona; and Cincinnati, Ohio; and an ongoing campaign in Providence, Rhode Island.

Jen Kern of the Living Wage Resource Center of the Association of Community Organizations for Reform Now (ACORN) says that the best campaigns are those that pursue an "inside track" and an "outside track." The inside track refers to the lobbying efforts directed at the city council. This includes sending delegates comprised of representatives from a variety of organizations to face-to-face meetings with each city councilor. Each visit with a council member has two purposes: first, to assess where that councilor stands on the ordinance and how strong his or her support or opposition is. Second, the meetings are meant to pressure and per-suade. To this end, the coalition wants to demonstrate its power to the council member. This can be done by involving a wide range of organizational leaders and community members (especially those from a councilor's district or ward), and a campaign endorsement list that grows over successive visits, representing a wider swath of that elected official's constituency.

The outside track of the campaign is the organizing that occurs out in the community. This also has several purposes: building ties between coalition members, informing the public about the issues, and demonstrating power to the city council. To demonstrate power on the outside, Kern recommends setting a timeline and engaging in tactics that escalate in terms of the engagement of coalition members and level of conflict with city councilors. For example, early tactics include holding public forums about working poverty, or getting people to sign postcards to send to their elected officials. Going door to door with a cell phone, getting constituents to call their council member before a vote is a higher-level tactic. High-pressure activities include rallies outside of the homes of councilors who oppose the ordinance or even civil disobedience at City Hall.

Coordinating the inside and outside tracks of a campaign can be difficult, and requires energy and planning. Some groups, such as certain labor unions, may be used to engaging only in inside track/lobbying efforts to get what they want, while other groups may have little to no experience with lobbying and prefer confrontational measures. Although ordinances have been passed without using an inside-outside approach, Kern feels that campaigns are more likely to win the ordinance they want and to achieve other campaign goals (such as public education), when both tracks are used. I argue that using both approaches also increases the likelihood of strong implementation and enforcement after enactment.

The following case studies show how living wage campaigns have or have not used inside and outside tracks to get ordinances passed. It's important to see how these dynamics work during the life of a campaign to understand how they might affect the likelihood of implementation, and how they can be utilized again if city officials resist implementation.

Victory in Boston

By the early 1990s, it was clear that the stagnant minimum wage was hurting workers in many cities. And it was also clear that the much-touted efforts at urban redevelopment of the 1980s were not bearing fruit for urban residents. After Baltimore won its living wage ordinance in 1994, followed by victories in Milwaukee, Portland, New York, and Los Angeles, word spread quickly among progressive community activists: "Here is an issue that you can build coalitions around; here is an issue you can win!" Polls consistently showed that a majority of Americans support an increase in the federal minimum wage, and experience with living wage campaigns suggested city councils would support them, too.

Leaders of ACORN knew about the movement as well—and had led one of the first campaigns in St. Paul, Minnesota, in 1995. ACORN had been organizing in cities around the United States on issues such as housing, jobs, bank redlining, education, and improving low-income neighborhood services for more than twenty-five years and saw living wage organizing as a natural extension of that work. ACORN organizers in Boston also saw a living wage campaign as a way to build ties with the local and state labor movement.

In late 1996 and early 1997, ACORN approached the Greater Boston Central Labor Council and the Massachusetts State Federation of Labor about launching a campaign and then quickly moved to bring other coalition partners on board to launch the Boston Jobs and Living Wage Campaign. Soon they had approximately thirty groups endorsing the campaign, including four Teamster locals, the SEIU local representing city workers, some building trades locals, the Immigrant Workers Resource Center, Jobs with Justice, and others.

Initially, it looked as if the ordinance would be difficult to pass. According to an article in the *Boston Globe*, the living wage "appeared to be neither an important nor a politically popular issue."[1] Although the coalition was able to find a council member, Mickey Roache, to sponsor and help shepherd the bill, other council support was lukewarm and Mayor Thomas Menino was noncommittal.

The coalition decided to utilize a variety of tactics to gain support. First, they made the strategic decision not to introduce the bill until they had significant input and buy in from a majority of council members. This proved key in besting the local Chamber of Commerce—which opted not to take a position until the bill was introduced. They then began a series of regular lobby visits to the mayor and council members with delegations of community, labor, and religious representatives of the coalition. With each meeting, they attempted to assess individual city leaders' level of support for the living wage, negotiate around specific concerns about the legislation, and persuade them to vote in favor of the proposal. Every week before the city council meeting, the campaign dropped off new petitions in support of the living wage to city councilors and the mayor.

The coalition also made the issue public. They kicked off the campaign with a Labor Day event where local and state politicians signed on publicly to support the principles of a living wage law for Boston. They put yard signs up around the city in support of the living wage, and passed out fliers in the neighborhoods letting residents know about the proposal and asking them to call their city councilor. After spending the fall and early winter meeting intensively with city councilors and the mayor, the coalition organized their first major public rally in February of 1997 at the electrical workers (IBEW) union hall. The event was a turning point in the campaign. Coalition leaders invited all city councilors and the mayor to the event—urging them to publicly declare their support for a living wage ordinance. Shortly before the event, however, the mayor came out against the ordinance and—although most of the city council members had agreed to announce their support at the rally—only Roache, the bill sponsor, showed up. Pressure from the mayor had clearly sent them scurrying.

According to ACORN, the failure of council members to show up angered their labor union partners, who understood they had been snubbed. As a result, the state federation of labor and labor council immediately stepped up their pressure on council members. They cast the living wage as "prevailing wage for low wage workers," knowing the rhetorical power of prevailing wage laws in the heavily unionized city. Labor leaders let city council members and the mayor know that labor's political support would be contingent on support for the living wage. The coalition deliberately had the sponsor introduce and schedule a vote on the bill at the last city council meeting before the Labor Council made their endorsements for the upcoming council elections.

When it was clear that the coalition had secured the votes it needed to pass the bill, they again approached the mayor, this time from a position of greater strength. In exchange for his support of the bill—and his commitment to aggressively enforce the law once passed—campaign leaders agreed to negotiate with the mayor on some of the details of the proposed ordinance before the final vote. In May 1997, the campaign held their largest rally yet at City Hall, followed by a boisterous public hearing on the issue inside council chambers. In the end, the city council passed the living wage with a 12–1 vote. Mayor Menino not only did not veto it but made a strong statement in support of the ordinance when signing it into law.

"Living Wage Walks" in Tucson

Organizers in Tucson had tried a few times to pass legislation mandating higher wages.[2] The Pima County Interfaith Council (PCIC), affiliated with the Industrial Areas Foundation (IAF), had attempted to put forth a living wage ordinance in 1996 but failed. That same year, a group called the People's Congress for Social and Economic Justice, with support of the Southern Arizona Labor Council, had introduced a ballot initiative to raise the city minimum wage to seven dollars per hour, but the state legislature stepped in to pass a measure banning city minimum wage laws. (Despite the state law, the vote went ahead as scheduled, and the measure lost by a large margin).

Around the time that the minimum wage measure was defeated, the national AFL-CIO began promoting a new educational curriculum on economic issues. After participating in the course, Ian Robertson, president of the Labor Council, began to go into the community to look for people who were like-minded on economic justice issues. Through this effort, the Labor Council reached out to about seventeen religious leaders, including some from the Interfaith Council. The Labor and Interfaith Councils came together to help form a new coalition called the Southern Arizona Alliance for Economic Justice (SAAEJ). Robertson states that "the group had two missions: to educate people on economic issues, and to build a group that could be mobilized around these issues."

With the groundwork in place, SAAEJ soon began discussing a new living wage campaign, one that built on the strength of its founding organizations. SAAEJ began with fifty to eighty members, about half from labor and half from the Interfaith Council. Soon, SAAEJ was working to build the coalition, holding study groups at churches and doing "Living Wage Walks" throughout neighborhoods in Tucson. The walks were a way to get rank-and-file members of both organizations involved in the campaign. According to Communications Workers of America Local 7026 organizer Rolando Figueroa, the group chose neighborhoods that were close to schools and churches, and volunteers went door to door, talking to residents about their work, concerns about their schools and neighborhood, and their opinions on the living wage campaign. SAAEJ grew rapidly, and over the course of the campaign more than one thousand volunteers did the Living Wage Walks. Robertson says that SAAEJ specifically tried to pair up people from the Interfaith Council and the Labor Council to deepen the ties between the groups.

In addition to the walks, SAAEJ organized face-to-face meetings with individual lawmakers. They held roughly one hundred meetings with council members, the mayor, and the head of the city procurement office. They attended numerous council hearings and fiscal subcommittee meetings. SAAEJ relied on existing research about the costs and benefits of living wage ordinances. They could point to cities with ordinances such as Baltimore, Los Angeles, and Milwaukee, and show that passing an ordinance had not led to economic ruin. But while statistics about poverty were important, firsthand stories had the most powerful impact on council members in meetings and hearings. Many of the workers who spoke to councilors had been identified through the Living Wage Walks.

The Living Wage coalition also sponsored two large group study sessions, one in a church and one at the Carpenters' Hall. To run the study sessions, SAAEJ worked with the group Scholars, Artists, and Writers for Social Justice (SAWSJ) to connect with two professors, a sociologist and an economist. The professors helped run the meetings to brief people on the issues. The first hearing had 450 people; the second 650.

Throughout the campaign, SAAEJ continued to build itself as a coalition, and eventually brought in more than fifty organizations. Ian Robertson describes it

> like a shopping mall, anchored by two big groups—the Interfaith Council (itself a coalition of fifty-seven religious groups) and the Labor Council; and then lots of small ones: Students against Sweatshops, Jobs with Justice, SAWSJ, Labor Party, Earth First, Southwest Biodiversity Center, Stop the School of the Americas, American Friends Service Committee, Primavera Foundation, homeless organizations, Community Food Bank, the labor liaison at United Way.

The campaign had opposition from the start from elements of the business community and the Chamber of Commerce. For example, city contract holder Lynn Kastella was a vocal opponent, stating that the ordinance would cost the city lots of money and would add an administrative burden. Furthermore, Kastella argued, "It's extremely unconstitutional to dictate to any private company what in the world they pay their people."[3]

However, the opposition to the campaign was never as organized as the supporters. Unlike the previous effort, this campaign came out of a broad community-wide coalition. Most of the city council members supported the effort fairly early on, once they were made aware of the breadth of support for the campaign. With thousands of residents demonstrating their interest in the issue, it was clear that public support was squarely behind this idea.

The education and organizing went on for about eighteen months, until the campaign felt it had built up enough momentum to push for passage. On September 13, 1999, with about 550 people in attendance at the hearing, the city council voted 5–2 to pass the ordinance. It required any firm with a city service contract to pay their employees, whether full- or part-time, eight dollars per hour with or nine dollars without health benefits. The wage is indexed to increase every year with the Consumer Price Index.[4]

A Noncampaign in Cincinnati

In contrast to the long-term efforts in cities like Tucson, where it can take years to pass a living wage ordinance, the city council of Cincinnati, Ohio, introduced and passed an ordinance in less than a month. On November 14, 2002, some city residents were surprised to read in the *Cincinnati Enquirer* that city council member John Cranley and Vice Mayor Alicia Reece were planning to introduce a living wage ordinance to the council.[5] Although a local group, the Coalition for a Just Cincinnati (formed in the wake of police abuse scandals in 2001), had been discussing a possible living wage campaign for some time, the local Labor Council president went on his own directly to his allies on the council to get an ordinance passed when he heard that the city was considering privatizing some services. While the coalition scrambled to comment on the ordinance and suggest improvements, the city council moved quickly. An ordinance was passed on November 27, to become effective three months later.

The ordinance covers city employees and those employed by service contractors (and their subcontractors) holding contracts worth twenty thousand dollars or more. Covered employers are required to pay $8.70 per hour with benefits, or $10.20 without (adjusted annually with inflation). Employers found to be in noncompliance are subject to penalties, which may include suspension or termination of the contract, repayment of the contract to the city, and disbarment from future contracts. Although the *Enquirer* reported that the ordinance was likely to be one of the first divisive issues to come before the council in some time—the six Democrats and two Republicans tended to be "remarkably united" on most issues—the ordinance passed with little debate, and almost no community input.[6]

Still Fighting in Providence

The Boston and Tucson campaigns are inspiring, both in the ability of the activists to create a solid and diverse coalition capable of winning an ordinance and staving off attacks, and in the impact the ordinance has had on workers' lives. But not all campaigns succeed. In Providence, Rhode Island, a group of supporters have been fighting for a living wage for more than four years but have yet to achieve victory.[7]

The Providence effort was spurred in large part by an established and thriving multiracial community organization—Direct Action for Rights and Equality (DARE). DARE was started in 1986 with the mission "to organize low-income families in communities of color to win economic, social and political justice." DARE is a community-based group that is not directly affiliated with a larger national organization. It is made up of individual members and families in the Providence area. As of 2002, approximately eight hundred families belonged to DARE. According to DARE, roughly 80 percent of its members are women, and almost all are low income.

In 1999, the Providence Central Labor Council (CLC) decided to build off of the success of the recent living wage victory in nearby Boston and mount a campaign of its own. The CLC pulled some people together, including Jobs with Justice members in the area. The Labor Council's approach was to simply substitute "Providence" for "Boston" in the Boston ordinance and put forth the proposal to the city. The mayor told the CLC that the time wasn't right, and that they should hold off on their demand.

While the Labor Council agreed to go with the mayor's request, others in the coalition were not ready to give up the campaign. Jobs with Justice members active in the effort went back to their organization and took the idea of pushing onward to DARE. According to DARE director Sara Mersha, when the DARE membership met in December 1998, they talked about how the idea was worth pursuing. Some DARE members were teacher's assistants—paid by city dollars, yet minimum wage and with no benefits. The living wage seemed like the perfect idea to raise awareness of low-wage work, and possibly win direct gains for some DARE members. As one bus driver and member of DARE remarked, "We transport the city's most important possession, its school children, and yet we are paid less than waste haulers. We work hard, and yet we're still falling behind. We deserve a living wage."[8]

The campaign officially began in February 1999. Soon after, Mersha and a DARE member and teacher's assistant Carmen Kunhardt went to Los Angeles to talk to the Los Angeles Alliance for a New Economy, to learn about their living wage campaign. They got ideas about how to run a campaign in Providence, and how to make sure that workers would see actual wage increases as a result. According to Sara Mersha, while many living wage campaigns start out of the desire of activists to find a winnable campaign, the Providence campaign came from real need. DARE members were active in the leadership of the group, and they saw higher wages as a key issue. DARE acknowledged that it was unlikely to be able to win the campaign on its own, and would need coalition partners to get something passed. The group immediately began to work with Jobs with Justice and other community allies to get the campaign moving.

The new coalition's goal was to win an ordinance in the first year, but it did not have a clear list of demands. They decided to work with Just Economics, a grassroots economic literacy organization based on the West Coast, to develop curriculum around living wage issues. Running workshops with community members, the living wage campaign was able to raise awareness about inequality and wages, as well as to work with participants to clarify the campaign's demands. The workshops had people work through living wage budgets, to determine for themselves what a real living wage level would be.

Out of this process, the campaign put together an ordinance proposal that included "everything we could dream of, and everything we felt we deserved."[9] That included a wage rate of $16.58, as well as demands for benefits and access to city jobs. As the coalition talked through their demands, they realized that they probably could not win a wage of more than $16 per hour. Nonetheless, they wanted to put this demand in the proposal and create an opening to talk to the community about the real cost of living. They decided to set $10 per hour as a minimum level below which they would not go. They chose to propose $16.41 per hour, which was 250 percent of the poverty level for a family of four, plus another $4.02 per hour for benefits, affirmative action requirements, and community hiring halls requiring employers to hire locally when possible.[10] The campaign also added a "labor peace" provision, which would allow the city to deny contracts or subsidies to employers with a history of labor law violations.

As the proposal took shape, the coalition went back to the Labor Council to persuade them to rejoin the campaign. Council leaders said the demands were too high, and said they would only sign on to the proposal if the wage was dropped to $12.30 per hour. The coalition agreed, and the group introduced their formal proposal to the city council in late 1999. Another interesting aspect of the Providence proposal was a clause outlawing discrimination in hiring against those with prison records. This was a result of DARE's Jobs Committee meeting with its Prisons Committee.

The campaign, now called the Providence Jobs and Living Wage Campaign, began to increase its visibility with rallies, press coverage, workshops, and actions. Jobs with Justice, which had been part of the coalition from the start, decided to increase its presence and put significant staff resources into the campaign. The evolving project created the space for some nominal members of Jobs with Justice to get more active, such as the public sector union AFSCME and various faith-based organizations. On September 26, 2000, the campaign joined an international effort to protest corporate globalization. On that day, protestors in Prague were attempting to stop International Monetary Fund and World Bank meetings being held there. Hundreds of rallies were held in solidarity around the world, including one in Providence. After a rally at City Hall, more than two hundred supporters marched into the offices of former Providence mayor Joseph Paolino Jr., now a major developer attempting to build a Hyatt hotel in the middle of downtown.[11] The coalition called for living wages and demanded that Paolino sign a neutrality agreement for the proposed hotel. Neutrality agreements are promises by employers or developers to not interfere with efforts to organize a union at a workplace. Unions have increasingly attempted to pressure employers into signing these agreements in recent years as a way to counter the pervasive use of anti-union tactics during unionization campaigns.

Paolino wouldn't agree to sign the neutrality agreement but in the end did consent to a meeting. Mersha believes this was one of the high points of the campaign, as it brought together a wide range of people, involved a lot of new activists, "was huge and fun," and was the biggest action Rhode Island Jobs with Justice had ever had.

Despite the success of the action, or perhaps because of it, just before the first public city council hearing, the *Providence Journal-Bulletin* editorialized against the living wage proposal, which they claimed was "bespeaking either a staggering ignorance or simply good old-fashioned demagoguery."[12] The ordinance was referred to as "almost incredible," "bizarre," and "deadly to the economy." Editors claimed that it would "sharply raise the Providence area unemployment rate, swiftly scare away business and send taxes into the stratosphere." Ordinance opponents, led by the Greater Providence Chamber of Commerce, pushed the city council to reject the measure.

Although it appeared that supporters outnumbered opponents, coalition members found themselves pressured to negotiate amendments to their living wage proposal as the city council appeared reluctant to sign on.[13] Some council members said they would support the proposal only if the clause prohibiting discrimination against those with prison records was modified. In the end, the coalition agreed to use federal Equal Employment Opportunity Commission policy language, which looked at the nature of the offense, time passed, and connection to the job. After some more time, the Laborers Union, part of the coalition and representatives of many city workers, notified living wage advocates that the Laborer's supporters on the council would only endorse the proposal if the wage were lowered to $11 per hour.

Meanwhile, as the campaign picked up steam and engaged in more actions such as door-to-door canvassing, collecting over twenty-five hundred postcards, and coordinating "living wage Sundays," the city council dragged its feet and called for more research. The Chamber of Commerce solicited a study that claimed the ordinance would result in $18 million in taxpayer costs and more than three thousand jobs lost. The business community organized the "Coalition to Keep Providence Working" and continued to speak out against the ordinance. Local newspapers published numerous negative articles about its potential impact.[14]

By early 2002, the campaign was feeling the pressure to win something. Organizers wanted to get some ordinance passed, yet have it be something that was still meaningful to those affected. The coalition was aware that their wage demand was considerably higher than the wage levels won in other New England cities. With Boston's living wage at only $10.25 per hour, activists began to see just how difficult it would be to win more in Providence. But when a suggestion was made to lower the wage level once again, to $10.19, there was dissension within the group. At the time that DARE members first agreed that they would demand $16 per hour but go no lower than $10, many members were still earning minimum wage and no benefits. But because of the living wage campaign and other successful organizing, a number of DARE leaders had themselves recently won raises. Most notably, substitute teachers' assistants in the Providence city schools won the right through collective bargaining to be converted to full-time positions (for the school year), and got their pay increased to $10.81 per hour.[15] Bus monitors had received raises as well, as a result of DARE organizing at the school board. Suddenly, reducing the living wage campaign demand to $10.19 seemed to some DARE members to be "selling out."

Deyanira Garcia, one of the teaching assistants who had been bumped up to $10.81, knew that even that was still too low—in part because the work was still only thirty hours a week, nine months a year. Garcia had seen firsthand that $10.81 was barely enough to make ends meet, even with a second job. It was hard enough for her to afford small treats like ice cream for her two children, let alone save anything for a college education.[16] In the end, after numerous committee and leadership meetings and one-on-one conversations, the desire for a victory won out. DARE members agreed to amend their proposal down to $10.19. This then went to the larger coalition, which adopted the change in March 2002.

Eventually the coalition agreed to drastically water down their demand for a community hiring hall—agreeing to a provision that would only require that jobs be posted through the state Department of Labor and Training and would urge (but not mandate) that three out of every four new hires be local residents. This set the stage for a minicrisis for the coalition. On April 15, the day of a scheduled city council hearing, a *Providence Journal-Bulletin* article quoted Jobs with Justice organizer Matthew Jerzyk criticizing the patronage in City Hall.[17] Jerzyk claimed that the campaign had to accept the watered-down hiring clause because the council and mayor refused to accept any reduction in their power to hire their friends and supporters. Jerzyk's comments angered one of the main coalition members—the Laborer's Union that represents most city workers. The union was so angered that they decided to pull out of the coalition for a year and tell their city council supporters not to approve the living wage proposal but to take up the issue again in 2003. Despite these obstacles and others—such as a the release of a report by the city's director of finance that claimed the ordinance would cost the city $16.3 million over a five year period—the campaign continues.[18]

What can be said about the Providence living wage campaign? Because it started in 1999 with the goal of winning something in the first year, should we judge the campaign a failure, four years later with no ordinance yet in place? The campaign has been rocky from the start, with several highs and lows. Numerous compromises have been made already, and others are likely necessary in order to get something passed. Living wage advocates have struggled against a city newspaper and business community that are especially opposed to the living wage, and a city council that has been slow to take a position. The campaign has also had a harder time than in some cities keeping together its tenuous coalition of labor and community organizations.

Yet it's clear that the living wage campaign has brought in new individual members for DARE, and new organizational members for Jobs with Justice—such as Sisters Overcoming Abusive Relationships (SOAR). The campaign gave energy to DARE's successful effort to win higher wages and permanent jobs for teacher's assistants and bus monitors. "I'm pretty amazed that people have stuck with it for so long," says Mersha. "That in itself is inspiring."

But perhaps most important, according to Mersha, is the impact of the campaign on worker organizing in Providence. While DARE kept a focus on the living wage campaign, it continued to keep worker organizing as a long-term and central goal. Throughout the course of the campaign, DARE's efforts led to victories for teaching assistants and bus monitors. In both cases, workers received wage increases and permanent jobs. While organizing bus drivers, DARE members happened to find out about fifty substitute school clerks making $7.65 per hour with no benefits. DARE introduced the clerks to an organizer with AFSCME Council 94, which represents the permanent clerks in the schools. A union drive was launched, and through house calls, a majority of the clerks signed union authorization cards. The school department has refused to recognize the union through the card count, so the union has filed for an election.

While the number of workers organized through the living wage campaign is not massive, the work has made a real difference for hundreds of people who provide essential services to Providence schools. In addition to higher wages, better benefits, and more permanent work, the effort has allowed workers to develop organizing and leadership skills and to build their own institutions.

Conclusion

The campaigns profiled in this chapter offer a few examples of tactics used, compromises made, and coalitions built in the living wage movement. Out of the almost two hundred living wage campaigns conducted as of 2003, including the successful, defeated, and ongoing, no two look alike. In every case, the actors in the coalition differ, as do the strategies employed. The broad-based and creative Providence living wage campaign has been going for more than four years and still the city does not have an enforceable ordinance. In Cincinnati, city council members introduced a living wage proposal with no campaign behind it and passed an ordinance within a few weeks. Because every campaign looks different, the cases profiled here are not necessarily typical. I chose to highlight them because they show the potential excitement and frustrations of a living wage campaign.

The cases are interesting for another reason. In chapter 3, I discussed the range of motivations that different organizations have for getting involved in the campaigns. The profiles presented in this chapter suggest some similarities and some differences in the motivations of the key actors. Labor and community groups in Boston and Tucson wanted to build coalitions that would act on behalf of workers' rights. DARE, in Providence, was less concerned about coalition building and more about winning concrete gains for members. In Cincinnati, the main advocates behind the ordinance were city councilors hoping to the allay concerns of their union allies about plans for privatization of city services. As I will argue, these different kinds of motivations can affect the likelihood of implementation success.

The tactics used in a campaign can be relevant in influencing implementation. In Boston, Tucson, and Providence, we see all campaigns utilizing inside and outside tactics. All three campaigns were highly contested—particularly in Providence, where the campaign is ongoing as of 2003. The Cincinnati ordinance passed with little controversy, and with only inside tactics.

To see how differing motivations for running campaigns and differing tactics and strategies can influence implementation, we now turn to a look at what happens after ordinances are passed. Many activists might decide that their job is over once they get the city council to approve the ordinance, and responsibility is handed over to city staff. As shown in chapter 5, this is usually not true.

5

LIVING WAGE OUTCOMES

We simply provided the information that they needed, documented it in the
files, and that was it. We didn't feel the need for a specific type of monitoring
system.

    Perlean Griffin, former living wage implementation officer, Toledo, as
quoted in Tom Troy, "'Living-wage' Questions Draw Blank at City Hall,"
Toledo Blade, April 4, 2002

Implementation struggles are far from the minds of most activists
at the start of a campaign. Their focus is on building a coalition, generat-
ing public awareness, and passing legislation. They generally assume that
if the law passes it will be implemented. If implementation doesn't happen
automatically, activists usually assume that city staff will be the ones who
work to ensure that the city enforces its own laws and they hope that the
city does so effectively. But it is not just activists that hold these assumptions: a central tenet of American liberal democracy is that our elected representatives pass laws the people want, and our civil servants carry out
those laws.

Unfortunately, living wage advocates have paid relatively little attention to what happens to the ordinances once they are passed. In many
cases, cities are ignoring the ordinances as well, leading to unsuccessful
implementation.[1] In this chapter, I profile a few examples of implementation outcomes, starting with an example of strong enforcement in Tucson,
Arizona, then turning to cases of less successful implementation in a
number of other cities. However, to begin this discussion we need to
define what is meant by "successful implementation."

Measurement of Success

Success in policy implementation can be measured in various ways. Policy outcomes are often judged by specific measures directly related to the law, such as, in the case of living wage ordinances, the number of workers eligible for wage increases who actually receive them or the number of firms who claim to be in compliance with the law. These measurements may not tell the whole story, however. For example, advocates of the 1990s welfare reform legislation claim these laws have been successful because the number of persons receiving welfare benefits has decreased since the enactment of the reforms. This type of statistic does not capture the full impact of such laws, since many of the recipients leaving the welfare rolls are not finding work or not finding work that pays family-sustaining wages.[2] For this reason, we must also consider implementation outcomes vis-à-vis the range of goals behind them.

In addition to looking at policymakers' goals, another way to measure success is to consider indirect benefits, such as how the living wage campaign led to outcomes desirable to the advocacy groups. For example, struggles over the implementation process may lead to an increase in citizen involvement in local government, the passage of other policies, or the restructuring of government agencies. Of course, these are just as likely to be negative outcomes as they are positive ones, depending on the goals of the advocacy groups. However, the positive indirect outcomes are sometimes a greater "success" than the direct outcomes of the policy implementation. As mentioned in chapter 3, for living wage advocates, these goals include influencing the public discourse on wages and work, organizing low-wage workers, and strengthening their own organizations.

As other implementation researchers have discovered, part of the difficulty in measuring outcomes is the difficulty in obtaining accurate data. As one example, a growing number of corporations, educational institutions, and nongovernmental organizations have begun to take concrete steps to eliminate the hazardous and abusive conditions of garment workers in the global South. Despite a growing number of experiments monitoring factories for labor abuses, the lack of consistent data hampers researchers' ability to evaluate the effectiveness of different mechanisms. Fung, O'Rourke, and Sabel write that the first step toward improving sweatshop monitoring is making the methods and results transparent. This means establishing monitoring criteria that are well-known and understood by all interested parties. Monitors then should evaluate compliance in a standard way, write up their results, and make those reports publicly available. Benchmarks should be established to compare the performance of manufacturing facilities and monitors.[3]

Access to data is a problem in measuring living wage implementation as well. In many cities it is difficult to find a staff person who can answer questions about the ordinance. In few cases can staff give data on number of workers and contracts covered by the ordinance, and the percentage of those workers receiving the living wage. For this reason, it is difficult to base an assessment on these quantitative measures alone. Therefore, I rely on various criteria to measure successful implementation, including an assessment of the implementation process. First, I divide the process into four steps: administration, monitoring, enforcement, and evaluation.

Administration refers to initial steps to implement the ordinance: assigning a department and staff person to be held accountable for implementation; establishing transparent rules and regulations to clarify which employers are covered and how the ordinance will be carried out; notifying relevant city departments and staff about the ordinance; and informing covered employers and employees. I have also included a measure that gauges how easy it is for the public to get information on the ordinance (see table 5.1). Monitoring includes taking steps to assess the degree to which firms are complying with the rules and regulations of the ordinance. This includes procedural changes that make it easier for the city to monitor compliance, such as requiring covered employers to submit payroll records, as well as active steps taken to monitor firm compliance, such as regular visits to workplaces. Enforcement refers to the actions pursued when employers are found to be in noncompliance with any of the provisions of the ordinance. Finally, evaluation refers to steps taken by city or county staff to assess the implementation process over time, including identifying loopholes and looking for ways to correct problems.

To determine which municipalities have been most successful in implementation, I rate each case along the fourteen dimensions listed in table 5.1. For example, a municipality is given a 1 if there is a department with one or more persons assigned to implementation, or a 0 if there is no one accountable. I gave a 1 for "waivers difficult to obtain" if I found at least one case where a request for waiver was denied by city officials. "Easy to get information" was scored as a 1 if the city had made information about the ordinance easily available on the city website, or if it was easy to reach a knowledgeable staff person by phone when contacting the city. (A full description of the measurement criteria can be found in appendix C.)

Table 5.1. Measurements of implementation success

Administration

City assigns implementation to a particular department and staff person
Rules and regulations are established to determine coverage and apply ordinance
Training provided for other city departments that let contracts
Ordinance language in Request for Proposals for contracts
Employers required to post notices at worksites
Easy to get information about the ordinance

Monitoring

Employers must file payroll records on request of city
Employers must file payroll records on regular basis
Contracts regularly reviewed by city staff
Worksites regularly monitored

Enforcement

Waivers from ordinance difficult to obtain
City applies penalties to those in noncompliance

Evaluation

City staff writes implementation evaluation reports
City attempts to close loopholes in ordinance

Based on the total scores, I classified cities into four categories: expansive implementation (those scoring 9 to 14), moderate implementation (5 to 8), narrow implementation (1 to 4), and blocked implementation (0). Although the specifics vary by location, in general implementation is strongest (expansive) where there is at least one full-time person assigned to oversee ordinance administration who can answer questions about the law and who can be held accountable for problems. In this setup, staff people actively monitor the ordinance by reviewing payroll records and inspecting worksites. The ordinance is treated as a living document designed to meet certain goals. Here, staff try to improve on the ordinance through regular evaluation and recommend amendments to the original language in order to best stay in line with the goals of the policy. Staff members attempt to create benchmarks by compiling data on contracts, as well as on the number of employers and employees covered by the ordinance. Information on living wage coverage and compliance is made available to the public. Under expansive implementation, employers requesting waivers must prove their case of economic hardship to the city.

At the other extreme, we have narrow implementation, where cities do the minimum to fulfill the technical requirements of the law. In these cases, there is not any full-time staff person assigned to administer the law. It is not always easy to find one person who knows about all aspects of the ordinance or can answer questions. Requests for proposals for city bids contain information about the living wage requirement, and employers are asked to sign forms saying they are in compliance with all regulations, but little more is done unless a complaint of noncompliance is filed. Under narrow implementation, it is easy for employers to receive a waiver from the ordinance. These were cities that scored between 1 and 4 of the 14 criteria.

In between broad and narrow implementation, we have "moderate" outcomes—those scoring positively for 5 to 8 of the criteria. Here, there is at least one accountable staff person who can answer basic questions about the ordinance and who reviews payroll records for compliance. However, no active monitoring is conducted unless a complaint is filed, and little effort is made to evaluate or improve the ordinance. Finally, we have "blocked implementation," where the city refuses to implement, the city or state legally challenges the ordinance, or employers threaten to sue the city, causing (sometimes permanent) delays in enforcement.

One challenge in classifying cities is that outcomes change over time. For example, as mentioned earlier, implementation in Boston, Massachusetts, was initially blocked. However, after a year of negotiations, the process began, and eventually the city became a prime example of expansive implementation. For purposes of classification, I rate cities on the implementation measures at one point in time: the end of 2002. While we lack solid measures of outcomes in many cities and counties, it is clear looking at table 5.2 that out of the scores of living wage ordinances, only 14 percent fall into the category of expansive implementation. One strong example can be found in Tucson, Arizona.

Expansive Implementation: Tucson, Arizona

By most measures, living wage implementation was working well in Tucson, Arizona, by the end of 2002. A long dynamic campaign led by the Pima County Interfaith Council and the Southern Arizona Central Labor Council resulted in the passage of a living wage ordinance in 1999. Responsibility for implementation was put into the hands of the Finance Department, in the Contract Administration division of the Tucson city

Table 5.2. Implementation efforts by cities and counties, ordinances passed through 2002

Blocked	Narrow	Moderate	Expansive
Buffalo, NY	Ashland, OR	Ann Arbor, MI	Alexandria, VA
Camden, NJ	Bozeman, MT	Baltimore, MD	Boston, MA
Hempstead, NY	Charlottesville, VA	Berkeley, CA	Los Angeles, CA
Monroe County, MI	Chicago, IL	Burlington, VT	LA County, CA
Omaha, NE	Cook County, IL	Cambridge, MA	Miami-Dade, FL
Pittsburgh, PA	Cumberland County, NJ	Cleveland, OH	San Francisco, CA
Santa Monica, CA	Dane County, WI	Corvallis, OR	San Jose, CA
St. Louis, MO	Denver, CO	Duluth, MN	Santa Cruz, CA
	Des Moines, IA	Hartford, CT	Santa Cruz County, CA
	Detroit, MI	Hayward, CA	Tucson, AZ
	Durham, NC	Madison, WI	Ventura County, CA
	Eau Claire County, WI	Miami Beach, FL	
	Eastpointe, MI	Minneapolis, MN	
	Fairfax, CA	New Haven, CT	
	Ferndale, MI	Oakland, CA	
	Gary, IN	Pasadena, CA	
	Gloucester County, NJ	Port of Oakland, CA	
	Hudson County, NJ	Somerville, MA	
	Jersey City, NJ	Suffolk County, NY	
	Meriden, CT	Toledo, OH	
	Milwaukee City, WI		
	Milwaukee County, WI		
	Milwaukee S. Board, WI		
	Missoula, MT		
	Multnomah County, OR		
	New York, NY		
	New Britain, CT		
	Oyster Bay, NY		
	Pittsfield Township, MI		
	Portland, OR		
	Richmond, CA		
	Richmond S. Board, VA		
	Rochester, NY		
	San Antonio, TX		
	San Fernando, CA		
	Santa Clara County, CA		
	St. Paul, MN		
	Warren, MI		
	Washtenaw County, MI		
	West Hollywood, CA		
	Ypsilanti, MI		
	Ypsilanti Township, MI		
8	42	20	11
(10% of total)	(52% of total)	(25% of total)	(14% of total)

Source: Author's analysis based on ordinances, interviews, and review of relevant documents.

government. The division, directed by Marcheta Gillespie, already had a full-time staff of seven people, who were charged with ensuring that the city's contracts were being responsibly let and fulfilled. Gillespie determined that it was necessary to have a full-time person in charge of living wage compliance, and a job opening was posted shortly after the ordinance was passed. Ray Valdez, who had been working in the city's affordable housing program, applied for and got the job in early 2000.

Valdez's work consisted of determining which city contracts were covered under the ordinance, developing procedures to notify contractors about the law, and setting up a system to determine compliance. When new contracts were let or existing ones rebid, Valdez worked with the department in charge of the contract to ensure that living wage language was put into the bid. Staff received a handout titled "Solicitation Language to Be Included in Special Terms and Conditions." Valdez then attended the "preservices conference" for potential bidders, where he covered the requirements of the law and made sure they understood the need to bid based on the living wage level, and handed out copies of the ordinance and other relevant forms. After the city awarded a contract, Valdez continued to work with the contractor to make sure they filed the appropriate paperwork—primarily, the contractor was required to submit payroll records for all covered employees to Valdez on a biweekly basis.

Valdez did more than work with other city staff and contractors to enforce the ordinance. He estimated that he also spent about 40 percent of his time each week at worksites, talking to workers to see if they were indeed receiving the living wage and benefits they were entitled to. Valdez developed a card with information about the ordinance and his phone number, which he handed out at worksites. In the few cases of noncompliance to date, Valdez generally corrected the problems immediately by talking with employers.

Representatives from the Interfaith Council met with the Procurement Department staff occasionally to check in on the status of implementation, but otherwise, Valdez did not work closely with the living wage coalition. Mostly he was on his own, given a fair degree of autonomy from his supervisors to implement the living wage ordinance. Living wage supporters noted that they were pleased with the city's handling of implementation and found no cause for concern.

Living wage implementation in Tucson appears to be a textbook case: this is how city bureaucracies should work. Unfortunately, this is not the standard outcome. As will be seen in the next section, city staff cannot be relied on to implement the ordinances on their own. What is happening in other cities?

Narrow and Blocked Implementation

About a year after the city of Toledo, Ohio, passed a living wage ordinance covering city service contractors and recipients of economic development subsidies, the city council was considering a request from a developer for a living wage waiver. The outdated Southwyck Shopping Center asked the city for a tax abatement in order to help finance a renovation, including converting the old Montgomery Ward's into a Sears. Under the ordinance, the abatement on the $100 million dollar renovation would require Southwyck and Sears to pay the living wage of $9.57 an hour with, or $11.31 without, health benefits. Both Southwyck and Sears argued that they could not afford to pay the living wage.[4]

To decide if he would support the waiver, city council member Louis Escobar asked the city administration for information on the living wage ordinance. To his surprise, the city could not tell him how many employers had been covered, the impact of the ordinance on employers, or even the fiscal impact on the city. In fact, when first asked, city administrators did not even know the living wage amount, and took two days to calculate it. City administrators admitted that no action had been taken on implementation of the ordinance. But they weren't the only ones who had forgotten about the living wage. Living wage supporters had also moved onto other things after enactment and had not been following the city implementation progress.

Unfortunately, Toledo's case is not unusual. In fifty cases, implementation of the ordinance has been narrow or completely blocked (see table 5.2). This can happen for a number of reasons, which we will discuss in chapter 6. In some places, implementation seems to simply fall through the cracks: there is no one person in charge, and no one who knows much about the ordinance. Beyond that, there are cities in which the staff are incompetent, ineffective, or personally hostile to the ordinances. Third, there are cities where the administrations are outwardly opposed to the ordinances and work to stall implementation or water down or repeal them, sometimes with assistance from employer associations. Finally, some city councilors and/or administrators continue to publicly support living wage ordinances but make it easy for employers to receive waivers or exemptions from coverage. I will briefly review each of these cases.

No One in Charge

Unlike Tucson, most cities don't have any one person assigned the job of living wage oversight. Instead, the job falls to a department, or departments, already doing other tasks. For example, in Toledo, the city council assumed that the Office of Affirmative Action and Contract Compliance was implementing the ordinance. However, no one staff person took charge, and as city staff turned over after an election, the job fell even further through the cracks. In the cities without staff, enforcement is complaint-driven, meaning that if workers call the city to say they are not receiving the living wage, the city has the power to investigate the claim and require compliance and possibly impose penalties. In the absence of complaints and assigned staff, it is highly unlikely that anyone will check payroll records or visit worksites. It is difficult for a worker to file a complaint if there is no department or person assigned to living wage implementation, so the absence of complaints may be an effect of poor implementation as well as a cause for it.

One might assume that once a city passes an ordinance, city staff would become familiar with its provisions. Unfortunately, this is not always the case. From 1999 to early 2002, I led a research team surveying all municipalities with living wage ordinances. We assumed the role of an average business owner or worker with questions about the law, and started by calling the city's general information number. In an alarming number of cases, the city operators had no knowledge of such an ordinance. Our effort to contact living wage officials in the city of Chicago was typical. We were calling in 2000, two years after Chicago had passed its ordinance. However, the person answering the phone insisted the city had no such ordinance, and that we must mean the minimum wage and therefore had to talk to the state Department of Labor.

In most of the calls, the operator transferred us to a department that might possibly know about the ordinance. In a few cases, usually after several transfers, we were successful in reaching the responsible department. Sometimes, the multiple transferring was not successful, and we ended up in an infinite loop with no one who could answer basic questions about the living wage. We then attempted to call back, this time looking up the number for the department most likely in charge of enforcement: procurement, finance, or contract compliance. Even in these cases it was sometimes a difficult task. For example, in Miami-Dade, which has active enforcement, the following account shows how difficult it was to find the person responsible for living wage implementation. The

Miami-Dade ordinance had been in effect for ten months when one member of our research team attempted to speak to someone about its impact. She reports:

> I called the Procurement Department, which was listed [in the law] as overseeing implementation. No one there knew what I was talking about, so I was transferred to "Action Metro." They didn't know what I was talking about, so I was transferred to the question desk of "Action Metro." They didn't know what I was talking about and after putting me on hold they transferred me to the local office of the Department of Labor. I [sent email to] Eric Rodriquez from Procurement and asked if he was the proper person to speak with. He emailed me and told me that the Office of Business Development and Alice in particular, dealt with the living wage. I called the office to get a copy of the ordinance and the woman on the phone didn't know what I was talking about. Finally, I was transferred to someone who knew what I was talking about but she had no access to the ordinance. [She said] my request would be forwarded to Alice.[5]

Alice Hidalgo-Gato did then contact our research team and was prompt and helpful. But the experience suggests how difficult it can be to learn about the living wage ordinance, particularly for someone who was not as persistent as we were, or someone who did not have access to phone and email, or who could not call during business hours. Miami-Dade is not alone: similar stories could be told about a number of municipalities, where we were transferred and cut off multiple times before reaching a person with information about the ordinance.

We also worked to find information about the ordinances on city web pages. The existence of information has improved over the past few years as web access in general has improved. But even as of 2002, for only twenty-two cities was it possible to easily get a copy of the ordinance from the web page, and even fewer had additional information, such as a contact name and phone number for questions.

Given how difficult it was for university researchers to obtain information about the ordinances in some cities, it is likely that low-wage workers would have much more trouble finding out about their rights under the ordinances and figuring out how to file complaints for noncompliance.

Understaffed

For those cities that do know about their ordinances and have at least part-time staff to monitor, the number of staff varies. In part, it varies due to political decisions over the availability of city funds to hire or assign staff to the work. It also varies due to the number of firms covered by and kinds of provisions included in the ordinance. Larger cities and cities where the scope of the law is broad will need more staff. In cities where the ordinance has narrow coverage, like New Haven, Connecticut, where only twelve to fifteen service contracts are covered in a given year, the city can manage by assigning implementation duties to a city staff member who spends most of his/her time on other work. Mark Pietrosimone, New Haven city controller, estimates that approximately a half day per week of staff time is needed for living wage implementation. This includes the time spent by Procurement Officer Michael Fumiatti, who informs bidders of the living wage requirement and checks basic compliance as part of his broader duties approving contracts, and by Internal Auditor Ed Zack, who reviews payroll records submitted by contractors. Whether this amount is sufficient remains to be seen, but at the minimum New Haven has city staff that can answer questions about the ordinance, provide copies of contracts, and conduct some payroll review.

Other cities have assigned one or more people to work full-time on living wage implementation. In Tucson, for example, one person oversees implementation on approximately fifty contracts, while in Los Angeles, four and a half staff oversee implementation on approximately a thousand contracts. There is no consistent formula for staff-to-covered contract ratios.

Because the implementation responsibilities are tacked onto the other work of procurement officers, they do not consider it a part of their job to enforce the law. If questioned, many of these procurement officers note that it is the job of the contracting personnel in each department to follow up with monitoring. But those department personnel don't know this, or don't have the time or inclination to do so. Again, enforcement doesn't happen.

The problems listed here are several. First, there is a lack of accountability: no one person is in charge of implementation and enforcement. There is not a city staff person who can answer questions about the ordinance, who can produce all relevant materials and paperwork, and who has access to employers and workers.

Second, even where one person may be accountable, he/she is usually overworked, with living wage enforcement being tacked onto the full-time job they already hold. Because they want to avoid the expense and don't want to be known as an administration that expands bureaucracy instead of shrinking it, most cities have been reluctant to hire new staff for the work. So, staff that have already been monitoring contracts for compliance with prevailing wage or affirmative action, or staff in charge of processing contracts, may be asked to take on the task.

In many cities, a decade or more of downsizing had already led to an overworked staff. During the Milwaukee campaign, city council member and living wage supporter Ruth Zubrensky raised the concern of adding more administrative tasks to the already overburdened prevailing wage monitors. She wrote in a memo:

> The DPW [Department of Public Works] has only one man, Dave Lewis, who analyzes payroll records. He is always a year or more behind (partly because he can't tell if there has been compliance until a contractor has completed the job—the department is hopelessly without computer capability in being able to analyze payroll information.) . . . Presumably, Dave Lewis could add on the administration [of the living wage ordinance] to his already burdensome responsibilities, I don't know.[6]

The Milwaukee activists also pursued other options, including working with the Equal Opportunity Office and the Equal Rights Commission to identify ways that they might be able to take on the compliance responsibilities. This was because of the city's refusal to add new staff to implement the law. In the end, the job in Milwaukee was split, with the DPW in charge of monitoring their own contracts, and the Standards and Procurement Division in charge of all other contracts.

Staff Resistance

Another way in which implementation gets held up was referred to in chapter 2. It cannot be assumed that city administrators are sympathetic with the goals of the living wage ordinance and will work their hardest to ensure enforcement. While there is conscientious staff such as Ray Valdez in Tucson, not all city employees share their commitment or dedication.

One example of this can be found in Los Angeles. Los Angeles has not suffered understaffing problems in the way that most other cities have. When the city council passed the ordinance, it included a directive for the Bureau of Contract Administration (BCA) to take charge of enforcement and to place five people on the job. BCA senior management analyst Jalal Sudan was put in charge.

Initially, living wage coalition members were enthusiastic about their chances to work with the staff assigned to monitor the ordinance. Coalition members wrote regulations to accompany the ordinance, which were adopted. Coalition leader Madeline Janis-Aparicio praised the process: "It really is a wonderful streamlining of a horrendously bureaucratic system, and that's being nice. We think they are model regulations. This is how the city should work. Everybody should know what to do, where to go, and everyone should know what their rights and responsibilities are."[7]

Once the ordinance and regulations were in place, the BCA began to focus on several aspects of implementation: determining which contracts were covered under the law and developing materials to educate department managers, contract administrators, and contractors about the ordinance. This step was contentious, as there were disagreements early on as to which firms were covered under the law.

Major disputes arose when airlines at the Los Angeles and Ontario airports claimed that the law did not apply to them or their subcontractors. After several months, the city had not yet reached a decision over the matter, leaving both sides frustrated. A *Los Angeles Times* reporter wrote: "The struggle to agree on a definition of the ordinance and to coherently implement it says much about the way business often is done in Los Angeles government—slowly, ineffectively and at cross-purposes, leaving almost no one involved in the process happy."[8]

Another area of contention involved the education and training of workers. Living wage coalition representatives managed to insert a provision in the regulations requiring the BCA to provide training to workers covered by the ordinances to inform them of their rights under the laws. However, the coalition found the BCA slow to develop and initiate the trainings, forcing the coalition to continue pressuring the BCA through city council member Jackie Goldberg's office.[9] The BCA soon declared that the coalition could not play an official role in the training, as it was not a neutral body. According to Janis-Aparicio, "They won't let any union people do the training, since they are afraid they will say the U word."[10] Coalition members then negotiated an arrangement for some lawyers associated with their nonprofit, the Los Angeles Alliance for a New Economy (LAANE), to take part in the development of educational materials and training.[11] Eventually an agreement was reached for LAANE to provide two training sessions per month for one year, to workers covered by the living wage law. However, disagreements over training materials, content, and process continued to arise. According to Linda Lotz of the living wage coalition, "This finally culminated in a series of disastrous sessions at the Los Angeles International Airport where the BCA basically allowed a dozen employers to intimidate workers." After awhile, LAANE decided to end their partnership to provide training with the BCA.

It is not clear what was behind the disagreements between the BCA and the living wage coalition, but the relationship had grown sour fast. After the first year of the ordinance, the living wage coalition submitted a "report card" to the city council on the implementation efforts of selected city departments and actors. The coalition gave the BCA a "C-" for its efforts, for the following reasons:

- their emphasis on contract eligibility rather than enforcement;
- insufficient efforts to educate and pressure departments to comply;
- inadequate worker complaint system;
- the difficulty the public faced getting this information about contracting, even though the regulations guarantee public access to such information.

But it was not only the living wage coalition that gave low marks for the BCA. UCLA law professor Richard Sander had been hired as a consultant by the city to act as a neutral outsider to evaluate the ordinance. Sander's report concluded that a thorough evaluation of the law was not even possible after one year due to severe problems in policy implementation. Sander outlined these problems in a memo:

- Most contracts entered into by the city were not being submitted to the BCA in the first place. This meant that the BCA could not make a determination on the contracts eligibility under the law, and the contractors were not being told to pay the living wage. Sander did not have access to complete data but estimated that only 38 percent of all contracts were submitted to the BCA for review in the first year.
- Although the law requires covered employers to submit compliance reports every six months, only a small percentage of employers did so. Sander stated that the BCA had been passive in requesting the reports.
- The BCA had spent little effort on enforcement in general, and most effort was placed on determining which contracts were covered by the law.
- Specifically, Sander found no evidence that the BCA had begun to determine which firms were covered under the provision of the ordinance covering economic development. No effort had been made to require these firms to comply.

- Finally, Sander wrote that the BCA's approach to implementing the ordinance has "tended to be mechanical and bureaucratic, rather than substantive and creative." For example, Sander argued that the form the BCA used to collect payroll information was "rigid and misleading" because it contained little instruction and left employers to interpret as much of the law as they wished. Furthermore, the form led employers to spend significant time calculating wages and benefits for employees not even covered by the law.

Sander concluded, "The BCA's performance in implementing LWO has been so dismal to date that I am not optimistic that it can be remedied." Speculation rose that Mayor Richard Riordan, who had vetoed the ordinance, was behind the weak implementation. Deputy Mayor Kelly Martin responded, noting that while the mayor continued to oppose the law, she had seen "no evidence the law is not being followed" and that "the mayor's personal opposition to the ordinance has not prevented city departments from implementing it."[12]

Whatever the reason for the BCA's performance, after several more months of back and forth reports and hearings, the city council took major steps to revise the law and improve implementation. In particular, at the urging of the living wage coalition, the council moved implementation from the charge of Sudan at the BCA to June Gibson, at the City Administrative Office (CAO).[13] The CAO's office had been cooperative with the living wage ordinance; Gibson had worked there for ten years and was considered an "experienced and widely respected City Hall insider."[14]

There is some disagreement about the causes of the problems with the BCA. Some in the living wage coalition felt that the BCA staff lagged on implementation because the BCA staff and management were opposed to labor's increasing political power, embodied in the passage of the living wage. However, former LAANE staff member Nari Rhee believes the BCA had done their job poorly in part because of "bureaucratic incompetence."[15] From the start, the BCA was plagued by staff turnover and had a hard time keeping all positions filled throughout their first year. According to Sudan, the BCA supervisor, this resulted in delays: "We can respond to our duties, but it would be more timely if we were at full staff." However, Rhee argues that the BCA's largest problem was not *understaffing* but a lack of *qualified* staff. She explains the hiring process:

The civil service system only takes in new people once a year, maybe. The applicants are graded on a list for hiring, for each job category. When any department goes to hire, they can choose off that list. When the BCA hired for monitoring staff, it was at the end of a hiring year so they really picked from the bottom of the barrel. The people they hired are very uninterested, and not at all motivated to work. Some senior management there have interest, have a stake in the work and the process but not the staff. One of them even slept through a meeting with us. These people have no idea of the political significance of the work.

In fact, many living wage coalition members and advocates noted problems within the BCA. Another former LAANE staff member, Julie Park, stated: "They are just incompetent, and don't care about the ordinance." Sharon Delugach, assistant to city council member Goldberg, referred to the BCA staff as "the flat liners," in reference to their failure to implement the law. LAANE argued that most of the staff were not even qualified to answer questions when workers call. For example, despite the fact that the majority of covered workers are Spanish-speakers, the BCA had no Spanish-speaking staff to deal with worker complaints.

LAANE staff thinks that some of the difficulties may arise from civil servants who are overly cautious about their jobs. Rhee comments, "I think that these departments are suspicious of all community groups and don't want to have any information used against them. They are protective and bureaucratic." Others also complained about the "sloth, resistance and caution" keeping the bureaucracy from adequately implementing the law.[16] For example, following up on Sander and Lokey's report about implementation problems, *Los Angeles Times* reporter Ted Rohrlich sought contact with the BCA. The following is his account of that effort:

Seeking comment, a reporter first called the agency's director, C. Bernard Gilpin, who was said by his secretary to be out of the office for an extended period. The secretary suggested an alternative, Bob Hayes, the director of public affairs and the usual media contact for the agency's umbrella organization, the Department of Public Works.

Hayes said he did not know enough to comment and suggested Ellen Stein, president of the Board of Public Works, who had been briefed by Gilpin. But Stein's secretary said she was on vacation; perhaps another board member would talk.

Board secretary James Gibson then called back to suggest that a reporter try Gilpin's underling, Dave T. Peterson. But Peterson would not come to the phone. His secretary said any request for comment would have to be submitted in writing—to Gilpin.

Two days later, Peterson called back, saying that unidentified people "higher on the food chain" had instructed him to talk.

Whether due to staff hostility, incompetence, or bureaucratic ineffectiveness, it is clear that the BCA's oversight of living wage implementation was seriously lagging. As will be seen in the next chapter, the situation in Los Angeles greatly improved once responsibility was moved to the Chief Administrative Office.

City Holds Up Enforcement

While it is not clear whether the BCA held up implementation for political reasons, or if they simply were not effective in doing their job, in a few cities implementation problems are clearly the result of ideological opposition to the living wage. The best-known example of this is in Buffalo, New York, where city officials simply refused to implement the law, claiming that they had no staff available to do so. Although the ordinance was passed by a unanimous city council vote, signed by the mayor in July 1999 and set to go into effect July 2000, by December 2000 the city had not acted to implement. Living wage advocates continued to try to meet with city officials, but it wasn't until February 2001 that the city designated a department to oversee the administration. After pressure, the mayor's chief of staff sent a one-sentence memo to all city departments, asking them to submit a list of their contractors to the office of contract compliance, but no department responded. Another memo was eventually sent, and after some time about two-thirds of departments responded to the memo but did not provide lists of contractors. As of July 1, 2001, two years after the law was passed, not a single person had received a living wage increase, and the city still did not have a list of covered contractors.

Living wage activists believe that despite the unanimous vote, the council and mayor were not behind the ordinance. In fact, the Buffalo law is weaker than many others: the wage is at a lower level and the contract threshold amount significantly higher than the average. Some believe that city leaders wanted to be known as living wage supporters but were unwilling to have an ordinance with teeth. In the end, two organizations joined to file a lawsuit against the city to push them to implement. In 2002 the state supreme court ordered the city to demonstrate compliance efforts. In response, the city council amended to law by a 12 to 1 vote to relieve the city of any implementation responsibilities and instead place the entire burden of enforcement on workers themselves. When the Coalition for Economic Justice held a public forum in early 2003 in order to develop a volunteer task force to administer the law, a hundred residents—but only four city councilors—showed up.

City opposition was also found in St. Louis and Detroit—two of the few cities where ordinances were passed by ballot initiative rather than council vote. In St. Louis, after 77 percent of voters approved a city living wage law in August 2000, the mayor announced that he would not enforce the law in the Community Improvement District located in the city center. Here, too, advocates were forced to bring a lawsuit against the city. Business groups countersued, claiming that a state law passed in 1997 prevented municipalities from setting their own wage floors. The courts ruled against this claim, stating that Missouri municipalities could enact their own wage laws. However, the courts set aside the ordinance, citing sections in which the law passed was too vague. (The St. Louis City Council came back to pass another ordinance in 2002).

Detroit voters also approved a living wage measure by a large margin (81 percent in favor) in 1998 but then faced a city government reluctant to enforce it. Soon after the ordinance was approved, a spate of campaigns developed around the state, prompting opponents to look for ways to stop the living wage movement. Their strategy was to work at the state level, pushing legislators to outlaw municipal wage ordinances. Detroit officials claimed that they needed to hold off on living wage enforcement until the state matter was settled. The mayor froze the account set aside to pay for implementation and refused to hire staff. Legislative sessions came and went, with living wage opponents unable to gather enough support to pass their state law. Living wage supporters began to push the city to move on implementation but found more resistance. As in Los Angeles, Detroit city officials were slow in their actions and narrow in their interpretation. A new mayor came in and agreed to hire staff, but although a call went out in January 2002, no one had yet been hired by late 2003, five years after the ordinance was passed.

In the meantime, city attorneys ruled that they would not apply the ordinance to any workers covered by a collective bargaining agreement. Although a number of ordinances have "collective bargaining supersession" clauses, the intent of the ordinance is to allow the living wage to be waived only in cases where both parties in the collective bargaining agreement agree. Once again, living wage supporters were forced to consider a lawsuit, with the Guild Law Center representing unions who claimed that their members had a right to be covered by the ordinance.

These cases illustrate what policy scholars Hill and Weissert call "the irony of delegation," where implementation fails because bureaucratic channels can be used to thwart initiatives.[17] In the case of federal radioactive waste disposal policy, cited by Hill and Weissert, the delegation of enforcement from Congress to states allowed a space for state leaders to stall implementation efforts. State officials found it was worthwhile to delay procedures that could be costly and burdensome, and hoped that changes in the federal policy would eventually justify their actions. In the case of living wages, the "irony of delegation" was used to delay implementation in Detroit. City administrators used impending changes in state law as a reason to delay living wage enforcement.

Omaha, Nebraska, presents the most extreme case of city leaders opposing a living wage ordinance. The city council adopted an ordinance in the spring of 2000, overriding a mayoral veto. Later that year, a city election was held, bringing in a new council majority who were committed to repealing the law. The ordinance went into effect January 1, 2001, so had only been partially implemented when the council took up the issue of living wage repeal. After some debate, they voted to rescind the living wage measure in August 2001. Interestingly, there was also a new mayor—one who supported keeping the ordinance and vetoed the new council's repeal. Once again, the council overrode the mayoral veto, repealing the living wage ordinance for good.

Waivers

The cases above show how poor performance or ideological opposition can weaken or stop living wage enforcement across the board. But in many cities, enforcement is watered down through the process of issuing exemptions. In addition to establishing general categories that are exempt from coverage (such as nonprofits), many living wage ordinances allow the city council or other city administrative bodies to grant exemptions or waivers from coverage in the case of financial hardship or other extenuating circumstances.

The exemption option has been exercised in numerous cities, often with little attention or fanfare. This has been most common in the case of economic development, where firms asking for subsidies say they will not come to the city if they have to pay the living wage. In some cases, the city officials argue that the project does not qualify for living wage coverage, either because there are not any city funds going into the subsidies, or the amount of the local funds is not enough to trigger coverage. Because many subsidy negotiations are held in private and information is not easy to access, living wage advocates outside of city government are at the mercy of city officials negotiating the deals.

One example of this was in Oakland, California, where the city council approved a plan to convert an old building into a hotel. The city claimed that the developers were not asking for a subsidy and would therefore not be required to pay the living wage. However, living wage supporters pointed out that the city sold the building for only $825,000, where a neighboring building sold for $1.7 million two years earlier. In addition, the city planned to provide the new hotel with parking spaces and the use of a rooftop garden on city-owned property nearby.[18] This, living wage proponents argued, amounted to a hidden subsidy that would easily be large enough to qualify the developers for the living wage requirement.

Similarly, although the St. Paul City Council unanimously approved a living wage policy in 1997, they were lenient with exemptions once the policy was in place. Soon after the law was adopted, the council, under the direction of then-mayor Norm Coleman, granted an exemption to a Minnesota Mutual development project.[19] In this case, it was clear that the city's subsidies would qualify the project for the living wage: the city set up a tax-increment financing arrangement whereby the city would borrow $15 million from Minnesota Mutual, which it would use to buy the property and prepare it for construction.[20] The city would sell the land back to Minnesota Mutual for $1, with the loan repaid over twenty-five years. The city argued that the project would create two thousand new jobs, of which only nine would be below the living wage, and therefore the project abided by the spirit of the policy. But living wage supporters didn't buy the city's argument, and filled City Hall to demand that the city do a better job with enforcement. While any one case may have had grounds for a waiver, advocates claimed the agency in charge of implementation, the Department of Planning and Economic Development, as well as the city itself, was not abiding by the spirit of the ordinance. The council had already exempted all small and new businesses, given a one-year grace period to all firms to implement the law, and refused to apply the ordinance retroactively. Supporters claimed the Department of Planning was actively encouraging businesses to use loopholes in the ordinance to avoid paying the living wage.

Despite the call from living wage supporters for tighter enforcement, St. Paul continued to use loose guidelines in applying the ordinance to subsidy recipients. In early 2001, the city council was asked to support a large renovation project by the Dayton's Department Store in the downtown shopping area, as it updated its look and converted into a Marshall Field's. Under the deal, the city would provide Dayton's parent company, the Target Corporation, with a $6.3 million loan (forgivable if the store stayed open for ten years) and $1.5 million for asbestos removal. Target would pay the remaining $12.7 million for the project but asked that it be waived from the living wage policy. Community members and some city councilors objected to the waiver, saying that Dayton's employees deserved a living wage. Council member Jay Benanav called on the company to explain its request, asking, "Are they going to ask for exemption from the human rights law or OSHA regulations? Why shouldn't Target be a leader in this area?"[21] When city economic development officials responded by saying that the company already paid a living wage or its equivalent with benefits, city council members demanded proof.

The Target Corporation refused to provide specific wage data, and in fact, refused to say much at all, including providing specific renovation plans. City officials claimed the waiver request was reasonable, as the company did not "want to set a precedent it might be asked to duplicate in dozens of other markets." In a memo to the council, St. Paul planning director Brian Sweeney and Port Authority president Ken Johnson defended Target's refusal to provide wage data: "We believe giving specific information on wages will put them at a competitive disadvantage not only in the Twin Cities market but also the national market in which they operate." Benavav suggested that the company provide the information privately to the city, but by the next day, the issue was pushed to a vote. The deal was approved 5–2, with Benavav and council president Dan Bostrom opposing. Target and city officials were pleased with the decision. Target "is truly the employer of choice, when you look at the combination of wages, benefits, and flexible working schedule," said Sweeney. Benavav agreed that Target was a crucial business in the downtown shopping district but added, "I think we are shirking our duties and our responsibility if we simply give them this money without the kind of information that any business or city council ought to be asking for." United Food and Commercial Workers union organizer Bernie Hesse noted that he worked harder to get his home mortgage than Target did to get their $7.8 million subsidy. A year later, the renovations were underway, and Target spokespeople announced that the new store would open with a streamlined staff, eliminating about eighty jobs.[22] Contrary to city officials' hopes, the Target deal failed to generate significant business expansion in the downtown shopping area.

These kinds of exemptions occur frequently with economic development projects but are found in contracting as well. After Boston, Cambridge, and Somerville passed their ordinances, the companies that bid
on recycling contracts in all three cities announced that they would not
pay the living wage and received waivers in the first year of coverage.
(An update on these contracts is provided in chapter 7).

In Milwaukee, when the contract for washing police cars was let, both
bidders submitted notes with their bids stating that they do not pay their
employees a living wage and would not comply with the city's living wage.
The purchasing department then simply went to the City Attorney and got
a waiver on the ordinance, exempting the contract from coverage.[23]

In some cities, administrators interpret living wage ordinances so that
current contract holders could renew or extend their contracts without
having to abide by the law, even though the intent of living wage activists
(and the laws themselves) is to apply the ordinance to any new or renewed
contract. Extending existing contracts when they expire is a way for the
city to essentially grandfather that employer out of the living wage law.
For example, in October 1996, Baltimore renewed a contract with Broadway Services for janitorial, cafeteria, and other service work in city-owned
buildings. According to an editorial in the *Baltimore Sun*, "The city
extended their existing contract so that it would not have to worry about
accepting a bid that included the higher wage scale." Although the president of Broadway Services had supported the ordinance publicly, he
decided that he could not pay his employees the higher wage. Because
the city would not open the contract for rebid, and the city refused to cover
the cost of the higher wage through a higher contract price, the 170
employees of Broadway Services did not receive the living wage they
were entitled to.

The process described here is not unique to living wage enforcement.
In the book *Dollars and Votes: How Business Campaign Contributions Subvert
Democracy*, Clawson, Neustadtl, and Weller argue that the process of
building loopholes into laws is commonplace.[24] This happens with all
laws, whether federal, state, or local. Loopholes allow politicians to pass
popular laws while allowing an out for influential corporations or industries. This way, the passage of the law seems like a victory to the public
and perhaps even to the activists who fought for the policy. But in reality,
once loopholes are taken advantage of, the victory is often a hollow one.
Loopholes are especially common in tax policy but can be seen in other
places. For example, economist Andrew Seltzer argues that many states
were only able to pass their state minimum wage laws in the early 1900s

because low-wage industry was assured that enforcement would be weak or nonexistent. He writes:

> Voters were sympathetic to low-wage female workers and thus preferred to have legislation but had little incentive to monitor the effectiveness of any law that was passed. Given voter preferences, it was in the interests of reelection seeking legislators to pass a law. However, due to the informational asymmetries between voters and interest groups, it was in the legislators' interests to make the law ineffective unless high-wage industry and labor advocates had more influence than low-wage industry.[25]

Another example of this is the Fair Labor Standards Act of 1938, which established a national minimum wage. As mentioned in chapter 2, in order to win support from key legislators, lawmakers agreed to include a number of exemptions and weak mandates for the implementing bodies.[26]

Explaining Failure

The stories above suggest that unfortunately, when living wage implementation is left to city staff, failure is more common than success. What insights can be gained from policy research in other arenas to help us understand why this is the case? What factors are most relevant in predicting success rather than failure? Living wage advocates are not the only ones who need to understand the implementation process. Throughout the country, thousands of citizens are hard at work, pressing their legislatures to adopt various laws, focusing their attention on enactment and not implementation. Policymakers and scholars can fall into the trap as well, treating lawmaking or policy formulation as the most crucial part of governance.

Implementation failures have serious implications. As social theorists Fung and Wright point out, the inability of governments to effectively administer the laws they adopt has provided ammunition for an ideological attack on the state, offering some evidence for those who argue that the state is inefficient, ineffective, bureaucratic, and corrupt.[27] Through these attacks, the right wing has built substantial political support for downsizing, outsourcing, and the defunding of social services administered by the state. This has also led to a wholesale political assault on the concept of an activist state, one that intervenes to correct market failures or enhance democracy.

While the assessment that the state has failed in policy implementation may be accurate, the causes for such failure are not necessarily the ones identified by the right. Perhaps the solution to weak enforcement should be more government employees, and more funding for social programs. Perhaps the solution is that the government intervene more, rather than less. Or perhaps the answer lies somewhere else: in new models of governance that combine the authority and resources of the state with the motivations and ingenuity of citizens. In order to discern the answers, we need a deep and thorough analysis of why and how implementation failure happens, a topic we explore in the following chapters.

6

IMPLEMENTATION

What Happens after Laws Are Passed?

For several reasons, the late-1990s are a particularly exciting time to examine policy implementation in the American context.

James P. Lester and Malcolm L. Goggin, "Back to the Future: The Rediscovery of Implementation Studies," *Policy Current*, 1998

Unfortunately, as research over the past thirty years has pointed out, policy implementation is not automatic. This is not only true of ambitious federal policy but some very mundane local level policy as well. Perhaps that comes as no surprise to the person who repeatedly has to call their city council member in order to get her garbage picked up on the right days. But most people would probably be surprised to find out about the gulf that sometimes exists between policy enactment and enforcement. In fact, when living wage supporters in Buffalo, frustrated at their city's lack of implementation, approached other organizations in the city for support they began to find that they were not the only ones whose proposals were enacted into law and subsequently ignored. Some city councilors told them that perhaps as much as 50 percent of all ordinances passed by the Buffalo City Council were never implemented.[1] There is no city documentation to back up this claim, and it may be overstated. Still, the living wage coalition was able to make alliances with dozens of other groups who had their own specific concerns about implementation of city policy, from recycling laws to welfare reform.

How is it that a policy can be passed with enthusiastic support (the Buffalo living wage ordinance was passed unanimously) and then never be implemented? We can answer part of this question with insights gathered from the last generation of implementation research. This scholarship has pointed out that key factors, such as the clarity of policy goals, number of staff and level of resources devoted to implementation, level of competence of public servants, incentives and penalties for compliance, and channels for evaluation, can make the difference between success and failure. In this chapter, I look at existing implementation research to isolate the factors that are relevant to predicting successful living wage implementation. In addition, I will add my own observations. What factors specific to the context of living wages do we expect would lead to more successful implementation, and which are likely to impair it?

Implementation Research

Researcher Sara McLanahan writes that implementation research is a subfield of organizational theory concerned with the period *after* a bill becomes a law.[2] It emerged in the late 1960s out of debates on why the "Great Society" programs failed. While conservatives argued that the programs failed due to "errors in social theory and to the 'inherent limits' to planned social change," implementation researchers argued that the programs could not be effectively evaluated without a thorough assessment of their execution.[3] Over the past thirty years, implementation researchers have come up with a long list of factors usually relevant in determining policy outcomes, but most fall into a few key areas: the *clarity* of the policy and its goals, the level of *conflict* surrounding the policy, and the *capacity* of municipalities and the staff in charge of implementation. I discuss each of these in detail below.

Clarity

Crucial to effective implementation is clarity, on a number of levels. First, the best policies are those that have a clear definition of the problem at hand and sound theory behind the policy proposal. Palumbo and Calista write, "Policy failure . . . is due as much to inadequate problem definition or policy design as it is to administrative misfeasance, malfeasance, or nonfeasance."[4] Definition and design can be an extremely difficult part of the process, especially with large federal programs involving multiple actors. Second, implementation is likelier to go smoothly when the goals of the policy are clear. Matland refers to this as policy ambiguity, which can refer to ambiguity of goals or of means for achieving goals.[5] This might occur when there are multiple goals for a particular policy, when there are uncertainties as to which organization or agency has responsibility for certain steps in implementation, or when the situation is complex and it is not clear which policy tools to use. Often, Matland argues, redistributive policies or large social programs, such as Headstart or the War on Poverty programs, suffer from this ambiguity.

Most living wage ordinances are relatively clear. The theory behind them is that poverty is a concern to municipalities, that cities should do their part to eliminate poverty, and that they can take a modest step forward by requiring firms they do business with to pay a higher wage. The goals are to get the covered employers to pay the higher wage. By no means is this a *simple* process, because it is not always clear which employers are covered, but relative to policies such as welfare reform, the living wage has little ambiguity.

What is less clear, however, is the administration of the ordinances. In chapter 5 we explained the difficulties that can occur when trying to locate those within city bureaucracies who are responsible for living wage enforcement. While most ordinances spell out the wage levels and coverage classifications in great detail, many fail to designate a particular person or office in charge of implementation. As of 2002, fewer than a dozen cities had drawn up regulations explaining the implementation process. This lack of clarity greatly hinders administrative efforts.

Conflict

A second factor relevant to implementation is the level of conflict surrounding the policy. Many implementation scholars focus on the conflict that arises between legislators and administrators. For example, Palumbo and Calista refer to tremendous conflict that occurred in the 1980s between the Reagan administration and the Environmental Protection Agency (EPA) over implementation of various environmental laws.[6] Reagan wished to quietly weaken the laws through underfunding and weak enforcement. However, most EPA staff were personally committed to the goal of environmental cleanup and also under external pressure from Congress to implement Superfund cleanup. The result was internal battling between the presidency, Congress, and a federal agency (the EPA).

Other case studies bring in the conflicts that can arise from external parties or forces, such as nonprofit organizations or other governance levels, or even from divisions within a particular community. For example, Giloth writes of how community resistance from certain neighborhoods in Baltimore, Maryland, was able to partially thwart the implementation of city efforts to continue economic development along the waterfront.[7] Goals for city development were not only ambiguous but contentious.

Matland states that policy conflict exists when there is "an interdependence of actors, an incompatibility of objectives, and a perceived zero-sum element to the interactions."[8] Simply put, it occurs when different actors want different things and at least some of their objectives are mutually exclusive. When there is conflict, actors must rely on bargaining to reach agreement and on coercive methods to ensure compliance. Some may argue that any policy is conflictual, especially since there are those who believe government should not intervene in most aspects of life. However, policies that might be less conflictual include those that benefit a very wide range of people, such as traffic safety, those that are very low cost, or some that are just symbolic.

Conflict may be less likely when there is more ambiguity since the differences between the parties are less clearly visible. Nakamura and Smallwood emphasize the importance of communication between actors when policy is formed, implemented, and evaluated, so that all actors are operating under similar assumptions and definitions. Weak connections between actors can mean less clarity and more conflict.

Perhaps more than other policies, living wage ordinances can cause conflict. Many (though not all) of the employers covered by the policies and their associations oppose them, either on principle or because they believe they (rather than the city) will have to bear the costs of the higher wages.[9] Even those employers who may already be paying the living wage rate often resent the ordinances for the potential extra regulations and paperwork. For these reasons, cities cannot assume employers will support the policies and pay the living wage voluntarily.

In addition, the "campaign model" of policy promotion common in many of the campaigns may itself create a conflictual dynamic. As mentioned in chapter 4, living wage advocates often adopt outside tactics as one part of their strategy to get the ordinances passed. These outside tactics may include rallies, marches, targeting particular employers and city legislators in the media, and in some cases, civil disobedience. Unlike the inside tactics of lobbying council members one-on-one and testifying at council meetings, outside tactics are more likely to arouse anger from living wage opponents and result in a sense of confrontation between the community and their elected officials.

Conflict does not only exist between advocates and the city, between employers and the city, or between employers and their employees. Conflict can also occur within the city, as the next sections will show.

Interests of City Leaders. Depending on the interests of each, city administrators and city councilors may be at loggerheads on living wage implementation. City councils may pass the ordinances, but support for policy passage is not the same thing as support for enforcement. While some council members may be proud to take ownership for passing a politically popular ordinance, their enthusiasm may dwindle when faced with applying living wage regulations to a developer planning to bring in new jobs to that council members' district, or forcing a large and politically influential service contactor to raise wages.

In a number of cases, council members who have sponsored or voted for the legislation have shown a level of personal investment in the ordinance after passage. Former LAANE staff member Nari Rhee explained that the Los Angeles ordinance was the council's "moral trophy."[10] After a protracted and public political battle with the mayor over the passage of the ordinance, the council took some responsibility for implementing it. For the most part, however, the level of attention the public gives to a campaign while in progress drops rapidly after enactment. Enforcement can be a tedious task. With little public attention at stake, council members have less interest in getting involved. The stories told earlier about votes on ordinance waivers and exemptions highlight this phenomenon. Although a city council may unanimously pass a living wage ordinance, that same council may turn around and grant a waiver or exemption to a firm with little justification (even with public attention on their actions, as in the St. Paul example).

In addition to the role of the council in policy implementation, the mayor or city manager can influence outcomes. City council members may enthusiastically support the ordinances, but it is the mayor or city manager that is the ultimate supervisor of the civil servants in charge of administering the laws. Although job security may be relatively well-protected through city government employment codes, it is the mayor's appointed administration that can reward or punish civil servants. This means that even in cases where city staff are sympathetic to the need to strongly enforce living wage provisions, it is possible that they will be prevented or discouraged from doing so by their superiors.

As mentioned above, in very few cases have mayors or city managers been strong advocates of the ordinances. These city administrators have various incentives to keep the ordinances from being passed and enforced. By the end of 2002, nine mayors had vetoed ordinances. Another set of mayors opposed but didn't veto. Many mayors who claim to support the ordinances have then worked to stall enactment, or weaken the agreement. For example, Baltimore Mayor Kurt Schmoke expressed general support but wavered on committing to an actual ordinance and living wage rate.[11] It was only after considerable pressure had been applied, and he'd become concerned about his upcoming reelection that he signed the ordinance. According to the *Baltimore Sun*, "In apparent deference to BUILD's presumed political strength, he relented."[12] Likewise, in Milwaukee, Mayor John Norquist expressed "support for [the] goal of creating family-supporting jobs in Milwaukee," but was noncommittal about the living wage due to his commitment to lower taxes and his concerns about a possible reduction in the city's competitiveness.[13]

There are exceptions to these stories, such as the Omaha, Nebraska, case mentioned in chapter 5. Support has also come from Boston mayor Thomas Menino. Menino was somewhat of an advocate of the ordinance when it was first passed but it wasn't until a few years later that his support helped improve the Boston ordinance. When the Boston Living Wage Advisory Board pushed the city council and mayor to amend the ordinance, expanding the coverage and raising the wage level, Menino agreed, making strong public statements in favor of a higher wage. After the Harvard living wage sit-in called for Harvard to match the Cambridge ordinance of $10.25 an hour for all workers at Harvard, Menino stated that he was embarrassed that his city's living wage level was only $9.11. He raised the Boston level to $10.25 (adjusted for inflation), and signed off on a host of amendments to broaden its scope.

However, these cases are rare. And it is not surprising that mayors would oppose the ordinances. As outlined in chapter 2, the dominant strategy for pursuing economic growth in cities has been based on an ideology that would reject increased labor standards such as those embodied in living wage ordinances. Employer's profits are partly based on paying workers as little as possible, so wage mandates are generally considered to run counter to a "friendly business climate." In fact, representatives from the Los Angeles administration stated that it didn't even matter if a living wage ordinance actually had a negative impact on the businesses affected: what mattered was the message it would send to the business community.[14] In their view, a living wage ordinance was a negative because of the "hostile business climate" it would create in the city, regardless of its actual impact.

As I argued in earlier chapters, one can't always assume that city administrators want to enforce all laws—particularly those progressive policies that run contrary to narrow city economic development strategies. While city council members subject to democratic accountability may pass popular legislation like living wage ordinances, city managers are likely to resist implementation when they perceive such laws as increasing regulation for business, harming to the business climate, creating higher costs for contracted out services, requiring more staff for enforcement, or hamstringing their use of economic development incentives to attract or retain business. Living wage ordinances, at least as perceived by many, go directly against current city management strategies such as outsourcing, downsizing, and awarding no-strings attached development subsidies.

What of the interests of city staff? Can we expect them to enforce the ordinances?

Interests of Public Sector Workers.   Conflict over policy implementation can occur not only between different branches of government, or between legislators and administrators, but between civil servants. Public sector employees may face structural constraints that keep them from enforcing living wage laws. They may also fail to enforce the ordinances for ideological reasons.

Structural constraints on city staff members come from several sources. If city managers perceive living wage ordinances as running against the economic development paradigm they ascribe to, city staff persons may be reluctant to actively pursue enforcement even when they are assigned the task. Even if they do not experience direct orders from their superiors to ignore implementation, they may simply find a lack of support for enforcement from above.

Another relevant factor has to do with where the city employee is working within the city bureaucracy. Those employees responsible for securing contracts for needed services are likely to see the living wage ordinance as just another hassle in their job. The living wage interferes with their main task, which is to find contractors willing to do the work for the city. On the other hand, city staff who are assigned specifically to monitor contracts will have an interest in making sure they do their job well. In fact, doing good work on enforcement might even be necessary for them to keep their job. As Ken Jacobs of the San Francisco Living Wage Coalition points out, there is a noticeable difference in the level of cooperation on living wage enforcement between different staff members at the San Francisco airport. The staff who are in charge of setting up leases for services in the airport (such as retail and restaurants) find the living wage ordinance an impediment to getting their job accomplished and have not been cooperative with implementation efforts. On the other hand, the staff at the airport who work to lease terminal space to the airlines are very cooperative. They see the living wage ordinance as helpful to getting their job done, because they believe it decreases employee turnover and makes the airport more secure.

A final structural issue that can be relevant is the ability of enforcement officers to levy fines for noncompliance. Again, the San Francisco case is instructive. Living wage enforcement is part of a larger contract compliance office within the city of San Francisco, which also includes staff who enforce prevailing wage laws for city construction projects. Prevailing wage violations result in a lot of fines, which come to the contract compliance office. This means that the compliance office is a money-maker for the city. The staff are highly insulated from debates over budget cuts or downsizing because of this fact. Where living wage enforcement staff are able to levy fines against employers in noncompliance, they could bring in enough money to politically insulate their position within the city administration.

While structural issues are key to understanding the incentives and constraints faced by city staff in charge of implementation, ideological factors may be equally relevant. Would we expect city staff to be in favor of living wage ordinances? Some insights into this question may be found in a subfield of sociology known as "state theory." Within this area, scholars have debated the importance of government structures and the ideology of different actors within the state (city officials, administrators, and staff) in policy passage and implementation. How much does the type of economy affect the ability of the state to pass and administer policies? Do the demands of a market-based economy or individual employer limit the state's autonomy to enact working-class reforms—that is, policies that favor workers over business? Do individuals within the state government have room to exercise their own judgment and preferences?

Some scholars have pointed out that governments should never be assumed to be a single, cohesive entity but rather an amalgamation of various interests. Jessop notes the potential for rivalries over resources and goals but also for deeper conflicts of interest within the state.[15] Wright finds that ideological differences exist between civil servants in different branches of government or from different class positions.[16] For example, working-class employees in the public sector are more supportive than middle-class employees of working-class struggles and of "an expansive role of the state in society." In addition, survey data suggest that public sector workers who work in the "decommodified services" (such as public health and education) are more likely to be critical of capitalism than are public sector workers in the "political superstructure" (the military, police, courts, and administrative and legislative sectors of government).[17]

One interpretation of the living wage is that it is a policy tool to correct failures of the market. Without mandated wage floors, competitive bidding leads to workers doing city work for wages below the poverty line. According to Wright's findings, we would expect that certain types of public sector workers would be more sympathetic to the goals of the ordinances: namely, those who are working in service provision sectors and/or are themselves working class.

The staff in charge of implementation varies by city. In many cases, the work is assigned to staff in a preexisting contract compliance department, usually located within a procurement division in the finance department. These departments would be considered part of the political superstructure of cities, as they are part of the administration. It is likely that staff in these kinds of departments have come to their work with training in mainstream philosophies of urban economic development.

The 1997 International City/County Management Association (ICMA) survey on "Reinventing Government" suggests the kind of ideology that is fairly pervasive among city managers. The ICMA asked city managers, city administrative officers, and finance directors—the people who usually supervise living wage administrators—in 1,276 cities questions about their management philosophies. In numerous questions, the majority of respondents indicated their support for greater competition in public service delivery, increased contracting out, and treating government like a business. When asked about their political philosophy, 46.7 reported that they were "very conservative" or "moderately conservative," as compared to only 19 percent that considered themselves "very liberal" or "moderately liberal."[18]

Interviews with city living wage administrators yielded similar findings: namely, an ideological opposition to the concept of living wage laws. In Duluth, Minnesota, Business Development Manager Tom Cortruvo stated, "When the law came up, our position was quite strongly that we agree with the concepts and the goals, but we didn't think it should be in the form of a specific law."[19] Ronald Guzi, director of purchasing in Warren, Michigan, added that he too was opposed to a living wage ordinance in his city.[20] In Eugene, Oregon, the city council asked the Budget

Committee to come up with recommendations for city action regarding a living wage proposal before the council. City staff Lauren Chouinard (executive director of the Human Resources and Risk Services Department) produced an astonishing one-sided and ideological set of materials for the Budget Committee to assess the options.[21] For example, he focused on unintended consequences and did not address potential benefits; the only study cited was funded by the anti-living-wage Employment Policies Institute that has been roundly critiqued (but the critiques aren't mentioned); and Chouinard predicts negative outcomes that are based purely on speculation without citing any research dealing with actual outcomes after living wage passage. Mr. Chouinard also pointed out that one of the negative aspects of an ordinance is that it would move away from a market-based system of pay. In numerous cities, city staff like Chouinard who are ideologically opposed to the concept of a living wage are asked to evaluate proposals for the city and later asked to administer the laws once they are passed.[22]

However, even within these kinds of departments, an outside person who has a different type of background may be brought in to do the job. In Tucson, while Ray Valdez works under the finance department, he states that he came into the job with a background in the city's housing division and also in community service work. In Santa Cruz County, Paul Campbell had been an active union member in the county public sector union before being moved into a management position in procurement.

In a few cities, the job of implementation is placed in departments other than finance or procurement. In Toledo, Ohio; San Jose, California; and Dane County, Wisconsin, the Equal Employment Opportunity/Affirmative Action offices are in charge. In Ann Arbor, Michigan, the Human Rights Commission oversees the law. Here, though the offices are generally part of the administrative structure of the city, staff in these departments are more likely to come from social service backgrounds and may be expected to have greater support for the living wage.

The likelihood that city staff will ideologically support the goals of the living wage movement could be expected to depend on several factors, including whether they come from the decommodified service sector or political superstructure of the state, their class location within city government, their union status, and their views about the link between living wage ordinances and union strength. However, given that most living wage administrators are located in the political superstructure sector, and that they are nonunion and not likely to be working class, we would anticipate that as a group, they would be less likely to personally sympathize with the goals of living wage ordinances.

This does not mean, however, that one should expect these employees not do their job. Many civil servants take great pride in their work and will carry out assignments regardless of personal ideology. "If I was on the city council I would not have voted for the living wage," said Steve Mermell, living wage administrator in Pasadena, California. "But now that it is policy it is our job to make sure it is enforced. We are serious about doing our work well."[23]

Capacity

A third factor that influences successful implementation is the capacity of municipalities and city staff. A number of implementation researchers have noted the importance of the level of resources available to administrators as a factor in determining success.[24] Matland claims that resources are *the* main factor determining successful implementation for policies that are unambiguous and have a high degree of consensus, such as the eradication of disease. Resources are not just financial but include information, skills, and technology.[25] The level of resources is important: in a 1997 survey conducted by the International City/County Management Association, city managers were asked, "How often could programs be implemented without some funding?" "Never" was the answer of 11.3 percent of the respondents, and 51.5 percent answered "seldom," suggesting that financial resources are key to successful implementation.[26]

Where do these resources and capacities come from, and why do they vary among governments and state employees? Gilbert and Howe argue that state capacities are not given but are, in part, the result of political contestation.[27] States depend on taxes and other revenues to operate, and the battle over who pays these taxes reflects the political power of different interests. According to Markusen, "The conflict over who should pay local taxes is an extension of the struggle between profits and wages. If the capitalist interests can arrange for the transfer of various costs of production to the city budget and escape the tax bill for them, they successfully enhance profits at the expense of wage-earners."[28] Wage-earners, on the other hand, wish to have city services provided to them at no or minimal cost.

Aside from determining the overall level of revenues, political struggles also influence how funds are disseminated between departments and programs. Again, capitalists and wage-earners will have different interests in terms of what is funded. When federal and state funds for cities declined dramatically in the 1980s, the battles over city budgets intensified, as different interests struggled over who should pay the taxes necessary to make up for the lost revenue and where the remaining monies should be spent. In addition, the downsizing efforts discussed in chapter 2 intensified struggles *within* the state as municipal employees were laid off, entire programs eliminated, and city managers were increasingly forced to behave like their counterparts in the private sector.

How does this affect policy implementation? Earlier in this chapter, I described how the interests of state actors couldn't be taken as homogenous: that various public sector employees are likely to hold different ideological perspectives on the role of the state and on working-class reforms. As such, there may be state employees who actively oppose or support the implementation of any given policy. Where these employees are situated within city government, however, could have a large impact on how policy is administered. For example, those employees with more authority may have greater access to resources that would allow for effective implementation (such as operating budgets, staff, and technical skills). Likewise, nonskilled working-class employees with little or no authority are not likely to have access to such resources, and may, therefore, be constrained in their ability to implement policy.

Number of Staff.   We've already discussed the issue of staffing in previous sections. In particular, in many cities there are no city employees in charge of living wage implementation. What is important to note is that this is not purely a technical issue but a political one. City administrators make decisions about hiring and firing of city employees based on priorities and budgets. Again, with pressures to keep city employment down, city administrators will resist hiring new staff to monitor the living wage ordinance. However, this is a political struggle that living wage advocates can engage in. In many campaigns, the question of staff availability for ordinance oversight is an element up for negotiation. For some campaigns, this is an area in which they have been willing to give up, and weaker campaigns have had to settle on a final ordinance that allocates no city staff. In other campaigns, living wage advocates have insisted on city staff for monitoring. For example, in Los Angeles, the coalition pushed the city to hire six enforcement officials right after the ordinance was passed.

Staff Responsibilities.   In cities with little staff time available, city capacity for enforcement is limited. The minimum activities include informing all contracting departments about the living wage ordinance and providing them with the language and paperwork necessary to include the living wage requirement in request for proposals or grant agreements. Most cities also mandate that covered employers post some form of notice of the ordinance within their worksite, letting employees know about the ordinance and the living wage level. City staff will tell employers about this requirement and provide necessary posters and answers to employer questions.

In a handful of cities, implementation administrators take a more active role by providing detailed information and sometimes training about the ordinance to city staff in other departments, bidders, and workers. In San Francisco, city staff have prepared extensive materials available from their office or website for covered employers and workers. Los Angeles and Alexandria, Virginia, have information sheets available in Spanish, and Los Angeles has Spanish-speaking staff available to answer questions by phone.

This brings up a crucial aspect of implementation: monitoring of employers. For those cities where staff have time to engage in active monitoring, the majority of efforts are put toward a systematic or random review of compliance forms and/or payroll records submitted to the city. In a few cases, staff make random visits to worksites to insure that posters are posted, and that workers agree that they are receiving the living wage. Ray Valdez of Tucson, who spends about 40 percent of his time at worksites, is on the high end—most city staff spend far fewer hours on this task.

Staff also spend a good deal of time working with employers to obtain compliance. This includes initial discussions about the ordinance, working with firms who may wish to apply for a waiver, following up with firms to be sure payroll and other compliance forms are turned in, investigating complaints, and finding solutions when noncompliance is discovered.

Many city administrators note that they prefer to take a "nonconfrontational" position with firms and work with them to solve noncompliance rather than immediately penalize them. Although provisions for large penalties exist in many cities, few administrators have used them. Rather, they believe that the majority of noncompliance cases to date have been due to communication problems and can be rectified on notification.

A final task of city staff is to evaluate the implementation procedure. Roughly a dozen ordinances mandate staff to write regular reports to the city council, summarizing the impact of the ordinance and effectiveness of implementation.[29] In some cities, no reports have been written, despite regulations requiring otherwise. For those who do write reports, the depth varies from a one- to two-page memo, such as in New Haven, to more extensive analyses providing detailed data on the number of contracts and workers covered, such as in Ventura County, California.

Other Resources: Information and Expertise. Other than staff time, resources include access to information about living wage ordinances and how they operate, experience in monitoring and enforcement for similar legislation, access to information within the city, access to information from covered employers, and financial resources to produce necessary materials (such as web pages and handouts for workers at worksites).

Our survey of city staff suggests that the key resource concern is staff time. Clearly, many cities are not able to focus on implementation because city administrators have not allocated money to departments to hire new staff. Beyond that, financial resources are not a large factor in implementation. Most staff feel they have enough resources to print necessary material. More important is access to necessary information. While some city staff were able to speak with prevailing wage enforcement officials in their city and apply lessons learned from that and other contract enforcement departments, a surprisingly few number of city staff speak with enforcement staff in other cities. In fact, it appears that many staff are working through implementation issues on their own, "reinventing the wheel" in each case. In some cases this is necessary, as the ordinances do differ in almost every city. But even where there is similarity, city staff aren't likely to turn to other cities for help. Take for example the question of how to calculate the annual increase in hourly wages for those ordinances that have an indexed wage rate. In some cities the ordinances are vague, creating several options for staff to adjust the living wage level each year. In Cambridge, it became clear that the staff was calculating the increase in such a way as to provide a lower increase for workers. In Oakland, staff chose the method that would give a higher raise.

Examples like these indicate that staff members are often left on their own to make decisions about implementation, with little guidance from their supervisors and no assistance from past precedent or other cities. When surveyed, a number of city staff have expressed interest in a national meeting for living wage city enforcement officials, noting that they would welcome a chance to exchange information. In January 2003, Gail Dance from San Jose, California, convened a "support group" meeting for northern California living wage administrators. Staff members from seven municipalities attended and planned to continue meeting on a quarterly basis.

In addition to lack of information sharing between city staff, a number of city officials are also hampered by their inability to get adequate information from other departments within the city. The first task of a living wage enforcement administrator is to gather information on the contracting patterns in the city. Especially in larger cities, this task can be quite challenging. In many cities, there is no centralized place in which contracting and economic development information is kept. In large cities such as Los Angeles it can take months to create a centralized database of current city contracts. In the case of subsidies, the work is even harder, as specific firm deals are usually negotiated on a case-by-case basis. Also, tax abatements are often separate from grants, loans, and bonds, so it may require getting information from numerous departments or agencies to understand one economic development deal.

Covered firms may also pose an obstacle to data collection. This is due to a few factors. First, the reporting requirements differ by city, and in some places employers have actively opposed strong disclosure provisions. For example, in Boston, the original ordinance passed in 1997 required employers to submit payroll records at regular intervals so the city could inspect for compliance. While many business leaders acknowledged that few Boston businesses paid much lower than the living wage rate of $7.49, the Chamber of Commerce threatened to file a lawsuit against the city if the disclosure provision was implemented. Jim Klocke of the chamber noted "that information is kept confidential for competitive reasons" and disclosure provisions could allow competitors to gain information about firms' internal finances.[30] In the end, a deal was reached where the reporting requirements were reduced such that covered contractors would be required only to make their payroll records for the work on the contract available to city staff for inspection if requested. (In exchange for this compromise the Boston living wage coalition won other provisions, such as a strong role for the Advisory Board).

In Toledo, Ohio, the Chamber of Commerce considered their role in the living wage deliberations to be a success when they managed to prevent strong disclosure provisions. According to the chamber's newsletter, the chamber's public affairs director worked to negotiate a change in the original draft, which would have required covered employers to submit payroll records to the city's economic development department. The final version approved by the city requires only that employers notify their employees of the ordinance's requirements.[31]

When cities are limited in their ability to access data from employers, it makes it difficult for them to do adequate enforcement. This not only affects their ability to actively seek out employers in noncompliance but also makes the decisions about waivers difficult. Most of the ordinances allow for firms to obtain waivers from the city council if they can prove that economic hardship would result from application of the living wage. But without access to full information from firms, cities are left to guess whether the employers' claims are valid. As we will see, this has been a serious implementation issue in some cities.

Conclusion

This chapter has presented factors that might help predict the outcomes of living wage implementation. Although the theory behind the ordinances and their intent are relatively clear, the proposed mechanisms for implementation are not always so apparent. Some cities designate a particular person or department to oversee administration, which helps provide accountability. But in other cases, there is not a single person or department in charge, making the implementation process ambiguous. In many of these cases, it is difficult to gather any information about the ordinance, let alone details about enforcement and impact.

Living wage ordinances are fairly conflictual. Many employers oppose the policies, if only on ideological grounds. But conflict is not confined to the employer/employee relationship. In many cities, one finds ambivalent attitudes toward the laws from mayors, city managers, and even city councilors, creating a situation where city staff do not always get the support and incentives necessary to thoroughly enforce the living wage. This is exacerbated by the fact that the majority of cities have assigned responsibility for enforcement to finance or purchasing departments, where city staff are less likely to be sympathetic to the goals of the ordinance. This does not mean these staff will necessarily shirk their duties but suggests that the living wage enforcement will not be a top priority.

Finally, we see a wide variation in the responsibilities, capacity, and resources of city staff. In some cases, the staff-to-contract ratio appears adequate, and staff feel they can do their jobs. In other cases, staffers are hard-pressed to get even the minimum amount done. These factors—lack of accountability, contradictory goals of city leaders and staff, and weak capacity—suggest that chances are good that implementation will fail, or will be narrow at best, in most cities. So what can be done to improve outcomes? Fortunately, living wage advocates do not have to leave implementation to city staff but can themselves play a role in the process, improving the chances for success.

7

FIGHTING FROM THE OUTSIDE

We did everything by the book. . . . We did everything right. We did everything
we were supposed to do.
Joan Malone, Coalition for Economic Justice, on the Buffalo living wage
campaign, *Buffalo News*, March 5, 2003

City governments are not the only force driving the implementation of living wage ordinances. Since most ordinances rely on a complaint-
driven model of enforcement, workers themselves are obviously a key part
of ensuring that employers abide by the law. But pressure on the state does
not have to rely on workers alone. In some places, the organizations or
coalitions formed to pass the ordinances are playing a role in implementation, sometimes formal and sometimes informal.

In earlier chapters I argued that policy implementation must be
analyzed not simply as a product of legislator and administrator
behaviors but rather as an interactive process that involves societal as
well as state forces. Community members, interest groups, and social
movements can influence policy formation *and* implementation. They can
influence enforcement outcomes by pressuring the state to act and by
directly altering the state's capacity and resources. In fact, some societal
forces—namely corporations and business associations—already play a
huge role in policy formation and implementation. But why is that input
usually limited to certain segments of society? This chapter reviews why
implementation has often excluded community input. I then discuss the
ways in which outside forces can affect implementation, through the
avenues of outside protest and pressure, giving examples from several
cities.

Implementation as an Arena for "Experts"

Previous implementation research has tended to focus on the legislators and administrators, leaving community actors out of the picture altogether or treating them as a fringe element. Government regulation expert Carol MacLennan explains some of the reasons for this.[1] She argues that in the years following the Great Depression, the thinking of Frederick Taylor and the scientific management school shaped the "philosophy of public management" by promoting the idea that politics could be separated from administration and that the goals of efficiency and greater productivity could and should be applied to governments. This school of thought helped create "an 'administrative orthodoxy' that holds certain key values and assumptions about how government organizations should work and, more importantly, about what the proper role of government in society should be."[2] According to MacLennan, the three main values held by this approach are:

1. The belief that administration is a *politically neutral* instrument of public policy-making.
2. The view that problems of bureaucratic unruliness can be cured through centralizing *managerial control* and strengthening hierarchical decision-making.
3. The assumption that *business principles* of management are directly applicable to the public sector and should be applied to public institutions.

The acceptance of these principles has created an atmosphere where policy implementation is considered to be separate from policy-making: specifically, that the administrative process can be designed to be efficient and rational if left to "experts."

Despite claims of neutrality, these values clearly bolster an ideological position supportive of dominant class interests. The status quo is reinforced when administrative decisions are treated as technical rather than political, because crucial questions of distribution and equality are not discussed. Hierarchical decision-making favors those currently in power and those with more resources. In addition, when city governments adopt the position that business principles of management should be applied to the public sector they have acquiesced to the idea that profitability should guide public decision-making. As mentioned earlier, this is a key question of problem-definition. Should cities make decisions based on meeting the "bottom-line"?

Some may argue that city administrators are simply doing their job when they work to ensure that the city is making decisions based first on financial considerations. True, a responsible manager must consider her budget—material constraints are real. However, not all social institutions make decisions based entirely or primarily on economics or "efficiency." We can find many examples where people act on other values and priorities, such as safety, security, love, charity, religious belief, guilt, fear, or anger. Families generally act on these values above the economic. Parents will try to feed their children no matter what the cost. It is conceivable that city leaders could incorporate humanitarian goals into their fundamental decision-making process.

In addition to entrenching the values of the dominant class, MacLennan asserts that this administrative orthodoxy has been responsible for "removing" government from the people it serves, leaving the wider public (those not in the dominant class) out of the implementation process altogether. MacLennan advocates a broader analysis of policy implementation that includes the political context of the implementation environment and the citizenry affected by the programs. State theorists Gilbert and Howe also recommend a broader approach to assess policy formation and implementation. Rather than putting all the focus on the state, they argue, scholars should focus their analysis on the interrelation of state and society.[3]

Returning to our measures of successful implementation from chapter 5, we can examine the relationship between implementation categories and societal input. As table 7.1 shows, when living wage implementation is left to the city alone, outcomes are weaker than in cases where community organizations are involved. I have left the cases where imple-

Table 7.1. Implementation outcomes in city-only versus community-involvement efforts, ordinances passed through 2001

	City-only implementation	Community involvement in implementation
Narrow	68%	24%
Moderate	27%	29%
Expansive	5%	47%
Total	100%	100%
	(Total = 56)	(Total = 17)

Source: Author's analysis based on ordinances, interviews, and review of relevant documents.

mentation has been blocked out of the table, since these cases mostly involve external forces, such as the courts, state legislature, or city referendums. But comparing city-only implementation to places where the community has been involved in some capacity, we see that out of seventy-three ordinances, the greatest numbers fall into either the city-only/narrow outcome, or the community-input/expansive outcome. When cities are left on their own to enforce living wage regulations, 68 percent (38 out of 56) fall into the category of narrow implementation. This is the case where cities do the minimal work to implement and no more. On the other hand, when community groups are involved in the process, 47 percent achieve expansive implementation, where waivers are difficult to obtain, and where staff monitors payroll records, evaluates outcomes, and makes recommendations to the city council on how to close loopholes. Another 29 percent of the cases involving community groups fall into the moderate outcome. Community involvement is not a guarantee that outcomes will be successful, but it greatly improves the likelihood. Likewise, it is possible, as with Tucson, to have broad results when implementation efforts are purely city run, but it is highly unusual. As the following chapters will show, societal influence on the state can dramatically affect outcomes.

Political theorist Paul Schumaker divides societal influence on the state into three types: electoral activity (voting), formal interest-group activity (lobbying), and protest politics.[4] He notes that voting is limited in its ability to convey to representatives the preferences of citizens. Interest groups and formal lobbying can also be limited in their effectiveness for certain individuals, particularly those with less education or money. Schumaker writes that interest groups tend to be the arena of "well-educated, high-income citizens," and their "heavenly chorus sings with a strong upper class accent."[5] Because of these drawbacks to electoral activity and lobbying, many people turn to protest groups, which he defines as

> groups of citizens who do not normally interact with government officials, but who, under certain conditions (when they perceive that their interests are threatened by the activities of others or that the political system can be of use in furthering these interests) organize on an informal, issue-specific basis to make demands on public officials through pressure processes.[6]

As other political scientists also argue, many Americans tend to turn to informal or protest groups as a means to make their political demands, particularly at the local level.[7] These protest groups utilize a range of tactics to influence governments to enforce the laws they have passed, including marches, rallies, civil disobedience, letter-writing and petitions. The ability of organizations to do this depends on their own resources and power. Their capacity relies on financial resources, information, technical skills, numbers of people, and the ability to mobilize those people. These factors strongly influence whether and how policy is implemented; therefore, any study of policy implementation must include an analysis of the strengths and weaknesses of relevant social forces before, during, and after the passage of policy.

Protest groups can also play a role in improving implementation by shaping state capacity—the ability of the state to do its job. Community organizations or social movements not only pressure states to adopt new policies but also to create new agencies and monitoring mechanisms. They might even impact the personnel selection to staff those new agencies. Their protests may also serve to give the state more legitimacy when it tries to enforce laws.

Gilbert and Howe also argue that the relationship can go the other way: state capacity can shape the capacity of class forces. They show that the federal Agricultural Extension Service was created and funding pushed by business organizations such as the Chamber of Commerce, which had stronger ties to larger and more prosperous farmers. Extension agents organized farmers into the American Farm Bureau Federation—a private organization that helped farmers adopt new farming methods and improve production. Its creation and subsequent growth precluded the growth of progressive farm organizations that served the needs of small and poor farmers. In this way, "as the state's *institutional capacity* created and built the Farm Bureau, it simultaneously strengthened the *class capacity*" of large farmers.[8]

Another state theorist, Jill Quadagno, offers another example of how states have affected the capacity of social forces. In the late 1950s, civil rights leaders began calling for the elimination of racial discrimination in the construction industries. After President Kennedy signed two executive orders barring discrimination by federal contractors and the unions working on their contracts, civil rights groups began organizing protests against discrimination at federal job sites. According to Quadagno, "The state's response to protest created a new 'political opportunity' by legitimating federal construction sites as an arena for protest."[9] The executive orders offered tools for civil rights groups to further their organizing.

Dara O'Rourke, who has studied policy implementation in various contexts, provides an example of the crucial links between state capacity and outside protest when he writes of the weak environmental legislation enforcement in Vietnam. Due to a variety of factors, including weak state capacity and contradictions and conflicts within the state, environmental legislation has tended to be enforced only when community groups apply outside pressure to state agencies.[10] O'Rourke calls this model "community-driven regulation" and argues that it can complement state activity and enhance the state's capacity to enforce controversial decisions against powerful polluting firms.

What about living wage implementation? Can living wage coalitions play an informal role in implementation by pressuring city governments to enforce the ordinance? Have coalitions been able to use protest politics to affect city capacity? In cases such as Toledo where implementation is weak, or even Detroit or Buffalo where the city actively resists enforcement, living wage activists have the option to remobilize their campaigns, using protest channels to pressure their cities to improve their enforcement efforts. Let us consider a few such cases.

Baltimore, Maryland

Baltimore, where the first living wage ordinance was passed in 1994 after a spirited campaign run by Baltimoreans United in Leadership Development (BUILD) and the American Federation of State, County, and Municipal Employees (AFSCME), provides an example of using outside protest to affect implementation. The Baltimore ordinance established a wage rate for service contract employees and assigned implementation responsibilities to the Wage Commission, which had already been enforcing the city's prevailing wage law. Although the ordinance required contracting agencies and the Wage Commission to collect full payroll data from contractors and subcontractors and to monitor these employers for compliance, it became clear early on that there were problems. According to a report on Baltimore's implementation, the information on contracts and payroll is "in theory publicly available but in fact is quite difficult to obtain. Contract information is often filed with other city documents with confidential information and would have to be laboriously separated in order to be made available. There is apparently no central file of contract specifications and costs."[11] In addition, not all employers were submitting the required records. According to Dana Wise, one of the authors of the report, "There is no doubt that the files were incomplete . . . 18 months after the ordinance was passed. There is definitely not full compliance with the reporting requirement and so chances are good that [the employers] aren't paying the higher wages either."[12]

A single employee of the Wage Commission was charged with the responsibility of receiving the reports from contractors and reviewing them. Wise describes the operation of that office:

> There was one guy [at the Wage Commission] sitting there in a bare room, with a file cabinet, a phone, and a bare desk. There were some reports there, but not all. This guy was new and he had no idea who the subcontractors were. The subcontracting is all decentralized—there are too many departments to keep track of—it is kind of comical. . . . There is just no information, and no structure to get the information.

The result was that no one was effectively monitoring the firms for compliance. The authors of the report noted, "Because of the voluminous data and the small staff, bus companies are as yet the only contracts which have been continuously monitored."[13] According to Wise, although the Wage Commission has the authority to do spot checks, they had not done any several years after the ordinance had been enacted.

In some cases, the living wage law was not fully implemented because it was not applied to contracts that were renewed after the ordinance was passed. This was the case with the Broadway Services contract in Baltimore, mentioned in chapter 5. Fortunately, living wage advocates were ready to step in to fight for better enforcement. The living wage campaign led to the formation of a new organization for low-wage workers, called the Solidarity Sponsoring Committee (SSC). Neither BUILD nor AFSCME had any official role in living wage implementation, and so SSC organizers decided to find out if workers were getting their mandated wage. They began to visit bus yards to talk to covered workers. When they found workers not receiving their mandated living wage, SSC helped them file complaints with the city and pushed the city to hold hearings over the case.

The Wage Commission held its first hearing on a noncompliance complaint in the fall of 1996 when two former bus aides employed by Eatman Transportation bus company claimed they had been paid $5.00 per hour for three months in 1995, when the required living wage was $6.10 per hour. Lillian Jackson, owner of Eatman Transportation, responded to the charges by claiming that she had paid the employees a higher wage but that she had falsified the payroll records she gave to the city, making it appear that the employees got a lower hourly wage.[14] Her explanation was that some of the bus runs were only forty-five minutes to an hour, but since no one wanted to work for that short of a period, Jackson would "round it off and give them $10 for two hours." A Wage Commission analyst questioned Jackson about the rounding off: "Your records are pretty specific. Here's 60.8 hours. That doesn't seem rounded off." The Wage Commission found that 17 workers had not received their mandated wage and ordered Eatman's to pay $5,100 in back wages. The commission decided to assess the company a fine of only $4,800, although under the law, which allows the city to assess fines of $50 per worker per day of noncompliance, the total charge could have been more than $48,000. The company appealed the decision to the Board of Estimates, and the board ruled that the company had to pay the back wages did not have to pay the fine.

A few months later, hundreds more school bus aides complained that their employers did not give them the legally mandated wage increase required in 1996. The twenty-six bus companies responded that they were paying the original wage of $6.10 per hour but that the city never notified them in writing that the wage minimum would increase to $6.60 per hour in July.[15] The mayor came out fully in support of the workers and said he would seek back pay for them. He rejected the employers' excuses that they had not been told about the wage increase: "That's an absurd position to take. That's just people trying to avoid their responsibility."[16] He added that it was fraud for the contractors not to pay the legally required amount and if they did not pay it, they would risk losing their contracts. The Board of Estimates ruled in favor of the workers and ordered the bus companies to pay back wages and raise the hourly wages to $6.60 per hour. However, once again the companies were not assessed fines.

In the process of the investigation, the Board of Estimates ordered a more thorough examination of the school bus contracts. In August 1997, a city audit report was released which found that "a pattern of mismanagement and nearly nonexistent oversight by Baltimore's public schools" led bus contractors to overcharge the city by at least $133,000 in 1995–96. These charges came primarily from the contractors billing the city for time and mileage on routes that they were not authorized to travel. In addition, the city was paying invoices without proper documentation. The report concluded that much of the problem was due to lack of city resources to monitor the contractors: "The Transportation Office is not requiring the contractors to adhere to the prescribed procedures and is not performing its monitoring responsibilities as set forth in the contract."[17]

Another challenge to the ordinance came in the summer of 1997, when the Maryland state legislature approved a city-schools reform plan that eliminated the Baltimore City Public School Administration and established a joint state and city group to run the schools. This meant that the city law affecting service contracts with the city did not legally apply to service contracts purchased through the state. As a result, about two thousand workers stood to lose coverage under the living wage ordinance. About eighty service contract employees and SSC members went to a school board meeting to demand that their right to the living wage be protected. The board did not offer a ruling, so the workers came back in two weeks to argue their case again. This time, the board promised to recognize the ordinance and require contractors to pay the employees $7.10 per hour. The Solidarity Sponsoring Committee continued its efforts to organize for the rights of the school contract employees, and in February 1998 the school board agreed to give the covered employees the living wage increase to $7.70 per hour as of July 1. Furthermore, SSC won the right for the workers to have money deducted from their payroll for the SSC health and life insurance plan.[18]

Throughout the hearings, SSC kept the pressure on the city to comply with the ordinance, turning out for hearings and rallies in support of the workers' claims. Although SSC did not have a formal role in implementation, their efforts helped workers learn about the ordinance and win the mandated wage level. However, other than informing groups of workers about the law, organizing supporters for rallies and hearings, and assisting some to file complaints with the city, SSC has not made any effort to become systematically integrated into the implementation process. Instead, they continue to deal with implementation failures on a case-by-case basis as they come up in other organizing work.

Chicago, Illinois

The Chicago living wage campaign was contentious and drawn out. An initial effort to pass an ordinance failed in 1997, but the coalition stayed active and kept the issue alive. They promised to make the living wage defeat an issue in the 1999 Board of Aldermen elections, targeting anti—living wage aldermen ward by ward. In 1998, the coalition saw their chance to push the campaign forward to victory when the Board of Alders was gearing up to vote themselves up to a twenty thousand dollar per year raise. The Chicago Jobs and Living Wage Campaign hit the streets with the message, "No raises for city officials unless low-wage workers get their Living Wage." Almost immediately, city alders contacted the campaign to negotiate an ordinance. This time the council approved the living wage ordinance by a 49–0 vote.[19]

However, city staff then attempted to limit coverage by using a narrow definition of eligible contracts. The living wage coalition, led by ACORN and SEIU Local 880, pressured the city to establish an informal living wage task force, composed of union, central labor council, and city representatives who met monthly for some time to address problems in implementing the law. When the city ruled that certain home health-care workers were not covered by the ordinance, the union representatives on the task force pressured the city to change the ruling, resulting in raises from $5.30 to $7.60 an hour and more than $30,000 in back pay for more than five hundred workers. According to Keith Kelleher of SEIU Local 880, which represents home healthcare workers, the pressure through the informal task force "was key to our getting that raise."[20]

Los Angeles, California

As mentioned in chapter 6, it was clear early on to the Los Angeles living wage coalition that the city staff assigned to monitor the ordinance was not doing an effective job. The main organization behind the coalition, the Los Angeles Alliance for a New Economy (LAANE), decided that they could not have a cooperative relationship with the city staff. According to Julie Park of LAANE:

> When they [the Bureau of Contract Affairs (BCA)] were first involved, they said they wanted to break all contact with the Coalition—they were afraid of negative publicity. We had had Marriott call the police on us for leafletting, and Marriott called [the BCA], saying they were thinking of suing the city, and accusing them of being pro-union. The BCA did not want the negative publicity. They told us they didn't want anything to do with us. [City councilmember] Jackie [Goldberg] got involved, and met with us and BCA, and told them that they had to cooperate with us. Now they are working with us, but reluctantly, and are very wary and mistrustful of us.

Instead, LAANE decided to work with unions to keep steady pressure on the city council from the outside to improve implementation. When airlines at Los Angeles International Airport refused to comply with the ordinance, the living wage coalition responded by using several channels to press for adoption of the ordinance at the airports. First, they hoped to push the airlines into voluntarily adopting the law by holding rallies at the terminals and building community support for their cause. After a rally in the fall of 1997, a security guard who was active in the campaign was suspended from her job with an airline for leafleting at the airport. A prominent local bishop wrote a letter on behalf of the woman, telling the employer that the workers had support from the religious community for their actions. The employee was reinstated that day.[21] A march and rally at the Los Angeles airport in March 1998 attracted more than five hundred people, including national AFL-CIO secretary Linda Chavez-Thompson. The coalition also worked to pressure the council and the mayor into asking the airlines to adopt the measure. Finally, they pursued legislative additions to the ordinance that would make it explicit that the airlines were covered.

In addition to struggling over the airport, the living wage coalition worked to ensure that the law would cover major development subsidies. In early 1998, coalition members got word of city negotiations over a large redevelopment project in Hollywood. The project was with major developer TrizecHahn, which had plans to develop a new entertainment/retail complex, including a new theater in which the Academy Awards would be held. Although the city was working to get almost $100 million in various subsidies for the corporation, none of the council members raised the issue of living wages at first, including Jackie Goldberg (the initial sponsor of the living wage), who represented the Hollywood district. When the coalition found out about the negotiations, they immediately made it known that they wanted the living wage to apply to the deal. In the end, TrizecHahn agreed not only to pay living wages and benefits to its workers but also agreed to require retailers leasing space in the development to pay living wages and give first priority in hiring to Hollywood residents. In addition, the living wage coalition won an agreement that required seven hundred to eight hundred of the staff positions at the new development to be unionized.[22] The coalition went on to win similar agreements for other major developments in the city.

Finally, the coalition pushed the council to improve implementation in general. In addition to getting the city to move implementation responsibility from the BCA to the City Administrative Office and to hire Spanish-speaking staff, LAANE also succeeded in getting the city council to unanimously pass amendments to the ordinance in 1998, closing a few loopholes and expanding the coverage.

Part of the amendments included provisions that stated clearly that subcontractors hired by the airlines would be covered by the ordinance.

Living wage advocates were pleased with the changes, as the airline industries had been resisting the law since it went into effect. Attorneys for the airlines had told the council that they believed that federal laws prohibited the city's right to impose local laws on the airlines and that they would consider litigation if forced to comply. According to the *Los Angeles Times*, city council members said that they were "more moved by the stories of workers such as Sonia Ramirez, who has yet to benefit from the ordinance" than by "threats of litigation from the airline industry."[23] This is an example of how a city council used criteria other than business profitability or city budget bottom-line to make a decision. LAANE director Madeline Janis-Aparicio commented on the importance of the council's vote: "This is very significant. It really puts the airlines on notice. This huge, national industry has drawn a line in the sand with the city of Los Angeles and the council is saying that they're not intimidated."[24] The changes in the law were expected to cover an additional twenty-five hundred to three thousand workers.

In January 1999 living wage supporters saw a tremendous break-through when United Airlines announced that it would not fight the changes and would comply with the law, resulting in wage increases for hundreds of security, baggage screening, janitorial, and other services. Although workers had been protesting at the airline for months, coalition members said that they were surprised by the airlines' announcement because United had been fighting the law for almost two years. However, a spokesman for United Airlines said that the airline had studied the issue and decided that it made "good business sense" to comply.[25]

Soon after, Host Marriott Services Corporation also agreed to increase pay and benefits for about seven hundred workers at Los Angeles International Airport.[26] Although the company operates about 60 percent of the food and beverage concessions at the airport, it was not required to pay the living wage as its current contract was negotiated before the law took effect. This contract with the city was not due for renewal until 2005. However, in negotiations with the hotel and restaurant union HERE, the company agreed to sign a three-year contract that assured the living wage rates and guaranteed full-time jobs to 70 percent of employees. None were guaranteed a full-time job under the previous contract.

It wasn't only the work of LAANE that led to the victories at the airport. The effort to organize the airport had received support and resources from area unions, the central labor council, the AFL-CIO, as well as groups such as Clergy and Laity United for Economic Justice, which had all been part of the living wage coalition. The persistent work of the coalition was instrumental in pressuring the airlines and other airport employers from all angles, including via the city council and the living wage ordinance.

Santa Cruz County, California

After winning a living wage ordinance in the city of Santa Cruz, the Coalition for a Living Wage turned its attention to the county, where the county board turned out to be less willing to pass an ordinance than the city was. Contentious issues included the establishment of a task force that would have the power to oversee the ordinance, as well as whether and how to apply the ordinance to nonprofits and recipients of economic development assistance. In the end, the campaign won an ordinance but did not win an independent task force, and administration of the law was assigned to the General Services Department.

At first this seemed like bad news. The head of General Services, Bob Watson, had personally tried to fight adding wage indexing (automatically adjusting the rate for inflation) to the ordinance. He had also been against the ordinance in general since it would mean more work for his department but no additional staff. But instead of Watson attempting to thwart implementation, he assigned staff member Paul Crawford to oversee the work. Crawford happened to have ties to a few coalition members already—he had known some of them when he was an active member of the public employees union before he had been promoted to management. Crawford seemed sympathetic to the goals of the ordinance, and coalition members quickly worked to develop a relationship with him.

The county had its first challenges early on. Its ordinance is only one of only two in the country that specifically requires any vendor with a county contract to pay all of its employees a living wage, not just those working on the contract. This provision led to two vendors immediately requesting an exemption. Although both companies held contracts with the *city* of Santa Cruz, and already paid living wages to employees on those contracts, they claimed that they could not afford to pay all employees a living wage to comply with the county ordinance. The first company was a small local firm that provided mailing services to the county, such as mailing absentee ballots and tax forms. The second vendor was a large private security firm, First Alarm. First Alarm had a $500,000 contract with the county but had seven hundred employees and said it could not afford to raise wages for all of them.

Crawford told the living wage coalition that the companies were applying for an exemption. The coalition mobilized to pressure the county to establish clear and consistent guidelines for granting exemptions. The county agreed and began to establish mechanisms for determining exemptions. Crawford notified both firms that in order to get an exemption, they had to prove financial hardship. In the case of the mailing services, the county decided to grant the vendor a six-month extension to its contract in order avoid service disruptions while the county decided what to do. First Alarm, however, made little attempt to prove its financial hardship. Instead, they argued that they should not have to pay the living wage because it was not the market wage.

In both cases, the firms had been the only bidders for the contracts for many years, so Crawford decided to begin talking to other firms to see if he could generate competitive bidding. He found another firm, National Securities, that appeared willing to bid on the security contract and to pay the living wage. When National Securities bid for and was awarded the contract, First Alarm threatened to file a grievance against the county and took their fight public, getting media stories about how the living wage ordinance had taken money away from a local company and given it to an out of area contractor (National Securities is based in San Jose, about twenty miles away). However, the county stuck with National Securities as the new contractor.

Meanwhile, the living wage coalition worked with Crawford in order to improve regulations for the ordinance. In particular, they were concerned about the worker retention provision—a clause that allowed workers to keep their job if the county changed contractors, by requiring the new contractor to give preference for any jobs to employees from the old contract. The coalition wanted to make sure that no one from the First Alarm contract lost his or her job when the county switched contractors. Crawford agreed to help out, and worked with National Securities to make sure that they would take on any employee who lost his or her job from First Alarm. The coalition also established contact with the First Alarm employees, making sure they knew about the ordinance and their right to keep their jobs. Most workers stayed on the job, taking a new position with National Securities and receiving a four dollar per hour raise.

In November 2002, living wage coalition director Sandy Brown noted that so far, implementation has gone well in the county. However, she felt that at any point, things could have gone differently. The coalition was lucky to find in Crawford a sympathetic staff person and to have cultivated a relationship with him. Although Watson initially opposed the ordinance, Brown thought that after losing the fight on wage indexing, Watson felt it was in his best interest to work with the coalition. Therefore, he did not stop Crawford from collaborating with the coalition. In this way, the living wage coalition enhanced the capacity of county staff to do its job. But as Brown noted, Crawford could retire, get transferred, or promoted at any time. His replacement might not be so sympathetic. The Santa Cruz coalition plans to continue to work behind the scenes to keep the pressure on for strong enforcement.

Ongoing Efforts in Other Cities

Living wage supporters in Baltimore, Chicago, Los Angeles, and Santa Cruz County have been able to improve implementation through outside pressure tactics, without a formal role within the city implementation mechanism. Activists in some other cities have begun similar efforts of their own. Although they have not yet come to fruition as of early 2004, their work has begun to raise public awareness about the difficulties of enforcing a living wage ordinance. What follows are examples of cities where activists have attempted to improve implementation through their own efforts, working through outside channels.

Buffalo, New York

Supporters have also been pushing for implementation from the outside in Buffalo. When activists realized that the city was not enforcing the law a year after it was unanimously enacted, the Coalition for Economic Justice (CEJ) and Citizen Action filed a joint lawsuit against the city in July 2001. Maria Whyte, executive director for CEJ, regretted that a lawsuit was necessary but felt there were no other options: "What are we to say about the state of our democracy when we have to sue our government in order for them to enforce the laws that hard-working citizens worked to pass!" Attorney Stephen Halpern added,

> The ordinance contains clear and specific measures that the City has a legal duty to take but has not for more than one year after the effective date of the ordinance. The leaders of the two organizations bringing the lawsuit have patiently but persistently advised the City of its continued failure to live up to its legal obligations.[27]

The living wage coalition did not limit itself to the lawsuit but used the implementation issue as a chance to do more organizing. They reached out to other social justice organizations around town and were able to strengthen ties with some as they discovered other policies had implementation problems as well. For example, environmental groups complained about the city's follow-through on recycling programs and expressed interest in working with the living wage group for better enforcement and governance in general. CEJ also developed connections with welfare rights activists who were themselves concerned that the city was failing in its efforts to create more living wage jobs. CEJ organized public rallies to get the word out about the city's implementation failures. They made a large reproduction of a check for $3 million, payable from the mayor to Buffalo workers, for the amount of wages that employees should have received under the living wage ordinance after its first year. They also delivered monthly IOUs to the mayor.

The activists had fought hard to get the ordinance passed originally. Given the unanimous vote, they did not expect the city to balk at implementation. "Even in my wildest dreams, I didn't think we would have to make sure this was implemented after it passed," said Citizen Action director JoAnn Cole.[28] Whyte added, "This is high school civics! Legislature passes laws, administration implements it. If the administration doesn't like a law they can veto it, they can fight like hell to keep it from getting passed. But once it passes, it's negligent not to implement it."[29]

In 2002, the city council amended the ordinance, removing their own responsibility for implementing the ordinance and putting the burden of enforcement on workers. CEJ has since worked with other organizations to develop a plan for a volunteer task force. In March 2003, approximately one hundred people attended a public forum to develop proposals for the new volunteer commission. The group continues to push for living wage implementation from the outside, by applying public pressure on the city and organizing on their own.[30]

Detroit, Michigan

In Detroit, living wage activists broadened their coalition after the ordinance was passed and the city failed to enforce it. In early 2002, three teams of volunteers visited worksites covered by the ordinance and found numerous violations. The teams collected formal complaints from six people and thirty petition signatures of workers "who were not making a living wage but were too scared to make a formal complaint as of yet."[31]

Although the ordinance required wages of $9.05 per hour with or $11.13 per hour without health benefits, the coalition spoke with workers such as those washing city vehicles making only $6.00 with no health benefits, and security guards at the Detroit Civic Center making $7.00 without benefits.

The group followed up the worksite visits with a labor solidarity action to support employees locked-out of their jobs at the Detroit-Windsor (Canada) Tunnel. The coalition helped mobilize about three hundred people and a caravan of cars to block the tunnel in June 2002. Although the tunnel workers were not covered by the living wage ordinance, the event was designed to bring public attention to the plight of low-wage workers around the city.

In October 2002, the Guild Law Center filed a lawsuit on behalf of workers at four worksites covered by the Detroit ordinance, including one worker still earning $8.35 with no benefits at a time when law required an $11 per hour wage.[32] In particular, contractor JOWA Associates, which supplied security guards to the Detroit Housing Commission and other city agencies, was singled out as a living wage violator. The lawsuit demands back-pay, and that the city require JOWA to post a copy of the mandated wage rate at any covered worksite.

Somerville, Massachusetts

The Somerville, Massachusetts, living wage campaign grew out of a discussion at a potluck for local progressive activists, an event held every month in the city for many years. After the ordinance was passed, the coalition stayed together, working on labor solidarity and related issues. Soon the coalition found out that the mayor was pushing for an exemption for one of the city's main contracts, for curbside recycling. They then discovered that nearby cities Cambridge and Boston, which also had living wage ordinances, had contracts with the same company, KTI. Activists in the three cities worked together to try to enforce the living wage ordinance for the recycling contract in each city. KTI was granted the waivers by Cambridge and Somerville. Rather than grant a waiver in Boston, the city chose to extend the contract until it could figure out what to do. The activists then moved to synchronize the contracts in the three cities so that they could run a coordinated campaign the next time the contract came up for renewal. Somerville and Boston activists succeeded at getting the contracts terms extended rather than renewed. Those in Cambridge did not—the mayor signed onto another contract with KTI.

Somerville activists continued work on the KTI issue. Their research uncovered the fact that while drivers were making high wages, a number of sorters at the recycling facility were making very low wages, as well as working under unsafe conditions. These workers were mostly Spanish and Portuguese-speaking immigrants, and many had second jobs in order to support themselves. Mary Jo Connolly, a labor educator from the University of Massachusetts-Boston and a member of the living wage coalition, began to research the recycling industry. She discovered that KTI's parent company was one of a handful of large, profitable companies that dominated about 50 percent of the nation's recycling market. It was clear that KTI did not deserve a "hardship waiver" from the living wage.

As the Boston and Somerville contracts approached their expiration date, KTI and the two other regular bidders for the recycling contracts announced to the cities that they refused to pay the living wage. If forced, they would not bid. Somerville activists stepped up their activities. They began looking into alternatives to the large recyclers: bringing the work in-house, to make it city work; or developing a worker-run cooperative that could take over the contract.

The Somerville coalition also forced the city to make the hearings about the waiver public, and then turned out a large crowd to attend. KTI appealed to the Somerville City Council for a waiver but refused to provide economic data to prove hardship. In the end, the activists convinced the city to extend KTI's contracts, rather than to make an immediate decision on renewal. This extension bought the coalition time to come up with alternatives and see what happened in nearby Boston.

Conclusion

Political theorists have differed on whether and to what degree protest groups can influence public policy. Here, I have shown that forms of protest or "outside" politics can in fact improve the implementation of living wage ordinances. This happens when coalitions maintain their ability to utilize "outside track" tactics that pressure city governments to act on their mandated duty. For example, living wage advocates in Baltimore and Los Angeles were able to use rallies and media attention to push their city administrators to improve enforcement efforts. Community groups can also use outside tactics to improve implementation by altering the city's capacity to do its job. Rallies, marches, and other forms of protest can bolster a city's capacity to govern, by getting the city to create new positions or add staff, add new resources, or give the city staff more legitimacy to do their job.

There are several crucial lessons here: first, nongovernmental organizations can affect policy outcomes, even when the policies in question are not priorities of the current government. In the case studies discussed above, city administrators had various reasons why they were not effectively enforcing the ordinances. Whether failure stemmed from a lack of political clout by the living wage administrator in Santa Cruz County, inadequate staff time and expertise in Baltimore, or ideological opposition from city leaders in Los Angeles, living wage advocates were able to push cities to do more on implementation than they would have done otherwise.

A second related lesson is that outside agitation on its own can produce desired outcomes. For some, this lesson may seem like common sense. Indeed, this point has been made by activists and social movement scholars alike.[33] But over and over again, citizens are told that creating a disruption can hurt their chances to have their demands met. Politicians may warn constituents that tactics like civil disobedience or public demonstrations will only "burn bridges," turning the public and legislators against their cause. While this may be true in some cases, it certainly does not hold across the board. Often protest politics are the most effective option. Finally, the cases of protest mentioned above suggest that outside tactics alone are not enough to guarantee ongoing implementation success. Protest can fall on deaf ears, or it could lead to symbolic changes that are quickly abandoned after the protestors leave. What can living wage advocates do to ensure more systematic improvements in implementation? We now turn to a discussion of the use of inside tactics.

8

COALITIONS PLAYING A
FORMAL ROLE

We are very fortunate in Boston to have this ongoing living wage work, and to
have this interest in living wage monitoring and enforcement. My perspective is
that of a lawyer, so I think the devil is always in the details. I believe there
needs to be a campaign, but then serious attention paid to follow-through
afterwards. Folks should figure out a way for continuous efforts at oversight.

Monica Halas, Greater Boston Legal Services

The previous chapters have illustrated a number of options for
enforcement. First, implementation may be completely the responsibility
of the city, left to the realm of "administrative experts." Given the
weaknesses of this model and its high potential for failure, citizens and
community organizations have looked to other means for improving
implementation outcomes. One option is to turn to outside protest.
Another option is opening up the implementation process to give those
directly affected by the living wage policy a role in enforcement. Yet
another option is to bring in third parties, such as a nongovernmental organization, task force, or review board, to assist in implementation. A fourth
option might be one with no role for government: voluntary resolutions,
enforced entirely by employers and employees. This option will be discussed in chapter 9. This chapter will review the ways in which living wage
advocates are playing a role in implementation from the inside, rather than
through outside protest politics. This includes creating structures to
enhance the ability of workers themselves to improve enforcement, as well
as forming task forces.

Workplace-Based Enforcement

Political theorists Joshua Cohen and Joel Rogers, among others, argue that it is desirable to involve nongovernmental organizations, or "secondary associations," in policy implementation because they can supplement the information gathered by state inspectors, frequently at a lower cost.[1] However, these authors caution that different groups have varying access to resources and to the state. Because government policy continues to be shaped by the push and pull of internal and external forces, Cohen and Rogers believe it is important to monitor the state itself, pressuring elected officials to serve the interests of those not in the dominant class. They note:

> Some groups, certainly, will seek to capture administrative agencies for private purposes. But others are commonly brought into service to act as "fire alarms," sending signals to legislatures about whether agencies are in fact acting on their legislative mandate. By sending them, they promote the accountability of bureaux to those mandates and reduce the costs of monitoring agency performance.[2]

It is instructive to consider the case of the federal Occupational Safety and Health Act (OSHA), which was passed in 1971 to establish and ensure health and safety standards in the workplace. The law mandated that federal inspectors examine all worksites for safety violations. OSHA has suffered in recent years from extreme budget cuts and a corresponding reduction in the number of inspectors. However, even when OSHA budgets were at their highest, because of an inadequate number of staff, health and safety laws were not fully implemented. By 1978, OSHA inspectors had examined less than 1 percent of all U.S. workplaces.[3] Cohen and Rogers argue that in the case of OSHA enforcement, worker committees would be more likely to expose safety and health violations than federal inspectors, as the inspectors are susceptible to "capture" by employers who can offer bribes or other incentives. Of course, workers can also be bribed—as well as threatened with job loss—so the proper protections must be in place for worker committees to function correctly. However, with these protections, workers whose safety and health are directly affected by violations will have a greater incentive to expose these violations. In this way, adequately empowered secondary associations can operate as a monitor of state enforcement mechanisms.

Part of the argument for worker committees also rests on the fact that the task is too big for state inspectors. Even several thousand inspectors would not be able to adequately monitor the several million businesses in the United States. According to Cohen and Rogers,

> So long as federal inspectors remain the chief enforcement mechanism, either the law will be—as at present—narrow in its objects and woefully under-enforced or the process of production will need to be more closely regulated through a qualitatively greater federal presence. The former is unsatisfactory, and the latter, whatever its merits (which are not obvious), is not in the cards.[4]

In addition, OSHA inspectors are limited in their ability to find all safety infractions in a workplace. Employers can hide violations when inspectors visit, and inspectors have legal restrictions on what they can search without a warrant. Finally, it is virtually impossible for any one inspector to have the technical knowledge necessary to examine all production processes. According to David Hemenway of the Harvard School of Public Health, the OSHA inspector "certainly has less knowledge about what he is inspecting than an elevator, restaurant, nursing home or meat inspector. He is thus more likely to miss important violations and to cite insignificant ones."[5]

Cohen and Rogers suggest that workplace safety and health committees could supplement the work done by federal inspectors. These "on-the-ground" committees would have a greater capacity than the inspectors to extract specific and current information about the safety and health conditions of the worksite. The committees might also be in a better position to search for solutions to problems, as they would have more time to develop education and training programs, consult with management about alternative production methods, and confer with other workers about potential problems that might emerge. In this example, state capacity could be enhanced indirectly through the development and integration of secondary associations.

Labor economist David Weil provides empirical results to back up Cohen and Rogers' argument. In an evaluation of safety and health inspection records, Weil finds that unionized establishments are more likely to receive inspections than nonunionized firms.[6] In addition, when a union is present, firms face greater scrutiny in the inspections and pay higher penalties for violations. Weil argues that unionization enhances the effectiveness of OSHA enforcement for several reasons. Because many unions have staff devoted to work on health and safety issues, and unions often disseminate information to members, unionized employees have greater knowledge of potential risks in the workplace and their rights under OSHA. In addition, unionized workers do not have the same fear of dismissal or reprisals for reporting health and safety violations as do nonunionized workers. In this manner, unions can enhance the ability of OSHA to do its job. Economists Hirsch, Macpherson, and DuMond make a similar argument about workers compensation, where they find that unionized workers are more likely than similar nonunion workers to receive workers' compensation benefits when injured.[7] They attribute this outcome to greater access to information and less fear of penalty for filing claims on the part of unionized workers.

Eric Parker provides another example of the role of secondary associations in policy implementation in his examination of youth apprenticeship programs in Wisconsin in the earlier part of the twentieth century. While the state tried to establish apprenticeships in various industries, it was only successful in "sectors where employers were somehow organized for apprenticeship."[8] While policymakers had attempted to establish broad training standards throughout industries, the state lacked the capacity to enforce and insure those standards. Instead, administrators spent their time trying to encourage employers and unions to assume more of the responsibility for the program. Eventually, as World War I led to a labor shortage that increased the bargaining power of craft unions, the Milwaukee Metal Trades Association began to invest in building an apprenticeship program with the assistance of their vendors and suppliers. Similarly, in the construction industry employers worked with the unions to establish and maintain training programs. Parker shows how it was only in those industries where employer associations and unions assumed responsibility for the programs that the apprentice policies were fully implemented.

All of these are examples of how nonstate actors can enhance the state's ability to implement policy. Particularly in larger cities, it is unrealistic to expect city staff to be able to continuously monitor workplaces. Some of the ordinances in cities like Los Angeles and Miami cover hundreds of employers and contracts, spread out all over the city (and sometimes even contractors located in other cities or states). It is easy to see that implementation could be improved if the workers themselves had a role in enforcement. As early as 1949, the Department of Labor had discovered that compliance was greater when employers were required to post notices letting workers know their rights under the Fair Labor Standards Act. According to the Federal Register, effective enforcement depended "to a great extent upon knowledge on the part of covered employees of the provisions of the act."[9] Some municipalities have taken a few steps in this direction, by making an effort to insure that employees know their rights. One common provision in living wage laws requires employers to post notices in the workplace, informing workers of their rights under the ordinance and telling them the current mandated wage. In Ventura County, as well as in several other cities, contractors are required to include an insert with this information in the employee's first paycheck under the county contract.[10] In Los Angeles, representatives from living wage advocacy groups are allowed to visit worksites to conduct trainings and tell workers their rights.

However, even when equipped with knowledge about their rights, workers often do not feel secure enough to act as whistleblowers against their employers. This is especially true in the employment-at-will system of the United States, where employers generally have the legal right to fire employees without cause. The kinds of workers covered by living wage ordinances are often among the most vulnerable to the threat of losing their jobs. Low-wage workers are more likely to be immigrants (some undocumented), people of color, and women. Many live in poverty and need every paycheck to survive.

In order to enhance workers' ability to push enforcement without fear of reprisal, many ordinances are including "anti-retaliation" language, which explicitly states that workers are protected from retaliation for asking about the living wage ordinance or complaining about noncompliance. In Los Angeles, for example, employers cannot

> discharge, reduce in compensation, or otherwise discriminate against any employee for complaining to the City with regard to the employer's compliance or anticipated compliance with this article, for opposing any practice proscribed by this article, for participating in proceedings related to this article, for seeking to enforce his or her rights under this article by any lawful means, or for otherwise asserting rights under this article.[11]

This kind of language has allowed at least a few employees in Los Angeles who had been fired after organizing around the living wage, to win back their jobs. However, language such as this is not always enough to protect workers. Kate Bronfenbrenner has found that in the case of union organizing, employers frequently violate labor law with few or no repercussions.[12] For example, in 31 percent of union organizing drives, employers fire prounion employees, despite the fact that this is blatantly illegal. These and other cases provide ample evidence that workers have reason to fear speaking out at work, even when they have legal protection to do so.

One solution to this is to protect the employees' identity. For example, in Oakland, California, the living wage ordinance states that employers do not have the right to know the identity of any worker filing a complaint of noncompliance. In fact, any complainant or witness must give written consent before the city will reveal their identity. Other ordinances also allow third parties to file complaints on behalf of the employee, without divulging the employee's name.

Another solution is to create conditions under which workers have more job security. As discussed in research on OSHA, unions are a principal way of getting that security, as they provide a contract as well as grievance structures for dealing with contract violations. With a union contract usually comes union staff who can work with employees to protect their rights. A union contract also brings the power of a collective voice. Some ordinances include provisions to strengthen union's ability to organize, thereby giving workers that job security. One example of this is also in Oakland, where the anti-retaliation clause is extended to cover union activity.[13] In San Jose, a "labor peace" clause gives the city the right to deny contracts or subsidies to any firm with a history of violations of labor law, or to deny them if the city determines that the funded site is likely to experience labor disruptions. This allows already-unionized or union-neutral employers to get higher priority for city dollars. Other ordinances have included language that protects existing unionized work forces. In cases where the city changes service contractors, a worker retention provision requires the new contractor to give the existing workers the right to keep their jobs if they want them, at the same level of wages and benefits. According to living wage attorney Paul Sonn, "Under NLRB doctrine, if a majority of the workers at the successor firm were members of a union at the predecessor firm, the management is required to recognize the union and cannot demand an election." In other words, says Sonn, worker retention provisions "effectively ensure the conditions where automatic recognition of the union is mandatory."

The point here is that some of the coalitions have included language in their ordinances to ease the barriers to unionization for the covered workers or to protect existing unions. Ideally, this would result in creating an environment where workers themselves could play a role in enforcing the living wage. With the protection that comes from a union contract, along with shop stewards and grievance procedures, workers might be more likely to feel they can file a complaint concerning noncompliance.

Chapter 10 will profile some of the outcomes of the effort to link living wage and union organizing, but the quick summary is that there are not many cases in which workers covered by living wage laws have been able to unionize their workplaces as a result of the living wage campaign. That means that with no protection, or the small protection provided from anti-retaliation clauses, workers are still unlikely to play an active role in enforcement. This is exacerbated by the problems of information discussed in chapter 5, which suggest that many workers may not even be aware of their right to the living wage. Therefore, living wage activists have also had to rely on other methods to improve enforcement, such as the implementation advisory boards we turn to next.

Community Groups Getting a "Seat at the Table"

Recent work in political theory has highlighted the role of nonstate actors in policy implementation beyond protest politics. Particularly in developing countries, much emphasis is placed on the role of nongovernmental organizations (NGOs) and civil society in creating new forms of governance.[14] Indeed, according to political theorist Paul Hirst, failures of state socialism and liberal democratic states have led some political theorists to focus more on the exclusive role of NGOs in policy formation and the provision of services.[15] Specifically, Hirst refers to the revival of the nineteenth- and early-twentieth-century notion of associationalism, or associative democracy. Associationalism calls for a decentralized economy and self-government. The model suggests that citizens, acting cooperatively, can create their own voluntary organizations and provide more effective forms of governance than a centralized state. Hirst asserts that associative democracy can provide a better alternative for the provision of services, as it is more democratic, less bureaucratic, and more accountable than previous systems based on capitalistic principles.

Fung and Wright examine four experiments in what they call empowered participatory governance—a model of governance that involves ordinary people at the local level, working with state administrators to solve concrete problems. They argue that such projects can enhance government efficiency and lead to more equitable and democratic outcomes, for several reasons. First, solutions to certain kinds of governance problems "may require the variety of experience and knowledge offered by more diverse, relatively more open minded, citizens and field operatives, than by distant and narrowly trained experts."[16] Second, incorporating civil society leads to greater accountability. When citizens are involved in decision-making, they bring new ideas and more information to the table, and are more invested in the outcomes.

Others have promoted the role of civil society in governance as a form of critique of the modern state. This includes libertarian organizations like the Reason Foundation and the Cato Institute, who call for a greater role for "noncoercive civil society" so that the role of government can be reduced.[17] It also includes "government reformers," such as David Osborne and Ted Gaebler, who wrote *Reinventing Government* in 1992. Osborne and Gaebler don't believe that civil society should replace government but that it can assist efforts to downsize bureaucracies. Whether the calls for greater influence from civil society come from the left or the right of the political spectrum, they focus on bringing nongovernmental actors in to enhance or replace traditional governance structures of policy formation and implementation.

One recent example of the reliance on nongovernmental organizations for functions traditionally considered part of governing is in the monitoring of factories for compliance with labor laws. With the development of the international anti-sweatshop movement of the 1990s, students, workers' organizations, and scholars noted that no government is particularly equipped to monitor the thousands of garment manufacturing factories in their country. Some observers called for NGOs to be involved in the process. In particular, the Fair Labor Association (FLA) and the Worker Rights Consortium (WRC) were established in the late 1990s as monitoring agents for the campus codes of conduct being pushed by United Students Against Sweatshops chapters and adopted by universities. The FLA and WRC were both meant to improve on voluntary compliance and internal monitoring, or monitoring by for-profit agencies such as accounting firms or by not-for-profit organizations hired directly by the company.[18] Many students charged that the FLA was still not truly independent, as corporate licensees are allowed to serve on the executive board. The WRC executive committee, on the other hand, is comprised of five labor representatives, five students, and five university administrators. However, both organizations assume that at least some external input is needed to conduct proper investigations of apparel factories for code-of-conduct compliance.

Another place where nongovernmental actors were called on to improve monitoring comes from the realm of city governance. Beginning in the 1960s, a growing movement in the United States called for greater public participation in local politics, both to improve the delivery of services and "the trust and confidence of neighborhood participants in local government."[19] This included neighborhood advisory boards but also citywide commissions and boards with citizen representation. A survey by the Advisory Commission on Intergovernmental Relations in the early 1970s found that more than two-thirds of responding cities reported beginning some form of citizen participation.[20]

Many of these experiments did not last or had little effect, but a few models in particular remained. One such model is the citizen review board often used to oversee community police activity. For example, one such police review board in Portland, Oregon, states:

> The police should be responsive to the desires of the community. In order to make community values a priority for the police bureau, there needs to be extensive training for officers and structures of responsibility. This includes impartial, independent investigations of police misconduct and the power to make policy changes to address recurring problems in police practice.[21]

Citizen review boards established committees of citizens who met regularly to monitor and sometimes investigate police actions and policy. Such boards exist in a number of communities. According to Human Rights Watch (HRW), "By 1997, thirty-eight of the fifty largest U.S. cities (76 percent) had some form of citizen review."[22] For the most part, these boards are established in response to ongoing and often egregious cases of police corruption, violence, or other forms of misconduct.[23] Police citizen review boards vary greatly in terms of their membership, authority, and scope, which leads to differing levels of effectiveness. In a comprehensive review of fourteen such boards, HRW concluded that in order to be effective:

> external review requires the review of police files about specific incidents, the ability to compel police cooperation, and the obligation to provide comprehensive periodic reports to the public about the types of complaints received, trends, and recommendations made to the relevant police department. Citizen review units must also have independence, civilian control, and some role in disciplinary proceedings.[24]

Under these guidelines, HRW found many of the review boards lacking but concluded that the structures should be revised rather than thrown out altogether. They concluded "external citizen review boards should be an integral part of police oversight and policy formulation" because "history has shown that police are not able or willing to police themselves in a manner acceptable to the public."[25]

A third area in which nonstate involvement is found is in environmental policy enforcement. Federal and state policies have allowed and sometimes even pushed for public participation in areas such as education, outreach, and evaluation of environmental policy.[26] The National Environmental Policy Act of 1970 did not include citizen participation but over the years as states moved to implement the act, citizen organizations pushed for, and won, a number of rights through court decisions. This includes the right of the public to have access to information about the environmental impacts of new developments on protected lands. It also includes the right for public input, or "commenting," through hearings and reports into decisions about awarding environmental permits that would allow developers to build.[27] Although public comment is now required for all federal regulations, most of the time the public does not get involved in this process. Corporations and industry associations are most likely to take advantage of the right to "comment."

The examples above show how nonstate actors can be brought into the implementation and monitoring process. This is sometimes done to enhance the capacity of the state to do its job, or because there is no clear or proper state authority to oversee implementation. Other times, nonstate actors serve as watchdogs on the state. The examples given are quite different in terms of the monitoring agents and types of programs covered, but all share a reliance on outside parties—often working as volunteers—to implement and enforce policy. We can also find this kind of enforcement agent in the case of living wage ordinances, in the form of implementation task forces or advisory boards.[28]

Living Wage Advisory Boards

In a few cases, living wage ordinances have established official advisory boards to oversee the implementation process. Advisory boards or task forces are generally promoted by living wage activists who want to ensure enforcement will occur, but sometimes cities support the idea as a way to decrease the administrative burden for the city staff and put some of the duties onto volunteer advisory board members. As of December 2002, eleven ordinances contained formal provisions for an implementation advisory board, including Boston and Cambridge, Massachusetts;

Cleveland, Ohio; Dane County, Wisconsin; Miami-Dade and Broward counties, Florida; New Haven, Connecticut; Warren, Michigan; Watsonville and Ventura County, California; and Suffolk County, New York. An additional three established some form of task force in the regulations or at some point in the implementation process—Santa Cruz and Los Angeles, California, and Chicago, Illinois.

An advisory board can provide coalition members with access to valuable information needed for policy implementation. Although cities may struggle getting accurate payroll data from employers, when citizens have an official role as part of an oversight committee it greatly enhances the chances that the public will get to see relevant material. A seat on a board also allows outside input into ongoing decisions in the implementation process. Even though living wage ordinances are relatively clear, they still are likely to involve dozens of questions for administrators, such as which contracts are considered service contracts, how to calculate the total value of a subsidy to determine ordinance coverage, and what criteria should be used to decide whether a firm is granted a waiver.

However, coalition members' possession of a seat or two on an advisory board is definitely not enough to guarantee that implementation outcomes will be more successful. Board members need to be motivated to participate fully in the work, even though it can be tedious and is almost always unpaid. Advisory boards also run the risk of diluting the power of coalitions, if the city uses them to co-opt activists who might otherwise be adversarial. Coalition members may feel less room to criticize city staff who serve on a task force with them or less able to pursue outside protest tactics at the same time. Cities in turn can shrug off criticisms, claiming that the implementation outcomes were an equal responsibility of all task force members.[29]

Having a formal seat on an advisory board is not only beneficial for the coalition members who can use it as a means to be a watchdog on the city. Outsiders can also bring additional resources to the city and improve the city's ability to enforce the ordinances. In some cases committee members are low-wage workers or union representatives who have better knowledge of the conditions of the covered workers than do city staff. In other cases, they can simply bring additional minds to work on problems that require time and creative thinking. For example, in Ventura County, the suggestion to include paycheck inserts came from an advisory board member. This is an example of how a task force can enhance the capacity of the city, even in a small municipality where few contracts are covered by the ordinance. This can allow the city to take an expansive approach to its implementation efforts, looking for ways to improve the ordinance and maximize its impact.

Given the potential pros and cons of implementation task forces, it is important to take a close look at how current committees are operating. What do the task forces look like, and what are their responsibilities? Have they worked in the cities where they are in place?

Advisory Board Composition

The size of the advisory board ranges from five to fifteen members, and in every case to date the ordinance spells out the various categories of members that should comprise the task force. For example, the Cleveland ordinance designates a task force of seven members, including two representatives from labor organizations, two from the business community, one from a community organization, one from the mayor's office, and one from the city council. The Santa Cruz Living Wage Advisory Body requires "one low-wage or minimum wage worker." All but two ordinances specifically create a position (or positions) for representatives from labor unions or community groups. The two that don't are Dane County, Wisconsin, which requires that a majority of the seven members shall be persons with an interest in or knowledge of business, labor, or economics; and Miami-Dade County, Florida, which says that no more than six of the fifteen members can be representatives of the business community or affected community groups. The Cambridge ordinance notes that no covered employer or employee is allowed to serve on its Community Advisory Board, to avoid conflict of interest.

Responsibilities

Most ordinances list the responsibilities of the task force, but the level of detail varies. In most cases, the board is charged with meeting regularly and reviewing city records to ensure that employers know about and are complying with the ordinance. They are usually required to conduct periodic reviews and report to the city council, including making recommendations for improvement. The advisory boards are also generally involved in any investigatory procedures regarding noncompliance.

The Cleveland ordinance has relatively extensive requirements regarding the board. The Fair Employment Wage Board is required to elect a chairperson and vice-chairperson by majority vote at the beginning of each year; to meet quarterly, and more as required; to have all meetings open to the public; to allow for public testimony on the issue of compliance; and to have minutes taken at all meetings. At the other end of responsibilities is the Warren, Michigan, task force, which is meant to serve primarily as a board to hear appeals from employers wishing to be exempted from the ordinance. The ordinance establishes only the number and composition of the Living Wage Appeal Committee. It is required to meet "as necessary." Below, I examine some of the city task forces in more detail.

Cleveland, Ohio.   Despite the level of detail in some ordinances, not all city task forces are meeting their requirements. In the case of Cleveland, the city did not hire a staff person until March 2001, nine months after the ordinance was in effect. The ordinance established a Fair Employment Wage Board with city staff and business and labor representatives to oversee implementation, but its first meeting, scheduled for September 2001, was canceled. By early 2002, the Wage Board had only met twice. Neither of the two labor appointees were connected to the campaign and had little personal investment in implementation. However, one of the main opponents of the ordinance, Gerald Meyer of the Greater Cleveland Growth Association, was appointed as one of the business representatives. At the first meeting, the group elected Meyer as chair of the Wage Board.

According to Dave Focareta, of Cleveland based think-tank Policy Matters Ohio, more than a year after enactment, the board had done little work on implementation.[30] Rather than develop the posters that employers are required to post in all worksites to inform workers of the living wage ordinance, the Wage Board focused its energies on developing a brochure directed at employers, explaining why Cleveland is still a good place to do business despite the living wage ordinance. Focareta notes that the posters for employees are especially important, because implementation of the law is almost completely complaint-driven. If employees don't know about the ordinance, they will not ask for the living wage, and there is no way to know whether employers are following the law.

Shortly after Policy Matters Ohio released a report critical of the city's implementation efforts, city officials announced that they were ready to start enforcing the ordinance, known as the Fair Employment Law.[31] The city's acting director of economic development, Greg Huth, suggested that the implementation lag had been due to a "wrapping up period" following the law's enactment. Huth announced that bidders for city contracts would now be required to attend sessions to learn about the law and to sign affidavits acknowledging that they understand the requirements. The city pledged to monitor payroll records on a regular basis. In explaining the city's turnaround, Policy Matters Ohio executive director Amy Hanauer notes that in addition to the critical report, the city also elected a labor-supported mayor around the same time as the shift in city policy. The Cleveland Central Labor Council has since pushed the mayor to improve implementation efforts, including designating a new labor appointee on the Fair Employment Wage Board who will take the job seriously.

Boston, Massachusetts.   Other task forces are much more active than Cleveland's. In Boston, the Living Wage Advisory Committee meets regularly and is active on a number of fronts. The ordinance specifically designates seats on the committee for ACORN and labor representatives. At the start, the Advisory Committee worked closely with the city to develop regulations. City staff and the Advisory Committee also noted early on that the ordinance covered fewer workers than it might, given that the eligibility level for service contracts was $100,000 (whereas in other cities it is usually around $25,000), and that nonprofit contractors were not covered unless they had at least one hundred employees. The Advisory Committee worked with the city's living wage coordinator to develop recommendations to the city council to lower the thresholds and increase coverage. In the wake of the much-publicized Harvard Living Wage campaign, the Advisory Committee also demanded an increase in the dollar amount of the living wage, from $9.11 to $10.25, indexed to inflation. Amendments comprising all these improvements were approved by the city council in October 2001, doubling the number of workers covered. In late 2003, the Advisory Committee enacted new and improved regulations to tighten implementation and monitoring.

City of Santa Cruz, California.   The Santa Cruz Living Wage Advisory Committee meets approximately once a month and makes its agenda, meeting, and minutes available to the public. The seven members work with city staff to review the implementation process, find solutions for problems, develop criteria for evaluation of the impact of the ordinance, consider applications for exemptions from employers, and look for potential funding sources in cases where nonprofit agencies are unable to pay the higher wage.

According to Sandy Brown, co-chair of the committee and staff member of the Santa Cruz Campaign for a Living Wage, the Advisory Committee has been a relatively effective mechanism for dealing with living wage issues. The committee allows the ordinance to be treated as an ongoing project, rather than a finished and complete law. The committee has addressed a wide range of topics since its inception, from dealing with administrative details such as getting materials translated into Spanish and calculating annual wage increases, to substantive and thorny issues such as how to find the money for social service agencies to help pay the living wage. The committee has also provided a forum in which to discuss such projects as getting media coverage of the positive impact the ordinance has had on workers.

Brown saw the role of the Advisory Committee as important enough to make its existence a demand in subsequent campaigns her organization ran in Santa Cruz County and nearby Watsonville. As discussed in the previous chapter, county supervisors were against the idea and insisted on eliminating the Advisory Committee provision in the final ordinance. In Watsonville, the city council decided by a narrow margin to allow a seven-person committee, rather than the city manager, to oversee the implementation of the ordinance.[32]

Miami-Dade County, Florida.   The living wage ordinance passed in Miami-Dade County, Florida, included an implementation Advisory Board to oversee monitoring. The Advisory Board has fifteen members: two appointed by the mayor, and one appointee from each of thirteen county board supervisors. There is one county employee assigned to staff the board, and two to three others who work on other aspects of implementation, including worksite investigations. The appointments have been slow in coming. Three years after enactment, the Advisory Board still only has ten members. Still, those ten members have had an active and useful role, according to Florida Legal Services' Arthur Rosenberg, a living wage proponent and Advisory Board member.

The board meets monthly to review reports from county staff. They also hear complaints from employees and employers. For example, they have heard from a number of employees who believe they should be getting paid a living wage but are not. They have also heard from employers who have questions about implementing the requirements, such as one who was concerned that the ordinance mandated he pay $1.25 per hour per employee in health care benefits, but he already provided a good plan that cost only $1.20 per hour. In each case, the Advisory Board hears testimony, then makes a recommendation to the County Attorney. The attorney makes a ruling, and the board reviews and responds. According to Rosenberg, the process has worked fairly well so far. Although he personally has not agreed with every decision by the attorney, he feels that the judgments have been fair and nonpartisan.

The Advisory Board has also worked on expanding the coverage of the ordinance. As in the Los Angeles case, the original ordinance was written narrowly so that many workers at the county airport were not covered. The board recognized that this was not the intent of the ordinance, so they worked with the attorney and county staff to rewrite parts. After a year, the county board approved the amendments and greatly expanded the scope of airport coverage. (However, in early 2003 the state passed a law negating all living wage coverage for economic development and airports). The board also discovered that the county was not applying the living wage to contract renewals. They succeeded in pressuring the county to amend the ordinance to close that loophole.

City of Los Angeles, California.   In Los Angeles, the Los Angeles Alliance for a New Economy (LAANE) was able to convert their informal outside pressure into a formal role for themselves on an implementation task force. Immediately after passage of the ordinance, LAANE representatives worked with city staff to write the regulations that would establish the implementation procedures. After relations between LAANE and the city implementation administrators became adversarial, LAANE pressured the city to establish a task force, allowing LAANE regular access to meetings about implementation. The task force included representatives from the City Administrative Office, the Office of the Chief Legislative Analyst, the City Attorney's office, LAANE, and from Councilmember Jackie Goldberg's office (the original sponsor of the living wage ordinance). Initially, the task force met on a regular basis to hammer out problems. According to June Gibson, City Administrative Office staff person in charge of implementation, now that the majority of implementation issues have been resolved the task force only meets on an as-needed basis.[33]

Are Task Forces Necessary? It's about Power

Although a task force can give legal standing and representation to living wage advocates in the implementation process, a few coalitions have shown how systematic involvement can be possible without such a body. The Santa Cruz County and Chicago coalitions were able to push for mechanisms for regular contact with the city even without a task force in place. This was also the case in Los Angeles, before the Task Force was established.

San Francisco is another example of how this can work. In that city, several of the key individuals from the campaign have played a regular role in implementation. After the ordinance was passed in 2000, activists played a large role in writing the regulations. They also pressured the city to create a new department, the Office of Contract Administration, which would oversee enforcement. They got the city to hire staff, and even had influence on which people were hired for the office. According to living wage organizer Ken Jacobs, while there is no formal task force, living wage advocates meet with city staff on a regular basis. Jacobs finds this mechanism to be sufficient and is not sure a formal task force would be an improvement. "We had an official task force created to get the ordinance passed in the first place, and that was a pain in the ass," he explains. "If you can get the regular contact with city staff and have a sympathetic ear then I don't see the need to create something more bureaucratic." The key here is that the San Francisco Living Wage Coalition had done effective organizing and demonstrated their power. In addition, Jacobs explains, the Board of Supervisors was already fairly sympathetic to the living wage. Under these conditions, living wage advocates may be able to play a large and systematic role in implementation without a formal task force. In cases where these conditions don't hold, such a body may be necessary.

Howard Greenwich, researcher with the East Bay Alliance for a Sustainable Economy (EBASE) in Oakland, California, agrees with Jacobs.[34] In the cities EBASE works with, such as Richmond, Berkeley, and Oakland, the living wage coalition has friendly relations with at least some city representatives. This allows EBASE regular contact with the city on implementation issues. Greenwich argues that EBASE and its labor allies have enough power and good relations with the city so that they can influence outcomes in their favor.

The difference comes in cases where the organizations do not have any inside connections. This is the case at the Port of Oakland, which is run by a board appointed by the mayor, which is therefore not subject to democratic accountability. In the case of the port, EBASE feels shut out from most living wage decisions, such as those over a firm's application for a waiver. In a case like this, where the coalition has no input, a task force would be desirable, as it would allow the advocates regular access to information (including the right to request information from employers), and would give them legitimacy in the implementation process. Indeed, in 2003 EBASE released a one-year status report regarding living wage implementation at the port. Among other recommendations, the authors call on the port to establish a public advisory committee to improve monitoring and enforcement.

Conclusion

In this chapter, I have shown that civil society organizations can fight for and win a role in governance structures, and the implementation process in particular. For example, several living wage ordinances have created a role for those affected by the policy, including informing workers about their rights and creating avenues of redress in cases of noncompliance. Given the tenuous nature of employment, however, I have noted that it is crucial that workers are protected from reprisals when registering complaints—otherwise, the opportunity to complain is of little use. There are direct ways to protect workers in the ordinance, such as nonretaliation language or the right to file anonymous complaints. Still, the strongest job security workers can have is a union contract, so living wage ordinances that assist union organizing efforts offer perhaps the best protection, albeit indirect, for workers involved in monitoring and enforcing living wage ordinances.

Another option is for civil society organizations to play a formal role in implementation, a situation akin to the citizen review boards created to enhance police accountability, and the NGO involvement in sweatshop monitoring. I have shown that in the case of living wages, advocates in some cities have pursued formal roles within the monitoring and enforcement process. Living wage advisory boards and task forces do not guarantee specific outcomes but greatly increase the likelihood of successful and expansive implementation.

Ideally, living wage ordinances would provide opportunities for both kinds of civil society involvement discussed in this chapter: language that creates protected opportunities for workers to enforce the law and task forces that regularly monitor employers. The first allows the best access to information, as it is the workers themselves who have the greatest incentive to monitor compliance. The second option provides systematic oversight by other stakeholders.

How do the findings in chapter 7—that outside pressure can effectively influence implementation—meld with our findings here? Specifically, how should living wage advocates best involve themselves in enforcement and monitoring? In the next chapter, I argue that in order to ensure the strongest implementation, community organizations who support living wage ordinances should utilize a combination of inside and outside tactics.

9

FACTORS NEEDED FOR SUCCESSFUL IMPLEMENTATION

Inside and Outside Strategies

Always assume more organizing is necessary.

Kirsten Cross, codirector, East Bay Alliance for a Sustainable Economy,
"Lessons on Living Wage Implementation"

The examples in chapters 7 and 8 show that living wage supporters can help improve implementation outcomes through various mechanisms. In chapter 7 I profiled cases of "protest politics," including rallies,
marches, and the use of media to push municipalities to improve enforcement. In chapter 8 I discussed inside strategies, including direct enforcement from the workplace and "third party" implementation. In this
chapter, I argue that the ideal form of implementation from the perspective of living wage advocates is a combination of inside and outside strategies. I discuss the factors desirable for successful implementation by
nongovernmental organizations (NGOs) pursuing inside and outside
strategies. These include access to information, incentives to do the hard
work of monitoring, systematic involvement in monitoring, decision-
making power over enforcement, and maintaining independence from the
city. I then look to other arenas in which nongovernmental organizations
have been involved in implementation and monitoring, using inside-
outside strategies. This includes enforcement of unemployment insurance
programs in several Scandinavian countries, environmental legislation in
Vietnam, and prevailing wage laws in the United States.

Finally, I discuss an alternative option: voluntary enforcement programs. As mentioned previously, failures in policy implementation have
led to serious critiques of the role of the state in monitoring and enforce-

ment. Some observers have proposed alternative mechanisms for policy implementation that do not depend on the state. These fall into two categories: policies that are legally binding but do not rely on the state for enforcement, and nonbinding policies that rely on mechanisms other than state law for enforcement. For example, in the arena of enforcement of international labor standards, some have called for mechanisms that rely on market-based incentives. Voluntary enforcement has not been popular in the living wage movement, although a few cities have experimented with the idea. This chapter will discuss the concept of voluntary monitoring systems in general, drawing out lessons for living wage ordinances and other labor standards.

Access to Information

The first factor that appears to have led to implementation success in specific cases such as Baltimore, Chicago, and Los Angeles is simply that the organizations had information about noncompliance. In Baltimore, the Solidarity Sponsoring Committee (SSC) found out during their organizing efforts that school bus drivers were not getting the living wage they were entitled to. In Los Angeles, the living wage coalition discovered various cases of noncompliance through worker trainings and organizing efforts at the airport. In Chicago, SEIU Local 880's own members would have been denied a raise had the city not changed its interpretation of coverage. It was this kind of information that spurred the organizations to protest before their city councils and push for covered firms to pay the living wage.

The need for information is itself a good argument for having a formal role in living wage implementation. A task force can provide the ideal mechanism to access information about compliance. In the best case scenario, all task force members would be able to view employer payroll records and even monitor worksites. However, the examples of Baltimore and Chicago show that a seat on a task force is not necessary to find out about noncompliance. In fact, the best method for gathering wage data is getting it directly from the covered workers. This means the workers themselves are active in enforcement efforts. The next best option is to have workers closely linked to organizations, such as unions or community groups that are working on implementation on their behalf. However, even with strong contacts in certain covered businesses, it is unlikely that workers or unions from every covered worksite would be active in enforcement efforts. A task force can help activists get information on a regular basis. Without this systematic access to data, activists must work much harder and will never have ongoing reliable information. Furthermore, systematic internal city information is needed to know which contracts or subsidized projects are going to be covered in the future in order to prepare to monitor them.

Motivation to Monitor

As the Cleveland case shows, it is not enough to have a formal seat on an implementation task force. Those serving on such a body should have incentives to insure that the ordinance is enforced. In Cleveland, although there were two seats for union representatives on the task force, one member never came to meetings, and the other attended but offered little input. Although the representatives were from labor unions, these were unions that had not actively participated in the campaign itself and had little or no incentive to put time into living wage enforcement. This may be because they didn't see the connections between the living wage and organizing opportunities for their union, or because they saw living wage enforcement as a low priority compared to their other responsibilities.

Even when a task force is not in place, living wage advocates will be more likely to put time and effort into implementation when they have an incentive to do so. In Milwaukee, for example, the living wage coalition never knew that workers were not receiving their mandated wage. The reason is that the living wage advocates in Milwaukee never attempted to establish contact with the low-wage workers covered by the law and, therefore, had no information about compliance. In Baltimore and Los Angeles, the associations—a low-wage worker organization (SSC) and a nonprofit representing unions (LAANE)—did have an incentive to seek out the covered workers, specifically, because they were trying to organize them. While the Milwaukee coalition had resources, such as paid staff, Progressive Milwaukee, a political party and the primary coalition organization, did not have such incentives. It did not directly represent covered workers and was not trying to sign up low-wage workers as members. The Campaign for a Sustainable Milwaukee, a community organization involved in the coalition, may have had the incentive to monitor the living wage but decided to focus its efforts elsewhere. No unions in the Milwaukee living wage coalition took up the call to organize these workers employed by city contractors because they were engaged in other campaigns.

For SSC and LAANE, the living wage campaign had specific goals: talking to workers and getting them to join SSC in Baltimore, or SEIU or HERE in Los Angeles. For this reason, finding cases of employer non-compliance gave SSC and LAANE greater organizing opportunities. They could use living wage implementation as a way to talk to workers, and a way to show the power and value of their organizations. Specifically, they could make the argument to workers that having a living wage ordinance is only useful if workers belong to organizations that can enforce the ordinance. In Milwaukee, where the advocate organizations were using the living wage campaign victory in a different way—to define the values of a political party and show voters that they were able to achieve legislative victories—there was no incentive to find examples of noncompliance.

Similarly, SEIU 880 in Chicago worked on the living wage campaign and then had an incentive to make sure its members were covered by the agreement. The union had had a hard time getting decent pay raises for its members directly through collective bargaining. When the living wage ordinance was passed, union leaders took the opportunity to meet with city officials to make sure that home health care workers got the living wage along with other workers. This meant that SEIU organizers fought to have the ordinance interpreted in a way that included home health care workers. The union was successful in winning significant raises for its members.

The Case of Subsidies

Nowhere is the importance of motivation to monitor more striking than in the case of economic development subsidies. While over 40 percent of living wage ordinances (as of 2002) include provisions that mandate that employers receiving grants, loans, tax breaks, or other public subsidies pay a living wage, very few cities can point to actual instances where the living wage has been applied to an economic development project. Why is this?

As Ken Jacobs, a San Francisco living wage organizer, argues, economic development projects usually do not have a natural base of support. Many new subsidies are for business recruitment, not retention. Therefore, they apply to proposed developments. There are no employees at the start of the project, and therefore no one with the motivation to make sure the living wage is applied and enforced. This differs from contracting, where the services in question are usually already provided by a service contractor or by public sector employees. In either case, there are existing employees who will benefit materially from the living wage law, and therefore have the incentive to fight for implementation of the ordinance.

Does anyone have the incentive to make sure the subsidy provision is implemented? In some cities, unions or corporate accountability watchdog organizations may have the motivation to follow city council deliberations about potential development. The hotel workers union HERE pays attention to the use of city tax breaks for hotel development because they can use the public process to demand card-check prior to the opening of a new hotel (a process which allows workers to more easily gain union recognition). But in most cases, it is only when tax breaks are granted to existing businesses for retention purposes that we could expect to find a natural constituency for living wage subsidy provision enforcement.[1]

Systematic Involvement

I just noted that in Baltimore, Chicago, and Los Angeles living wage advocates had the motivation to monitor the implementation of the ordinances. But earlier, I argued that of these three cities, only Los Angeles could be considered to have expansive implementation. What distinguishes the Baltimore and Chicago cases from the Los Angeles case? Baltimore's access to information and incentive to organize the workers covered by the city's living wage led to successful implementation of the ordinance in a few cases. However, the living wage organization (SSC) did not have the desire or the means to integrate themselves into the implementation process. By contrast, in Los Angeles the living wage proponents' close ties to city government employees and city council member Jackie Goldberg opened up a space for them in the implementation process itself. Through these connections, the living wage coalition was able to assist in writing the regulations, to gain a role in official worker training, to access inside information about upcoming contracts and subsidies, and to work with city staff to develop the legal language necessary to close loopholes in the law. This was important for two reasons. First, it gave LAANE enhanced and systematic access to workers (through the training) and, therefore, to more comprehensive information about working conditions and living wage compliance. Second, it gave them a chance to develop and promote specific suggestions for altering the city's mechanisms for enforcement.

For example, by suggesting that the BCA hire Spanish-speaking staff to answer worker questions, and by developing worker training, LAANE influenced the state's capacity to monitor the law. By steering the city toward adopting stronger mechanisms, such as having the City Controller withhold checks from employers in noncompliance and tying department managers' level of cooperation with the ordinance into their performance evaluation for merit pay, LAANE was able to affect the system of incentives for enforcement within the state and compliance among covered firms.

Without having a role in the city's implementation, SSC in Baltimore was not able to alter the state's capacity to monitor the law or to systematically improve the process by changing the incentives for city employees or covered contractors. Rather, they were only able to exert influence on a sporadic, case-by-case basis. In part, this was because SSC did not have the desire to integrate themselves into the process but also because they did not have the strong alliances with city council or staff. The result of this was that even though SSC helped certain workers get the living wage and receive back pay in 1997 and 1998, the city did not improve its monitoring.

Five years later, staff from HERE discovered that Aramark, a large concession vendor, was not complying with the Baltimore living wage ordinance. Although the company had signed a contract with the city in 1999 to provide food and beverage concessions at the city convention center, it had failed to submit any of the required payroll records over the years and failed to pay its workers the time-and-a-half overtime pay mandated by the living wage ordinance. HERE was surprised to find that although city staff were friendly and willing to help get the law enforced, they had little knowledge of the case. "No one was minding the store," said HERE Local 7 organizer Nick Weiner. Again, HERE was motivated by one specific instance of noncompliance because they represented a particular set of workers. They did not have the motivation to take on a larger implementation campaign or suggest an institutional role, which meant the city returned to its weak monitoring.

To avoid that outcome, a few coalitions profiled in this book have pursued systematic involvement in implementation through seats on a task force. Not only does this help improve access to information, but it can create an institutionalized set of actors committed to preserving the ordinance. Paul Pierson's research on welfare state retrenchment in Britain and the United States suggests this is true. In his book *Dismantling the Welfare State*, Pierson argues that the creation of social programs estab-

lished a specific set of loyal actors willing to fight any attempts to eliminate those programs.[2] This includes the direct beneficiaries of the policies
as well as those hired to administer the programs. In this way, it becomes
harder for state leaders to take away programs than it is to enact them.
Similarly, the creation of implementation task forces expands the constituency of those invested in keeping the ordinance in place.

However, as discussed earlier, a body of this kind is not necessarily the
only way for community groups to play a role in a city's process. As Ken
Jacobs of the San Francisco living wage campaign explained, when your
coalition is well-organized and has demonstrated its power, and when
there are sympathetic ears within the municipal government, it is possible to have a regular role in implementation through informal means.[3]
"They call us as much as we call them," says Jacobs of the San Francisco
city administrators.

Unfortunately for living wage supporters, the San Francisco case is not
typical. It is not common in most U.S. cities for city administrators to call
community activists on a regular basis to get input about their policy
implementation. This is true not only for living wage ordinances but
progressive policies in general. However, that doesn't mean that city
administrators and elected officials don't make calls.

Research on general government functioning suggests that it is much
more likely that officials will call living wage opponents before they call
advocates. As shown by the research of Dan Clawson, Alan Neustadtl,
and Denise Scott, due to the structure of campaign financing, the power
of political action committees, and business hegemony, elected leaders
and the civil servants they employ are generally financially dependent on
and socially connected to corporations and not workers. As the power of
money in elections increases, so does the power of those who have it. As
one political action committee officer noted, "In the past we have always
gotten calls from the administrative assistants to congressmen. Now the
congressmen are so hungry for money they are calling themselves. I had
two congressmen call last week."[4] This kind of power creates a sense of
entitlement among business leaders. Clawson, Neustadtl, and Scott write:

> Corporate PAC officials sometimes talked as if it were normal that
> anyone who wanted to see a member of Congress could do so—even
> if the person didn't live in the member's state or district. One executive
> saw this as a right, not a privilege: 'You want to have access to the member
> so you or your experts can tell your story. That's what the Constitution
> guarantees.'[5]

The power of money to gain access to elected representatives is greater at the federal level, where elections are more costly. In fact, this is one reason why living wage campaigns focus on the local level, where money is less important and elected representatives have greater accountability to voters. However, in large cities where elections are costly, and even in smaller cities where more and more money is being spent on campaigns, living wage supporters still must struggle to get the ear of their elected representatives. In some places, successful organizing can result in the situation in San Francisco Jacobs describes, but that remains an exception.

Decision-Making Power

A key aspect of an effective task force is decision-making power. While most of the task forces discussed here have the ability to make decisions on some aspects of implementation, none have ultimate authority. In Cambridge, for example, the ordinance established a Community Advisory Board to hear petitions for waivers from employers. The board is charged with analyzing supporting documents, holding public hearings, and offering a recommendation on the waiver to the city manager, but the city manager has the final say in all decisions. Similarly, in Boston, while all waiver request materials must be given to the Living Wage Advisory Committee, the ultimate decision about granting them is made by the mayor.

This issue became important in the struggle over granting waivers to recycling companies holding contracts in Cambridge, Somerville, and Boston, discussed earlier in chapter 7. Although the Cambridge Advisory Board wanted to extend rather than renew the recycling contract, the city manager said no. She granted the waiver, and then signed a four-year contract, saying the city could get a better deal with a longer time period.

In Boston, the contract came up for renewal the following year (2002). Again, in that case it was the mayor—rather than the Advisory Committee or the city's living wage coordinator—who made the final decision. Living wage advocates had to resort to outside track strategies, including pickets at the recycling plant, op-eds, and mobilizing community members for hearings. The mayor eventually decided to grant an indefinite month-to-month extension of the recycling contract, and the case is still pending.

Ventura County living wage administrator Cheryl Monzon noted that the county task force has the power to make decisions on administrative issues, but any substantive decision must be made by the Board of Supervisors. Task force chair Murray Rosenbluth explained,

> We have been a data gathering and watchdog group. I just initiated a forward-looking proposal to increase the living wage. One conservative member strongly objected saying that is beyond our allowable scope. I took the allowable scope question to the County CEO. He said that since we are an advisory committee our scope is whatever a majority of the committee says it is. I read that to mean, have fun but you have no real power. The County Board of Supervisors has the ultimate power.[6]

This suggests that living wage advocates cannot rely on their internal role as a guarantee for enforcement. A strong task force can accomplish much and have significant impact but in the end is limited to the power with which it is invested.

Maintaining Independence

The recycling example discussed earlier raises the final concern for living wage advocates, which is the ability to maintain independence while serving on a formal implementation body. This is a difficult yet crucial challenge for living wage advocates. While holding a seat on a city-sanctioned body allows the advocates access to inside information and a voice in decisions about implementation, it can also serve to close off the outside channels of protest mentioned in chapter 7. In part, this is because advocates may feel invested in the formal system and become reluctant to disrupt it from the outside. But it is also because task force engagement is one step removed from the political dynamic of implementation. In cities where there is no task force, most decisions are made by city council members—making it clearly a political decision, and one that should be open to public input. Putting the decisions onto the task force makes the decisions more technocratic, and not as likely to be open to public input.

In the recycling company case, it was only in Somerville, where advocates have no formal role in implementation, that some mobilization was done initially. When the Somerville coalition learned that the city was considering a waiver, they began to organize people to pressure the city. They made contacts with some of the workers at the recycling facility, and when the press began to represent the issue as recycling versus living wages, the coalition reached out to environmentalists. The Somerville activists did extensive research on the city contracting, on the recycling company, and alternative recycling options. They mobilized crowds for public hearings and pushed the city to listen to their arguments. In the end, they got the city council to grant a short-term extension of the contract (rather than a renewal) in order to buy more time to do research about recycling alternatives.

According to Somerville living wage advocate Mary Jo Connolly, this kind of organizing was possible in part because Somerville does *not* have a strong implementation system. "There is no question that Mimi Turchinetz [the city of Boston's living wage coordinator] is doing a much better job on implementation than the staff in Somerville or Cambridge— there is no doubt about that," Connolly said. "But, in some ways Somerville activists have more wiggle room because everything is public and a political decision. In the other cities, it is all done on the inside."[7] Eventually, the Boston living wage organizers resorted to outside activities as well, to pressure the city to deny a waiver to KTI recycling.

Despite the potentially dampening effect that task force participation can have, advocacy groups can maintain a role in the formal process and keep their outside protest channels open. This is the case in Los Angeles, where LAANE works closely with the city on their task force, yet maintains its base in the labor movement. This allows LAANE to mobilize when necessary. Rather than alienating allies on the task force, in the LA case the ability to mobilize in the streets appears to actually help city staff do their job. At the early stages of implementation, LAANE's work on the task force was helping to improve enforcement of the ordinance on several contracts. However, there were still employers at the airport who resisted compliance. LAANE and the Los Angeles County Federation of Labor kept up a steady stream of media attention, rallies, and actions at the airport and in city council hearings in order to keep the pressure on the council to demand that the airports pressure the companies into compliance. LAANE used the same tactics effectively to insure that the living wage was applied to large new developments in the city.

This was also the case in Boston, when the living wage coalition had to fight requests for waivers from the living wage ordinance from child care agencies and the recycling company. Although the city staff is sympathetic to the goals of the living wage ordinance, it is clear that the power of that staff only goes so far. In the case of the Boston waivers, the living wage coalition pressured the city from inside and outside. Outside pressure included pickets, talking to workers to get their stories, and letters to the editor. It also included mobilizing people to attend hearings and provide testimony against the waiver. According to Greater Boston Legal Services attorney Monica Halas, who sits on the Advisory Committee, the strength of the alliances built in Boston has really been apparent in the cases of organizing around waivers. For example, in one case, the city set a date for a hearing on the KTI waiver for a Wednesday. They didn't announce this date until the previous Friday, after 6:00 p.m. on a three-day weekend. Despite the short notice, the living wage coalition was able to mobilize dozens of supporters and a range of testimony.

In these cases, outside protest and community mobilization can provide political "cover" for staff or even city administrators who wish to enforce the ordinance but feel they can't. Public rallies can help a mayor tell a contractor that the living wage must be enforced. Ken Jacobs of the San Francisco living wage campaign notes that even in San Francisco, where staff are very supportive to the living wage, there is a need on occasion for outside mobilization to pressure the city on enforcement. Jacobs notes, "If you need to utilize outside pressure in a city like San Francisco, I can only imagine what other [living wage coalitions], where the city staff don't support the ordinance, need to do."

Balance of Forces?

Although task forces are one tool for living wage advocates to insure that ordinances are implemented, it should not be assumed that they need to be stacked with living wage supporters to accomplish this. Arthur Rosenberg, who sits on the Miami-Dade Advisory Board, noted that having business people on the board is useful. "No one side should dominate," he said, because then the board would lose credibility.[8] Rosenberg has also seen the business side appointees change their perspective over time, after serving on the board. After working on an issue for awhile, "You tend to become invested in making sure the law that was passed is upheld."

Boston city staff person Mimi Turchinetz also sees the value in a balance of forces working to implement the ordinance. In fact, Turchinetz explains some of the success of implementation in her city. In testimony to the Providence, Rhode Island, City Council, Turchinetz remarked:

> One of the factors that works in Boston's favor is our ongoing collaboration with the Greater Boston Chamber of Commerce. The Chamber has been at the table. Additionally, the Advisory Committee created by Mayor Menino includes representatives from both the Greater Boston Chamber

as well as the Neighborhood Chamber. This collaboration has served the city well. In fact, last year when we increased the living wage amount from $9.11 to $10.25, the Chamber lobbied the Boston City Council on behalf of that increase and went on the record stating that the increase would be good for business. Jim Klocke of the Boston Chamber stated "that paying workers a decent wage is good for retention and good for business."[9]

Of course, the Chamber of Commerce had initially vigorously opposed the Boston ordinance. It was only after the first ordinance was passed and business leaders threatened to sue the city over it that negotiations between the city and the chamber began. After a year or so of negotiations, a compromise was reached. This may support Rosenberg's claim that investing time in a project increases personal investment in its outcome.

Murray Rosenbluth, chair of the Ventura County Advisory Committee, concurred with Rosenberg: "When I speak to the [County] Supervisors as the chair of a balanced committee they are more likely to listen."[10] In addition, Rosenbluth feels that having pro– and anti–living wage forces on the same committee creates a place to discuss differences of opinion more openly and productively, because they are not happening via the media. "Thus our discussions are more rational and professional without public pandering to the media," says Rosenbluth.

However, Jen Kern of ACORN points out that the investment of the chamber in the Boston Advisory Committee is not as virtuous as it seems, as their supposed commitment to the ordinance became evident only after the ordinance was watered down to address their concerns. For example, the real estate industry representative on the Advisory Committee—who had been an active opponent of the living wage both publicly and on the committee—stopped coming to meetings after the city agreed to remove economic development subsidy recipients from coverage. The ordinance that was eventually implemented also removed most of the reporting requirements that the business community so forcefully opposed. Kern also suggests that the utility of a balanced task force may be overstated:

From our perspective, the goal of a living wage advisory committee is to insure that the ordinance covers as many workers as possible. Almost without fail, business representatives will have the opposite goal. By the time we get to the advisory committee stage, we've won the battle for our living wage law. At that point, we're not seeking "credibility," we're seeking to raise worker's wages as the law intended.

Besides, she adds, "The whole question of equal representation is kind of a moot point because the chances of a city creating an Advisory Committee without business representation are nil."

This again raises the issue of the political ideological hegemony of business interests in city management. Business power is not absolute and can be challenged, which the San Francisco and Oakland cases highlight. Here, labor and community movements have worked for years to build a power base that enables them to get the ear of city council members and at times, the mayor. But it isn't just that they can get elected officials to talk to them: they have succeeded, to some degree, in getting the cities to redefine the problems of the community. Due to many years of relentless organizing on behalf of worker and community organizations, the city of San Francisco does not always prioritize business climate above all else. However, cities like San Francisco are the exception rather than the rule, and even in San Francisco, ideological battles still must be waged to promote workers' rights. The challenge remains for all communities in the United States to redefine city priorities around human rights and community well-being.

Inside-Outside Strategies

Given the factors listed above as necessary for successful implementation activism on the part of living wage advocates—motivation to monitor, systematic involvement, decision-making power, and maintaining independence—it is clear that a combination of inside and outside strategies are generally the most effective for advocates who want to ensure strong policy enforcement. Gaining systematic access to information and resources requires working from within, and although few task forces have been granted decision-making power, this too represents an inside strategy.

However, in order to maintain independence from city staff and avoid being held captive to task force guidelines and procedures, advocates need to keep open the possibility for outside strategies—namely, protest politics. These channels can involve a larger group of people, such as the covered workers and concerned community members; push the city into making hard political decisions such as mandating compliance from powerful employers; keep the living wage issue alive in the media and the public eye; and serve as an organizing tool (more on this in the next chapter).

In chapter 4, I explained the ACORN campaign strategy of pursuing both an inside and outside track to getting living wage ordinances passed. Not only does this strategy help in the passage of a law, but it can also set up the conditions needed for more effective implementation. The outside track tactics of the campaign are similar to the outside tactics that can be used to pressure cities to improve enforcement efforts. In fact, Maria Whyte of Buffalo acknowledges that the lack of a more visible outside track of their campaign may have hampered implementation: "Perhaps the Buffalo campaign went too fast, and didn't build up enough support, or a climate of enforcement."[11] The implications of this are interesting and important. This suggests that those ordinances that are passed quickly and without an active community campaign will be less likely to be enforced.

Contentious Campaigns

It is not only community mobilization itself that is important. Our cases suggest that the level of opposition or conflict also matters. Specifically, the more opposition a campaign encounters, the greater the likelihood of successful implementation down the line. This finding appears counterintuitive at first glance. I have already argued that city managers will most likely oppose living wage ordinances because they run against mainstream economic development strategy. This alone may suggest that implementation will be difficult. Wouldn't even more open, political opposition suggest that implementation is even less likely, especially since that opposition often comes from city political leaders?

The reason that the level of opposition faced during a campaign matters is that it forces the living wage coalition to test itself. It forces the coalition to build much broader alliances, persuade city leaders of its position, educate the public, counter arguments against the ordinance, and demonstrate its power. Testing these inside and outside tactics during the campaign helps to insure they can be utilized when needed for enforcement. Of course, the level of opposition is related to the level of campaign mobilization. Jen Kern comments, "You might think that a bigger fight would intimidate people, but it doesn't. When they have to fight harder they get more energized."

In an effort to test this claim, I rated each campaign passed through December 2001 as contentious or not contentious. I considered a campaign to be contentious if there was active opposition from the city administration and/or an organization such as the Chamber of Commerce. While

Table 9.1. Implementation outcomes in contentious versus noncontentious campaigns

Implementation outcome	Noncontentious (did not face organized opposition)	Contentious (faced organized opposition)	Total
Blocked	5%	15%	10%
Narrow	70%	34%	52%
Moderate	20%	29%	25%
Expansive	5%	22%	14%
Total[a]	100%	100%	100%
	(Total = 40)	(Total = 41)	(Total = 81)

Source: Author's analysis based on ordinances, interviews, and review of relevant documents.
[a] Totals may not equal 100 percent due to rounding.

Table 9.2. Likelihood of implementation outcome based on level of contentiousness in living wage campaign

	Blocked	Narrow	Moderate	Expansive
Noncontentious	25%	67%	40%	18%
Contentious	75%	33%	60%	82%
Total	100%	100%	100%	100%
	(Total = 8)	(Total = 42)	(Total = 20)	(Total = 11)

Source: Author's analysis based on ordinances, interviews, and review of relevant documents.

this is a crude measure, it enables us to compare the strength of implementation outcomes in cities with active opposition versus those with relatively little opposition. The results, presented in table 9.1, are striking. We see that of the noncontentious campaigns, only 5 percent ended up with expansive implementation, and another 20 percent as moderate implementation. On the other hand, of the contentious campaigns, 22 percent resulted in expansive implementation. An additional 29 percent resulted in moderate outcomes.

We can also turn these numbers around and examine the relationship from the other direction. For example, when we look at the cases of narrow implementation in table 9.2, we see that 67 percent did *not* have contentious campaigns. On the other hand, most of expansive implementation cases (82 percent) *did* have contentious campaigns. Moderate implementation cases were split roughly evenly. The numbers suggest that a having a contentious campaign does not guarantee expansive implementation. In fact, note that contentious campaigns are also more likely to end up as blocked implementation than noncontentious campaigns. However, cases of expansive implementation are quite likely to have followed contentious campaigns.

These numbers are backed up when looking closely at specific cities. For example, enforcement has been weak in Cook County, Illinois; West Hollywood, California; Des Moines, Iowa; Meriden, Connecticut; and Jersey City and Hudson County, New Jersey. In all of these cases, there was virtually no campaign and little opposition to the ordinance. In contrast, implementation appears strongest in places like Los Angeles, California, where there was a hotly contested campaign that drew vigorous and public opposition from business leaders and the mayor. Implementation is also strong in Boston, where an ordinance was passed initially with little organized opposition but then was attacked by business. It took a year of threatened lawsuits and negotiations before the final ordinance was agreed on. In Tucson, city staff appear to be doing a successful job of implementation on their own. However, in that city a broad-based coalition worked for four years and turned out hundreds of people for multiple town hall meetings to get the ordinance passed. Tucson living wage administrator Ray Valdez noted that members of the Pima County Interfaith Coalition (PCIC), a major player in the living wage coalition, occasionally came to meet with Valdez and his supervisor to see how the implementation was going. PCIC visits to the city may have served as a simple reminder that the coalition was watching the city and was ready to mobilize if necessary to ensure enforcement.

It is possible that there are other explanations for these findings. For example, is it the case that some campaigns were noncontentious because the coalition wasn't asking for much in the first place, or that the coalition never intended to have an ordinance that was strictly enforced? Likewise, are the contentious cases those where the coalition did have a clear intent to pass and enforce a meaningful ordinance? If so, this would imply that coalition objectives are the key causal variable, resulting in a certain level of contention and degree of enforcement. While this theory may apply in some of the cases, a closer look at the data shows it does not hold throughout. For example, in Cleveland, implementation outcomes have not been strong. However, the living wage coalition in that city did fight a contentious campaign, attempting to include ambitious provisions and a strong living wage advisory committee. On the other end, the city of Santa Cruz living wage coalition worked very hard to pass a strong ordinance that allowed for tough enforcement and active participation in that enforcement effort through a Advisory Committee. Yet the campaign did not provoke opposition from the city or employer associations and is now one of the cities with the strongest implementation.

Although there are exceptions like Cleveland and Santa Cruz, these stories suggest that "outside track" tactics employed in the campaign demonstrate the power of those behind the ordinance and give the city greater incentive to insure that the ordinance is enforced. These tactics also help the coalition maintain its independence from the city. However, an outside track alone is not enough. Throughout most campaigns, activists must work with city councilors to negotiate details of an ordinance. Kern suggests that coalition members meet with every council member at least once, and most of them several times, even if that member is believed to oppose the living wage. Council members must hear from multiple constituents and community leaders, be presented with facts and research, and have a chance to ask questions and have their concerns addressed. This process can take time but can result in the council members changing their minds, or at least becoming willing to adopt a modified version of the ordinance. The more they are consulted, the more they feel ownership over the law and the more comfortable they are standing up to opposition and voting yes.

The inside track process can build support needed from city council members for the implementation phase. After months or even years of hearing about the ordinance and having their concerns allayed, council members will be more likely to put their weight behind enforcement. Paul Sonn, an attorney who advises living wage coalitions around the country, notes that this may be another way in which greater opposition during a campaign is linked to stronger implementation outcomes: "Where campaigns face strong opposition, they're forced to engage city leadership and ultimately work out a compromise that the city can live with and therefore is more willing to take seriously and implement."

Pursuing an inside track during the campaign primarily refers to working with city council members and city administrators. However, it can also include working with city staff to generate information about city employment, contracting and economic development subsidies, and to conduct research on the estimated impact of an ordinance. This collaboration with city staff during the campaign can be transformed after enactment, when coalition members establish inside mechanisms such as task forces. This gives coalitions the opportunity for ongoing, systematic involvement in implementation, including reviewing requests for granting and rejecting waivers. Although living wage ordinances are not as complex as many other kinds of legislation, there is a need for ongoing evaluation to make sure the ordinance's goals are being met.

Returning to our campaign profiles in chapter 4, we would predict that the contested campaigns in Tucson, Boston, and Providence would be more likely to have successful implementation outcomes. This has proven to be the case in Boston, and we will have to wait to see if the Providence ordinance is passed to evaluate it.

The city of Tucson did achieve expansive enforcement initially, despite the lack of community involvement. However, in 2002, due to budget cuts, the city decided to eliminate the position of living wage contract compliance officer. Ray Valdez was transferred to another position, and the city did not replace him. The director of procurement tried to save the position but was unable to do so. Would the director have had better luck had there been a community advisory board? Would the position remain if living wage advocates launched an "outside" campaign, pressuring the city to maintain the position? We can't know the answer to these questions. But the experience of Tucson does suggest the potential weaknesses of relying on a city-only model of enforcement.

We could also predict that the Cincinnati ordinance, which was passed in a period of two weeks at the end of 2002, with no public input or campaign, will be poorly enforced. Although it is too early to make a final assessment, the Cincinnati City Council was criticized in the fall of 2003 when it granted a living wage waiver to a car wash contractor with little investigation into the employer's claims of financial hardship.[12]

Inside-Outside Strategies in Other Arenas

Using inside and outside strategies to enhance policy implementation is not unique to the living wage movement. In fact, it is an approach used by political groups across the spectrum, normally referring to a way of achieving change through electing representatives to office and continuing grassroots activism. This strategy has been espoused by organizations ranging from the Christian Coalition, to the New Party, to the National Organization for Women (NOW). For example, Patricia Ireland, former executive director of NOW, commented in a 1999 interview in *The Progressive* that progress for women is only likely to come when combining grassroots activism with working with mainstream politicians: "I don't think that we can make change only from the outside. I think we have to get some people inside. And getting people inside means that they're going to have to be willing to fight as hard as they can, with us perhaps strengthening their hand by being as rowdy and obnoxious as we can." Ireland also notes that "some of the liberal guys are strengthened when we get more feminists or people who identify as women's rights supporters," in office.[13]

Some of the organizations involved in the living wage movement have themselves long been advocates of an inside-outside strategy to build a powerful grassroots base. ACORN, for example, has worked in recent years to elect representatives to local and state office through the New Party and the Working Families party in communities such as Little Rock, Arkansas; Chicago; and New York City. ACORN chapters work to recruit and train members to run for public office but then do not rely on those members to push their platform through. Rather, ACORN will keep up its grassroots organizing efforts, mobilizing community members to visit or write letters to their city council, attend rallies and marches, talk to their neighbors, and send letters to newspapers.

In these cases, "insider" politics focuses primarily on elected officials and ignores the role of nongovernmental organizations operating in a formal governance role. Emphasis is also usually placed on the passage of policy, more than on implementation. In this chapter, I put forth a model of "inside" strategies that can be pursued by citizens or the organizations to which they belong to pass and implement living wage ordinances but also a range of progressive policies. This does not exclude the option of living wage coalitions electing their supporters to office but does not rely on it. I also focus on the routine administrative work of policy implementation, rather than policy formation.

Another clear example of the inside-outside strategy is the case of unions that engage in collective bargaining yet maintain the threat of striking. The ability to mobilize rank-and-file union members to engage in job actions that could harm productivity or an employer's reputation is a powerful weapon for unions. Yet constant agitation is not sustainable and does not provide systematic improvements. Contracts can codify certain rights, providing a legal basis for workers to have demands met. But contracts on their own are simply a piece of paper; they are unlikely to be enforced if there is no active organization behind them. Thus, the ongoing and interactive utilization of inside (bargaining, signing contracts, and filing grievances) and outside tactics (rallies, work slow-downs, strikes, show of community support) affords unions the greatest chance of winning and sustaining their demands.

Another variation of an inside-outside approach can be found in the unemployment insurance programs in Belgium, Denmark, and Sweden. As Bruce Western shows, the unions in these countries were able to maintain a strong influence over the disbursement of unemployment benefits and over the job placement of the unemployed after World War II.[14] Called the Ghent system, union membership brought individuals into the unemployment insurance program. The union controlled the disbursement of funds but also referred unemployed workers to jobs. They could direct workers to union jobs, and in Sweden, a job offer was considered suitable only if the wages and benefits are comparable to those in collective bargaining agreements. This system allows the unions to maintain membership during recessions and higher unemployment and reduce the wage competition from the unemployed. The Ghent system is an example of an inside-outside strategy on a national level. In this case, unions are able to exert their usual influence on employers and labor markets through workplace negotiations and power on the shop floor. But they have also institutionalized an outside pressure group, through the organizing of the unemployed.

In O'Rourke's example of environmental legislation enforcement in Vietnam, discussed in chapter 7, the community-driven regulation model includes some forms of inside and outside implementation. While the role of citizens is fairly limited, they do have the legal right to register complaints against polluters. This gives them a systematic channel through which they can push the state to act. This is supplemented by protest politics—complaint letters to local government agencies, letters to the polluting firm, public demonstrations, and use of the media.

O'Rourke acknowledges that limiting the role of formal community participation to complaint registration has weaknesses. "With little data and no training, community members often end up only complaining about pollution problems that they can see, smell or feel," writes O'Rourke. "This results in a focus on purely localized, short-term, acute impact of pollution." In short, while having the legal right to register complaints has improved environmental legislation implementation, a more systematic and thorough method of community input could result in more effective, longer-term results.

The results of an alternative approach, favoring inside strategies at the expense of protest politics, are well-documented. In fact, a common outcome of social movements is for the movement to dissipate or to move on to other arenas once desired policies are passed. The social movement participants may move on completely, or may leave behind some institutional legacy: elected officials, permanent organizations, or representatives on implementation task forces. This leaves the new policy with little support, or backup, should implementation fail. The police civilian review boards mentioned in chapter 8 are a common example of this, where a high-profile case of police abuse will lead to community protest. A mayor or council may create a civilian review board as a response, but by the time the board is functioning and the next incident of police abuse occurs, the community is demobilized, having put their faith in the review board. Citizen member representatives have a formal role on the board but have few resources and power, and often no community movement behind them.

In some cities, however, community involvement remains high after the review board is established. For example, according to Human Rights Watch, community involvement has been crucial in sustaining the work of the Police Advisory Commission in Philadelphia, which has fifteen civilian members who meet once a month to review police activity.[15] Because the commission has the right to review police documents, it has been challenged from its inception by the Fraternal Order of Police, which has filed numerous lawsuits to disband it. It is only because of the constant community support and pressure that led to settlements in the lawsuits that the commission continues its work. Human Rights Watch concludes, "The leadership of the oversight system must actively educate the community about the merits of civilian oversight. This education must demonstrate that citizen review is useful; only with public support will external review agencies be able to survive during political or funding disputes." This is perhaps another example of where higher levels of sustained conflict lead to more successful implementation.

Prevailing Wage Enforcement

An area similar to the living wage movement that has required an inside-outside approach to implementation and enforcement is prevailing wages. Prevailing wage laws exist at the federal, state, and local level and require building and other contractors that are subject to the law to pay their employees the average wage for that industry in the area. There exists much debate about the best way to measure prevailing wages as well as their impact on construction contracting patterns, business climate, and employment (particularly of African Americans). Little analysis has been conducted, however, as to how well these laws are enforced.

Despite the lack of academic research, those most affected by prevailing wage enforcement—construction workers and their unions—know firsthand about the weaknesses of relying solely on governments to implement the policy. As with other policy arenas, prevailing wage enforcement divisions are often understaffed, underresourced, and subject to capture by builder associations. Building trades unions often take it on themselves to visit worksites to check for compliance, often finding numerous violations. According to the Building and Construction Trades Council of San Francisco, common violations found on construction sites include "misclassification of workers to lower paid crafts, wage payments in cash at substantially under the prevailing rate, manipulating the apprenticeship to journeyman ratios, not paying health and pension benefits, and the use of undocumented workers who, because of their work status, have no legal recourse."[16]

In response to the weak enforcement, unions have pursued several routes to strengthen prevailing wage laws. First, they have lobbied at the local, state, and federal level for legislation to increase resources for enforcement and close loopholes in existing laws. Second, they have established their own organizations to enhance existing monitoring. These organizations are state based and affiliated with the National Alliance for Fair Contracting. The associations are usually joint union-management projects, because contractors who work with union labor also have an incentive for prevailing wage laws to be enforced so that they do not have to compete with low-wage employers. According to prevailing wage expert Peter Phillips, a number of associations focus on large projects such as highway construction, but they also monitor building construction (less systematically).[17]

According to Karen Courtney, director of the Foundation for Fair Contracting of Massachusetts, the first state Foundation for Fair Contracting was started in California in the 1970s, and the idea then spread to dozens of other states over the next few decades. The foundation in Massachusetts was established in the early 1990s. Courtney states that the unions in the construction industry were concerned that for economic, staffing, and political reasons, prevailing wage laws were not being enforced in the state. The unions felt they needed someone to advocate on their behalf and worked to establish their own Foundation for Fair Contracting. After a few years, they were able to bring on their management counterparts. A joint union-management trust was established to fund the foundation.

Today, the organization has a director and four field monitors. The foundation targets approximately three hundred projects a year for close inspection. The state prevailing wage law, which covers construction, trash removal, office cleaners, furniture movers, printers, and bus drivers, requires employers to submit weekly payroll records to the state, with names and addresses of all covered employees. The submissions then become part of public record. The foundation files a Freedom of Information Act request and obtains copies of the payroll records, and then sends letters to all covered employees to notify them of the prevailing wage law and give them a contact number to call if they aren't being paid adequately.

Once they are contacted by a worker, the foundation helps the worker to figure out if they have a legal case against the employer. The foundation acts as the workers' advocate, helping them build and pursue their case and win back wages where appropriate. All of this work is external to the work of the state Attorney General's office, which is formally in charge of enforcement. According to Courtney, the relations between the foundation and the Attorney General's office were somewhat strained initially, but the two have developed a natural division of labor. Courtney notes that the state only monitors payroll records in the case of a complaint and does not systematically monitor worksites like the foundation does. In addition, the Attorney General must remain neutral and is not allowed to serve as an advocate for workers. Despite relatively stable relations, there can still be some tension between various foundations and their state employee counterparts, because part of the work of the foundation involves pointing out when the state is not doing an adequate job of enforcement.

This example of prevailing wage enforcement is primarily one of an outside strategy, because the Foundations for Fair Contracting have no formal statutory role within the enforcement mechanism. Although the foundation does not rely on protests and media, they will utilize these avenues when necessary.

Courtney says that there are advantages to "being 'not the government,'" because workers have a general reluctance to contact government agencies about wage issues until they are sure they have a solid case. "We're that first, confidential step," says Courtney. However, after playing a role in monitoring for several years, the foundations have become somewhat institutionalized. They have found ways to gain systematic information about compliance and have become an integral part of the prevailing wage implementation process. Courtney remarks, "After ten years, I feel people are very aware of who we are and what we do. We got the word out, and people know who we are and that we are paying attention."

Business and Inside-Outside Strategies

The use of an inside-outside strategy for implementation is not unique to progressive organizations. Certainly, business lobbies utilize both strategies on a regular basis. While it is rare to see business leaders in rallies or marches in efforts to persuade their representatives to adopt or enforce policy, a great deal of business influence goes on behind the scenes. First, as political scientists such as G. William Domhoff and Thomas Dye have shown, in many cases businesses leaders are the people occupying the top positions in government.[18]

Second, business leaders use various tactics to influence governmental decisions. As Clawson, Neustadtl, and Scott write about the formulation of tax policy, "One of the best indicators of the power of business is that not only are corporations able to win themselves billions of dollars through tax loopholes, but they are able to do so without much public exposure or blame."[19] The same is true for a range of other policies, at the federal, state, and local level. Business leaders use outside tactics such as lobbying, media, and threats (such as the threat to relocate business out of the town if a certain ordinance is or isn't adopted). Increasingly, corporations also work from the outside by hiring private consulting firms to generate "grass-roots" campaigns for them.[20] For a fee, the consultant can set up a front group that will send thousands of letters or make phone calls to Congress, or simply mobilize constituents on behalf of a particular corporation or industry association.

In addition to their outside tactics, business interests are able to work from the inside to influence policy through appointments to boards, commissions, and "blue-ribbon panels," through public-private organizations such as the economic development agencies mentioned in chapter 2, through fundraising committees, and through formal participation in political parties and administration decision-making.

A wealth of studies have shown the ways in which business interests played a dominant role in local politics, through direct and indirect means.[21] In addition to economic development, business has been active in local zoning and city planning, anti-smoking, homelessness, wetlands protection, alcohol access, and health and safety policy formation.[22]

An example on the municipal level can be found in the history of the Chicago Façade Inspection Ordinance. As the city of Chicago began to see the proliferation of high-rise buildings around the turn of the century, labor unions succeeded in getting the state to pass a Structural Works Act in 1917. The act stated that workers injured or killed on or near scaffolds, cranes, ladders, or other structures would, in addition to the worker's compensation provided by their employer, be entitled to sue any other company involved with the construction. In 1978, following the death of pedestrian killed by falling tile, Mayor Richard R. Daley passed a city-wide façade inspection ordinance which required regular inspections of building exteriors every five years. The city law was repealed a few years later, and in 1995, Republicans took control of the state legislature and repealed the state Structural Works Act.

Consumer and labor groups fought back and got the Chicago Board of Alders to consider adopting a city Structural Works Act in 1996. The Structural Works Ordinance would have allowed workers and their families to sue companies for costs related to injury or death on the job, increased safety regulations for building construction and demolition, and imposed fines on construction firms found not in compliance with safety measures. Business groups quickly mobilized. The Chamber of Commerce organized a twenty-seven-member coalition. Using lobbying, city council testimony, and media channels, the business coalition succeeded in stopping the passage of the act as proposed.

However, the council instead passed a new version of the Façade Inspection Ordinance. The new law as passed simply required building owners to get their buildings inspected by a licensed architect or structural engineer every few years (either a cursory inspection every year, or an in-depth inspection every four years).[23]

Within the city council, work on the ordinance is overseen by the City Council Committee on Buildings. The committee is made of up ten members appointed by the mayor, including city staff, architects, and engineers. Although the Structural Works Ordinance was designed to protect worker's safety, and the Façade Inspection Ordinance to protect the safety of pedestrians and workers, no labor unions, workers rights, consumer advocates, or other public protection representatives have a seat on the committee. Rather, committee membership represents those interests that had initially opposed the ordinances on the ground of high costs and damage to the city's business climate.

Over the next several years, a number of building-related accidents caused attention to return to the Façade Inspection Ordinance. In most cases, pieces fell from buildings and luckily missed hitting passers-by, but in several cases pedestrians and construction workers were killed. The weaknesses of the Façade Ordinance became evident. The city did not have enough staff to inspect buildings on its own and could not even say how many buildings had been inspected or how many building owners were in compliance with the ordinance.[24]

In 2002, three more people were killed when a scaffold fell from the John Hancock Center onto cars in the street below. At the time of the accident, the company that had built the scaffold was under investigation for the death of a worker in San Francisco. The company that operated the scaffold, AMS, already had been found guilty of twenty-two OSHA safety violations in other places.

The public outcry over the incidences forced the city council to consider new revisions to its building codes. Yet, City Council Building Committee alderman Bernard Stone was more concerned about protests coming from building owners about the cost of the stricter amendments passed in 2000. As a result, the law was amended again in 2002, this time *weakening* the inspection requirements. A number of key provisions were modified to give building owners more leeway in complying with the ordinance.

This example shows how building owners, engineers, architects, and other business interests managed to use inside and outside tactics to influence the Chicago building code. Through lobbying and media attention, the Chamber of Commerce was able to pressure the city council into adopting weaker versions of ordinances than they had originally considered. As representatives on the City Council Building Committee, business interests were able to push for lax enforcement of existing laws and to influence from the inside the discussions around amendments.

Voluntary Enforcement

The inside-outside strategies discussed above all rest on the model of nongovernmental organizations pressuring or working with municipal governments who are ultimately responsible for policy enforcement. In this model, NGOs can work with governments to enhance state capacity to monitor regulations.

In this section, I discuss voluntary models for monitoring and enforcement. This includes mechanisms to better enforce legally binding mandates, as well as programs that exist entirely outside the realm of the state. I begin with the former case, of legally binding policies.

Given the lack of state capacity to enforce a range of regulations, in some policy arenas people are experimenting with alternative models to monitor and enforce laws. For example, employers may decide to actively participate in self-monitoring. Jill Esbenshade has studied voluntary systems of monitoring in the U.S. apparel industry. In particular, she analyzes the practice of "social accounting" among garment firms in Los Angeles.[25] Due to public outcry over the conditions of work in the industry, a number of garment manufacturers have signed agreements with the Department of Labor promising to hire outside consultants to verify that the firm is complying with government regulations. Utilizing Department of Labor records and interview data, Esbenshade finds that this private monitoring is erratic, incomplete, and in the end, ineffective. Worse, she argues that it may do more harm than good, as it allows firms to present themselves as good corporate citizens, taking the pressure off of consumer demands for more substantial reform. In addition, private monitoring can undermine workers' efforts to win change through self-organization. Esbenshade found examples of private monitors that were relatively ignorant of labor law and had negative views of unions. Esbenshade concludes, "Private monitoring is not only paternalistic but statistics show that it is also ineffective. More significantly, it may well substitute for, cover up, or obviate workers' own organizing."[26]

The second form of voluntary enforcement is found in cases where policies have no legal teeth behind them but rely on either the good will of employers or consumers or on market incentives for enforcement. This is not a new strategy: indeed, for a period in the late nineteenth and early twentieth centuries, the American Federation of Labor (AFL) promoted a strategy of "voluntarism" for enforcing labor contracts between employer and unions. The AFL believed that the state was not neutral and could not be trusted to mediate labor disputes fairly. In many cases, the AFL had seen the state bring in federal or state troops to break strikes, issue injunctions, and imprison or hang unionists. Labor leaders believed they were better off on their own, head to head with employers.

More recent discussion of voluntary policies can be found in the debates about international labor standards. While some workers' rights advocates argue for the establishment and enforcement of stringent labor laws in all countries, others point out that the difficulties of monitoring, rapid changes in the global economy, including new kinds of production relations and the uneven distribution of power and wealth between countries, makes "hard law" (legally enforceable) options neither feasible nor desirable. Rather, instead of establishing provisions such as minimum wage laws and penalties for employers who don't pay the wages, countries should establish "soft" options such as a reward system for firms that pay higher wages.

In the case of the living wage movement, voluntary programs have been pushed not by unionists or living wage advocates but by employers and government administrations reluctant to add more business regulations or more bureaucracy. An example of this is in Tucson, Arizona, where the mayor established his own "Good Business Partnership" program to recognize businesses that voluntarily pay a living wage and provide benefits. Membership in the program means that businesses get a sticker to display in the workplace and a logo they can add to company letterhead.

Another kind of voluntary program—an ordinance with voluntary enforcement—exists in Northampton, Massachusetts, where the city council passed a Living Wage Resolution in 1998 that gives "preference in its business dealings to those businesses that provide assurances to the City that they will pay their employees a living wage" and encourages local businesses to do what they can to pay the living wage. Des Moines, Iowa, and Charlottesville, Virginia, have similar ordinances. Other city leaders have called for voluntary programs in lieu of mandated wage levels, claiming that mandates interfere with the market and are costly to the city.

Research suggests that the voluntary living wage programs have minimal impact. When asked about the impact of the living wage in Des Moines, Iowa, Tom Turner, director of Human Resources, responded: "We do not keep track of firms complying or not complying as . . . it is a resolution and not an ordinance. There has been no impact study nor is anyone assigned to monitor as this is a resolution and not an ordinance—no active enforcement."[27]

In Tucson, 111 businesses, employing a total of 10,092 workers, have joined the mayor's Good Business Partnership program.[28] In 2002, researchers at the University of Arizona conducted a survey of a random sample of 57 of these firms, and got responses from 41. These respondents report that "virtually every worker (99.4 percent) was already being paid a living wage before their company joined the program."[29] Many respondents reported ambiguous feelings about the program, stating that they had seen no benefits from their membership. Seven percent of those surveyed opposed continuation of the program, and 29 percent were unsure whether it should be continued.

In the case of living wages, it does not appear that voluntary monitoring is an effective strategy. Although there are too few cases to draw definitive conclusions, it seems that voluntary programs do not raise wages for workers and do not lead to enforcement by workers, consumers, NGOs, or firms. Of course, some of the advocates calling for market-oriented, nongovernmental standards and monitoring systems would say that the voluntary living wage ordinances are not designed properly to create incentives for any group to monitor or comply, and do not meet the criteria established by public policy analysts. But proponents of some of the "soft law" programs acknowledge that even the best-designed voluntary programs of international labor standards are criticized by some as "a corrupt attempt to free industry from the last vestiges of state regulation and union organizing."[30]

Conclusion

Despite evidence that many municipalities fail to implement living wage ordinances on their own, examples from the previous two chapters show that living wage advocates can greatly improve monitoring and enforcement. Outside tactics, such as rallies, press coverage, external reports, and grievances, can push the city to remedy instances of noncompliance. Working from the inside, through task forces or other formal systematic channels such as worker education programs, can also improve implementation. I argue here that combining the two will lead to the greatest chance of success.

Outside tactics can mobilize the community, create opportunities for new coalition building and public education, and provide city staff and city council members the political cover they may need to enforce the law over the objections of opponents. Yet these tactics are not systematic and require great energy and effort on the part of living wage organizers. Inside tactics provide advocates the ongoing access to information they need to improve enforcement and can provide living wage supporters the legitimacy they need to solicit data from employers and the city. It is through this kind of involvement that advocates are more likely to find loopholes that need closing and flaws that need amending. Yet working only from the inside can lead to a loss of independence and power for living wage supporters, particularly if they are politically weaker than living wage opponents who wish to hamper enforcement. Advocates who work within the system must be careful not to be co-opted; maintaining a mobilizable coalition on the outside will help to keep those inside advocates accountable to their mission of enforcing the living wage.

The use of inside versus outside tactics has been long debated within academic and activist circles. In their path-breaking book *Poor People's Movements*, Frances Fox Piven and Richard Cloward argue that most major social change comes from protest movements rather than institutionalized organizations. Indeed, the authors assert that social movements fail when they attempt to transition into formal structures. They fail in part because institutionalizing the movement demobilizes it and robs it if its power. They also fail because they rest on a fundamentally flawed assumption: the assumption that they can win concessions from elites when operating from the inside.[31]

Piven and Cloward's assertion that major social change cannot flow from inside tactics alone makes sense. However, critics have pointed to numerous weaknesses that arise from relying only on outside tactics. Institutionalizing some aspect of social movements can create stability, resources, credibility, leadership development, movement continuity, and systematic access to information. As discussed in chapter 6, sociologist Jill Quadagno argues that interventions from within the state can also create further opportunities for protest.[32]

The findings in this chapter suggest that living wage campaigns that are more contentious may be better able to win expansive implementation after victory. In short: what you win easily may be harder to enforce. This is because where living wage coalitions face organized opposition, they are forced to develop their skills and demonstrate their power. Through conflict, they test themselves and learn their own strengths and weaknesses. Conflict also helps build institutions that can be utilized down the road. A contentious campaign itself does not guarantee a victorious campaign or successful implementation. In fact, a contentious campaign may just as likely end in blocked rather than expansive implementation. However, this only highlights the finding that implementation is itself a political struggle that is an extension of the initial fight to adopt the legislation.

At the same time, the case studies in this book highlight the need to keep outside protest options alive in order to make implementation success more likely. However, observers have noted the tendency of social movements, for various reasons, to die out over time. If living wage advocates manage to win access to inside strategies for monitoring and enforcement, such as through an implementation task force, how can they be sure that interest in the issue will not die off? Can the individuals sitting on those task forces be sure that living wage activists remain ready to mobilize when needed?

It is unlikely that living wage campaigns can maintain their intensity on their own for the long term. For this reason, it is crucial for this movement to continue growing in new directions—merging with other causes while maintaining a commitment to wage fairness and worker justice issues. It is also important that workers have the opportunity and capacity to enforce the laws themselves, most effectively through worker-run organizations. To what extent have living wage campaigns aided unionization? To what extent have living wage coalitions been able to move from campaign to victory to new campaign? Have they merged with other organizations and movements? In the next chapter, we take a look at the answers to these questions.

10

OTHER OUTCOMES BEYOND IMPLEMENTATION

The labor unions have been very clear about why they are actively promoting living wage campaigns. They hope that by increasing the private sector's labor costs, the living wage can reduce the privatization of public-sector jobs.

Employment Policies Institute, *Living Wage Policy: The Basics*, 2000

Living wage campaigns create legal, economic and political environments in which workers and entire communities can fight the power of money.

The Black Commentator, "The Living Wage Movement: A New Beginning: Bread, Power, and Civil Rights in 19 Languages," May 8, 2002

Supporters and opponents agree: the living wage movement is about more than just pay raises for a subset of low-wage workers. While the actual ordinances may cover fewer than a hundred workers in some cities, hopes and fears about larger implications run rampant. These other implications include discouraging privatization and outsourcing of public services, creating standards for the way public money is spent, and developing tools for organizing workers in nonunion service jobs. Some see potential for the movement to build coalitions, foster new organizations, and create political power. Others see living wage campaigns changing the way communities talk, think, and deliberate about wages, inequality, poverty, and economic development. It is important to assess some of these indirect outcomes of the living wage movement. Other than raises for those workers directly covered by the ordinances, what has been the impact of living wage campaigns and efforts to implement these laws? Has the implementation process created an opportunity to organize low-wage workers? Have living wage laws proved valuable in other ways even if they are poorly implemented?

Impact on Organizing Low-Wage Workers

Although opponents fear that unionizing efforts are the true motive behind some living wage campaigns, the evidence about the link between the two is mixed. According to Ken Jacobs of the San Francisco living wage campaign, the determining factor is whether unions want to use the campaigns as part of a larger organizing plan. He argues that where unions have been strategic about involvement in campaigns, they have seen positive results. Where unions are neutral or even skeptical of the campaigns and stay out of them, living wage ordinances can in fact be a detriment to new organizing. In this section I review the ways that living wage campaigns have been used help organize low-wage workers into unions.

From a union organizing perspective, ideally, living wage ordinances would contain specific language or tools that would make it easier for unions to organize low-wage workers. Union organizers believe these tools could be a useful antidote to weak labor law combined with the pervasiveness of anti-union activities by employers. In chapter 8 I referred to research by Kate Bronfenbrenner, who finds that in addition to employers illegally firing workers in organizing drives, other activities press the limits of the law: "91 percent of employers, when faced with employees who want to join together in a union, force employees to attend closed-door meetings to hear anti-union propaganda; 80 percent require immediate supervisors to attend training sessions on how to attack unions; and 79 percent have supervisors deliver anti-union messages to workers they oversee."[1]

To counter the anti-union behavior of employers, unions sometimes try to include provisions for card check and/or neutrality in living wage ordinances. This was part of the initial proposal in Providence, Rhode Island, as mentioned in chapter 4. Neutrality agreements require the employer to stay out of union elections—no captive audience meetings, no harassment or intimidation of organizers. With a card check agreement, the employer agrees to bypass a National Labor Relations Board election and to recognize the union once a majority of employees sign a card saying they want a union. The Taft-Hartley Act prevents cities or states from requiring firms to honor card check and/or neutrality agreements outright.[2] Instead, campaigns rely on a precedent that has allowed some cities to require card check or neutrality from firms on a contract or development project if it can be shown that without such an agreement strikes or labor disputes on that project would jeopardize the city's investment. Using this logic, a handful of cities have passed a weaker form of neutrality clause in their ordinances, known as a "labor peace" provision that allows cities to deny contracts or subsidies to firms with poor labor relations history.

Other ordinances include language that gives preference on handing out economic development monies to businesses that "engage in responsible labor relations." In Minneapolis and St. Paul, Minnesota, responsible is defined as "neutrality on union organizing, providing a complete and accurate list of names and addresses of employees, reasonable access to employees and facilities during non-working periods, voluntary recognition based on card-check demonstrating that a union represents a majority of employees in a bargaining unit, and binding arbitration on the first contract." In a growing number of cities, labor was able to win language that prohibits the use of public money for anti-union activities.

Another provision that some ordinances have included to help union organizing is the "union opt-out" or collective bargaining supersession clause. This allows wage and benefit levels set by collective bargaining agreement to supercede the living wage ordinance if both the employer and union agree. The provision is included to give unions some flexibility in negotiations. Workers may be happy to take a lower wage—even temporarily—in exchange for more benefits and the job stability that comes with a union contract. However, others argue that when unions "opt-out" of the living wage, they undermine the movement's claim that this wage is necessary for survival. Still others critique the use of the union opt-out clause because it can be a dangerous tool in the hands of undemocratic unions. It is possible that union staff may accept the lower wage level against the wishes of employees, simply to get a union contract signed.

Many ordinances also contain language that explicitly prohibits employers from disciplining or firing workers who exercise their rights under the living wage law. This can aid union organizing efforts because workers who speak out about their right to join a union will be protected from job loss if they are also speaking about their right to receive a living wage.

Has there been success? To date, the efforts to use ordinance language to directly assist new organizing has resulted only in modest gains. For example, the neutrality clause in the Santa Cruz ordinance led to a card check agreement with an anti-union employer that held a contract to drive city buses and vans. Subsequently, the 150 workers won a contract with United Transportation Union Local 23. In addition, the campaign also won a card check agreement with the city to cover its 550 non-union temporary workers, who are now represented by SEIU Local 415. In a few cases, in Los Angeles and Berkeley, California, the Hotel and Restaurant Employees union (HERE) has been able to use the opt-out clause and the anti-retaliation clause to assist organizing drives, some of which have resulted in victory.

Greater success has come in indirect organizing victories, where the campaign has in some way spurred a new drive or assisted an existing one. For example, after the city of Tucson passed a living wage law, nonunion city workers began to demand that they too receive higher wages. Communication Workers of America Local 7026 organizer Rolando Figueroa, who had been active in the living wage campaign, approached the workers and launched an organizing drive. Eventually, fifteen hundred workers won recognition and a first contract with the city.[3] Figueroa asserts that the communication workers campaign might never have happened without the living wage campaign because the victory gave workers confidence to take on the challenge of a union drive. Figueroa notes that "many workers are reluctant to join unions because they are afraid to make the commitment, or think the effort is futile. But seeing a living wage coalition join together to fight for and win a living wage ordinance opens their eyes to the power of collective action, and the potential power of working with other workers in a union."

Other organizing drives related to living wage campaigns are ongoing. The Sacramento campaign helped the International Longshore and Warehouse Union launch a drive at a local recycling plant, where a city contractor was paying some of its employees minimum wage. Similarly, in Alexandria, Virginia, the coalition assisted an effort by the Amalgamated Transit Union to organize city bus drivers. The Vermont National Education Association has also incorporated living wage work into new organizing. The union averages between five and ten elections for their low-wage school support workers each year, and according to Jason Winston, "It is not uncommon for these workers—before they begin organizing a union—to have already pushed their school board for a livable wage and better health care. They often have the Vermont Livable Wage figures, usually off the web."

In a few cities, momentum from the living wage campaign has led to success in winning card check or neutrality agreements from employers or city agencies. For example, the San Francisco living wage coalition won card check requirements for airport contractors from the airport commission. As a result, more than two thousand workers have organized in the last few years into the Service Employees International Union, International Brotherhood of Teamsters, International Association of Machinists, Office and Professional Employees International Union, and the United Food and Commercial Workers locals. (However, a court ruling overturned the legality of the card check agreements in 2003).

University living wage campaigns have been closely tied to efforts to create or strengthen campus unions. In the 1990s, students at Wesleyan University in Connecticut returned to campus after participating in the AFL-CIO's Union Summer program and formed a student-labor solidarity group (University Student Labor Action Coalition, or USLAC).[4] In the spring of 1999, USLAC members learned that their university had privatized campus janitorial work, converting union jobs to low-wage, nobenefit, nonunion jobs. Luckily, when students sought out a union to work with them and the janitors in gaining union recognition, they found SEIU Local 531, a Justice for Janitors Local that was receptive. Local 531 helped the students talk with the janitors and introduce the idea of unionizing. After most of the thirty janitors signed authorization cards saying they wanted to have SEIU as their bargaining agent, the students pushed the employer, Initial Cleaning, to recognize the union. With students pressuring the administration, Wesleyan agreed to remain neutral, and Initial recognized the union. However, the workers then had to get Initial to agree to a contract with higher wages.

In order to insure that Initial Cleaning could pay the higher wages, USLAC mounted a campaign to pressure Wesleyan to pay living wages to all campus workers, including the newly unionized janitors. The campaign went on for several months, with USLAC holding rallies, meeting with administrators, contacting alumni, and pursuing all channels they could think of. When no progress was made by spring of 2000, students took over the Admissions Building until after twenty-four hours the university president gave in. Wesleyan signed the union contract giving janitors higher wages, benefits, and a grievance procedure. University administrators also agreed to negotiate a Campus Code of Conduct, which was worked out over the next few months.

Other successful efforts to link living wage campaigns to unionization have occurred in cities such as Berkeley and San Jose, California; Chicago, Illinois; and Miami-Dade, Florida. Perhaps the most extensive connection between the living wage and union organizing has occurred in Los Angeles. In Baltimore, the campaign has also been successful in organizing workers into a nonunion, low-wage worker organization. We review these cases in some detail below.

Los Angeles

After the Los Angeles ordinance was passed, the Los Angeles Alliance for a New Economy (LAANE) and the living wage coalition worked closely with local unions and the County Federation of Labor to turn the passage of the living wage ordinance into an union organizing opportunity.[5] LAANE staff would actively monitor all city meeting agendas, to see what contracts were coming up for bid or what subsidy projects were proposed. This information would be shared with unions, who would then attempt to work with the bidding employers in the hopes of obtaining card-check/neutrality in exchange for helping the employer's chances in getting awarded the contract.

The unions also pursued independent organizing because of the timing of the phase-in. As mentioned earlier, some contracts were not due to expire for up to ten years. In these cases, union staff hoped to build labor organizing efforts substantial enough to pressure the employers to adopt the ordinance voluntarily. According to Ed Iny, an organizer for SEIU and member of the living wage coalition, "We want to channel anger over living wages into organizing. This allows us to phase-in the ordinance and bargain over other issues as well, such as job security." Union organizers felt that the opportunity was there to agitate over the living wage issue at worksites that were due to be covered by the ordinance.

Meanwhile, unions worked to get unionized and nonunionized workers to pressure the airlines into paying the higher wage. In one case, the Living Wage Coalition and the Hotel and Restaurant Employees (HERE) union were successful in getting the city council to hold up the approval of a concession contract for Host Marriott until the company wrote a letter to the Department of Airports, assuring that they would comply with the living wage ordinance and not harass union organizers who talked to workers. This company, who organizers considered to be very anti-union, went on to sign a three-year contract with HERE at the Los Angeles International Airport, guaranteeing living wages and full-time employment to a majority of workers in January 1999, six years before they would be required by the law to pay the living wage.

Los Angeles unions have had a number of other organizing victories related to the living wage, with perhaps one of the biggest coming in 2002. When employees at several McDonald's restaurants at the airport complained of numerous labor law violations, including intimidation and harassment of workers trying to form a union, LAANE produced a report on the corporation to show to the Board of Airport Commissioners.[6] McDonald's had not been in compliance with the living wage ordinance because the city had signed a ten-year concession agreement with them to operate four restaurants in the airport in 1995, just before the ordinance was passed. But with outside pressure and reports of labor law violations, and with McDonald's looking to sign an extension of their contract expiring in 2005, the airport commission and city council got the corporation to amend their existing contract and to agree to follow the living wage and other city laws. While employees had not yet unionized by the end of 2003, their chances of doing so without intimidation are bolstered by the anti-retaliation provision of the living wage law. Furthermore, the city council sent the corporation a clear message that it would be watching its behavior in the area of labor relations.[7]

Baltimore

In Baltimore, the main organization advocating for the ordinance—the community based Solidarity Sponsoring Committee (SSC)—had always considered the living wage as only one step in their larger "social compact campaign," and in their effort to organize low-wage workers. After the living wage law was enacted, the SSC continued its organizing by targeting areas to which the living wage ordinance could be extended. The group made itself into an official membership organization and developed a benefit plan for members. Since its inception at the beginning of the living wage campaign, SSC has developed into an active organization with more than one hundred dues-paying members and several working committees.

One organizing priority after the initial ordinance was passed was aimed at contract workers in state-owned buildings. An SSC organizer, Kerry Miciotto, began talking to workers in the state-owned World Trade Center in the Baltimore Inner Harbor. According to an article in *The Daily Record*, Miciotto "stood on city street corners through snow and sleet last winter, serving hot tea to workers, getting to know them, introducing them to each other. She called it 'knitting and purling,' showing workers the common thread that runs through their lives and uniting them." Miciotto commented, "Many times they sat on a bus stop right next to each other and never knew that they worked together in these jobs."[8] Many of these workers that Miciotto spoke with were surprised to find out that they worked in state-owned buildings and some of them joined SSC. Soon, there was a core group of seven workers who formed a committee to get the living wage ordinance extended to cover their building. They worked for about a year and a half to sign up other workers into SSC and to get the ordinance adopted. The result was a three-year "pilot program" instituted at the World Trade Center in July 1995 that paid a living wage. More important, perhaps, was the result of the organizing efforts at the World Trade Center. According to Miciotto, over 90 percent of the workers signed SSC membership cards.[9]

SSC was also forced to address the challenges facing their organizing efforts as a result of the 1996 welfare reform. SSC saw that twenty thousand welfare recipients were coming into the workforce and possibly displacing public sector workers, or workers working for contractors who had just won living wages. Subsidized welfare recipients were brought in to work for thirty dollars per week as housecleaners at the large Inner Harbor Omni Hotel, where the existing unionized housecleaners had "been embroiled for a year in an acrimonious labor dispute over wages."[10] SSC worked for another year to get the governor to support an executive order preventing welfare recipients from displacing people already in jobs, making Maryland the first state to forbid employers from using workfare programs to displace workers.[11] SSC and BUILD also worked to get the School Counts bill passed, which allows women to stay in community colleges to fulfill their workfare requirements. As many as five hundred women at the Baltimore City Community College would benefit under the program. SSC member, college student, and welfare recipient Deborah Phillips said about the effort: "This is the first time that I have been a part of something that has affected the lives of so many people."[12]

SSC also worked to extend the living wage concept to the private sector. Their first target was the Johns Hopkins University and its private cleaning service company, Broadway Services, Inc. According to former student activist Dana Wise, living wage organizers decided to try to unionize Broadway Services and worked with students and faculty at Johns Hopkins to build support for the effort on campus.[13] The result was the formation of a campus-based living wage campaign, which worked at getting the university to adopt a living wage ordinance and also helped SSC off-campus in their efforts to organize school bus aides. Hopkins eventually adopted an ordinance that will set a living wage of $7.75, phased in over three years, although the student group is now pushing the university for a wage of about $9.00 to more accurately represent a "living wage."[14]

Winning Raises for Unionized Workers

Beyond showing up for picket lines, some living wage campaigns have fur-
thered the cause of organized workers in other concrete ways.[15] When
Alexandria, Virginia, passed its living wage law, the ordinance resulted in
raises for parking-lot attendants at city-owned lots, represented by HERE.
The union had only been able to win wages around $7 per hour, which was
higher than the wage paid to other parking lot attendants in the area but
still below a living wage. With the ordinance in place, wages jumped to
$10.21 an hour. Similarly, in Chicago, living wage advocates made sure that
that city's ordinance covered home health-care workers represented by
SEIU Local 880. The ordinance gave those workers raises from $5.30 to $7.60
an hour.

An interesting outcome of the statewide Livable Wage Campaign in
Vermont has been the support it has provided to employees in contract
negotiations. The Vermont National Education Association (NEA) not
only uses the living wage concept in new organizing, as profiled above,
but to raise the wages of already unionized employees as well. School
support staff (including bus drivers, teachers assistants, custodians and
kitchen staff) represented by the NEA have adopted the Livable Wage
materials and momentum to boost their arguments for a better contract.
These workers start as low as $6.17 (in 2001), and many need to take on
second or third jobs to survive. They have built a contract campaign
around the demand for a livable wage ($9 or $10 per hour, plus health
benefits). According to NEA organizer Jason Winston, the campaigns have
used livable wage language "at the table, in petitions, going to the school
board, buttons in school, calls from parents to board members, and newspaper ads." The NEA also relied on the living wage campaign model.
Even some of the same people active in the city living wage campaigns
came out to provide community support to the NEA contract campaign
under the living wage banner.

Gains for the already organized can be won on campus as well. In fact,
the Harvard students' demands included raises for some workers cur-
rently represented by HERE and SEIU, as well as a call to bring subcontracted service work back in-house and back into the union.

Ripple Effects?

Beyond winning raises for workers directly covered by the law, supporters and opponents both point out that living wage ordinances are likely

to have a so-called ripple effect. When employers raise wages for the lowest paid workers in a firm, they are likely to give raises to higher wage employees as well. Some argue that this is because those higher wage employees will demand raises out of fairness. Others claim employers need to maintain adequate wage differentials in order to keep in place incentives for lower-wage workers to work hard. Some have pointed out that certain employers and employees may wish to keep racial and gender pay hierarchies intact. Students fighting for a living wage for workers at Swarthmore College in Pennsylvania faced this issue. In response to the student campaign, the college created a committee charged with developing a proposal for increasing the wages for the lowest wage workers that also considered the needs of workers much higher up the wage scale. Andy Zuppann, a student representative on the committee, remarked on the ripple effect:

> It seems almost an insurmountable problem . . . it's hard because a lot of people are going to be really resentful and angry towards any increase in lowest compensated workers. It seems that there's almost nothing we can do, but, at the same time, there's a strong feeling that we have to do something because people are going to be so angry.[16]

In addition to the upward ripple effect, wage increases may spread to other low-wage workers in the firm that aren't technically covered by the law. Most living wage ordinances only apply to those employees working on the covered city contract or subsidized site. This means a janitorial firm that cleans City Hall must pay those janitors on the contract the higher wage. If the firm employs janitors who don't work on city sites, it is not legally obligated to pay those employees the living wage. However, a number of employers have argued that they would have to pay all their employees in the occupational category the higher wage out of fairness: another form of ripple effect.

Finally, wage increases may spread to noncovered employers in similar industries. For example, if a number of the largest security guard firms in Los Angeles raise their wages in order to comply with the city's ordinance, other security guard firms in the region may find they need to raise their wages in order to compete for employees. This phenomenon is sometimes referred to as a spill-over effect, where wage increases in one firm spread to others in the same region or industry.

Most observers note that ripple and spill-over effects do occur to some degree with living wage ordinances. Supporters claim that these effects are just another reason to pass the laws: not only do they help the targeted workers, but they can provide upward pressure on wages in the community at large. Opponents say the ripple effect is just another cost that employers can't afford. In fact, some of the most intense debates over whether to pass an ordinance or not have turned on the predicted size of the ripple effect. Unfortunately, there is very little research on the magnitude of ripple effects. How far up the wage distribution will the ripple effect go? How many workers will see indirect wage increases? How broad does living wage coverage have to be before it begins to impact a local labor market? Research by Card and Krueger and by Wicks-Lim suggests that ripple effects resulting from a minimum wage increase reach workers earning approximately 120 to 130 percent of the minimum wage.[17] For example, Card and Krueger found that when the federal minimum wage was increased from $3.35 in 1990, workers who had been earning up to $4.50 experienced ripple-effect wage increases.

These findings on the minimum wage may not apply precisely to living wage ordinances, but initial research on living wages suggests that ripple effects have also been observed. For example, in a study of the lower Rio Grande Valley in Texas, Paul Osterman found that living wage campaigns provided direct wage increases to 4,546 people, ripple effect raises to 1,859, and spill-over raises to 1,019.[18] This implies that, based on Osterman's study, for every hundred people covered directly by a living wage ordinance, an additional thirty-nine people will receive ripple or spill-over wage increases.

Osterman also calculates the size of the wage increases for the different groups. While the direct living wage recipients received an average raise of 81 cents per hour, ripple effect wage increases averaged $1.09 per hour, and spill-over raises 73 cents. These findings may suggest an adverse outcome of the living wage campaigns: an expansion of the wage differential between the lowest paid employees and those in higher wage categories. However, this data runs contrary to the findings of Card and Krueger, as well as Wicks-Lim, who find that the size of the wage increase for ripple effect recipients is smaller than that for direct recipients.

Reduction in Contracting Out

Another potential outcome of living wage ordinances, other than direct wage increases for some workers, is the impact on contracting out. It is not clear how much living wage ordinances have helped to slow down or reverse the process of contracting out, though organizers suggest that there has been some effect. Tammy Johnson, one of the lead organizers for the Milwaukee living wage campaigns, states, "I think our biggest victory at the city level has been the chilling effect on contracting out. There had been a lot of talk about privatization, etc. The mayor wanted to go hog-wild, but that is not happening now. Things have calmed down a lot."[19]

In training workers about their rights under the ordinance, the Los Angeles living wage coalition discovered several cases of janitorial contractors who were violating living wage and other labor laws. The coalition worked with SEIU and the workers to file complaints with the city, and to notify the city council about the violations. In two cases to date, when the contractor continued to defy the ordinance, the city chose to take the work back "in-house," making the employees city workers again.

The city of San Jose had engaged in privatization efforts with little public debate through much of the 1980s and 1990s. However, after the living wage campaign helped build a powerful coalition and educated the public on the issue of outsourcing, when the city of San Jose attempted to privatize the public water system in 1998, it was immediately criticized by city residents. Relying on the city's living wage ordinance, the Central Labor Council and their living wage allies were able to mount a successful campaign against the effort.[20] According to Amy Dean, formerly of the South Bay (California) Central Labor Council, it is possible that the issue of privatization and contracting out will become more of a concern in the next few years, as city and state budgets feel the impact of the recession.

Privatization was the key issue in the Cincinnati campaign mentioned in chapter 4.[21] It was the city's interest in privatizing services that motivated labor council president Dan Radford to push for the quick adoption of the ordinance. City council member John Cranley sponsored the ordinance, saying that he wanted to have a living wage ordinance in place before the city went forward with privatizing services. The cosponsor, Vice Mayor Alicia Reece concurred, commenting on the upcoming debates over managed competition, "If we're going to be contracting out jobs, the city has to make sure these jobs have a livable wage."[22] The ordinance went into effect in February 2003, and it is too early to estimate its impact on contracting out. However, having an ordinance in place with minimum wage and benefit requirements would certainly reduce the cost saving potential of contracting out in Cincinnati.[23]

A few ordinances contain specific language pertaining to contracting out. The living wage regulations in Oakland, California, mandate the city to do a cost-benefit analysis prior to any new privatization. The Minneapolis ordinance states, "Work presently being performed by City employees may not be contracted out unless the contractors pay employees performing that work a living wage or the current city wage and benefits, whichever is higher."

However, beyond a few concrete cases, it is unlikely that the ordinances have had a significant impact in reducing the level of contracting out in the cities where they exist. For example, in Baltimore, it appears that the living wage ordinance did not diminish city administrator's interest in privatization. In the years after passing the living wage, Mayor Kurt Schmoke met regularly with private companies that expressed interest in taking over the city's water and/or sewage service, stating "We are open. We invite people to come in [to discuss privatization]."[24] In 1998, Schmoke convened a "city efficiency task force" called the Millennium Group and commissioned studies from outside consultants to look into privatization opportunities. The task force and studies were to develop proposals for privatization in the areas of worker compensation, personnel, solid waste collection, fleet management, building maintenance, and trash collection.[25] While school privatization plans have been scaled back, the city has dramatically increased its contracting out of educational services, such as tutoring and test administration. These stories suggest that living wage ordinances may not ultimately stop privatization efforts. However, it seems that they at least slow down the pace of privatization efforts, as well as serve to protect contracted workers from rock bottom wages (which may in turn benefit private sector service unions).

Worker Self-Organization

Although the living wage movement has won raises for many low-wage workers, it is rare that the workers themselves are leading or even involved in the campaigns. There are reasons for this that make sense: the workers affected often have two or three jobs, leaving them little free time for sleep, let alone organizing. Some of the workers are immigrants without documentation who fear calling attention to themselves. Even those with documentation may fear discipline or firing for speaking out about their wages, as it is common for employers to fire workers who are considered to be agitators or are seen as pro-union.

In some cities, especially those with a high cost of living, the workers covered by a living wage ordinance might not even live in city borders.

This was the case in the Santa Monica, California, campaign, where high-priced real estate and steep rents meant that most workers had a long commute to the luxury hotels and restaurants covered by the living wage proposal. In cases like this, the workers' voices have less weight with city councilors, who tend to want to hear only from their own constituents.

Finally, turnover is high in many of the jobs covered by ordinances, precisely because of the low wages and poor conditions. Without the right to sick leave, workers who get ill or have sick children may be laid off. Without enough money for a car, workers who rely on public transportation may miss a bus and lose their job. When wages are so low they can't even cover basic costs of living, workers will always be on the lookout for a better job and will leave when they get the chance. This high turnover can mean that people are less invested in organizing, since they hope to leave the job soon.

These conditions are not unique to the living wage movement. In fact, there are many examples of individuals fighting on behalf of or alongside workers who find it hard to fight for themselves, including the abolitionist movement of the nineteenth century and the anti-sweatshop movement of today. For those who believe that an injury to one is an injury to all, these forms of solidarity are promising. But their challenge is to make sure that these movements in solidarity with workers do not forget the workers themselves.

In some of the strongest campaigns, low-wage workers have been involved in the effort for higher wages. Airport workers were active in the campaigns in Los Angeles, San Francisco, and Oakland. Employees working for hotels and restaurants at the Berkeley Marina were involved in developing demands and organizing. Chapter 4 showed how the living wage campaign in Providence, Rhode Island, arrived at its living wage level from workers' own experience, where they developed budgets for a realistic amount needed to survive. Workers also came up with a list of other demands to include in their ordinance based on their own experiences, including nondiscrimination based on prison records, and affirmative action guidelines for city and contracted workers. At Harvard, cafeteria workers and janitors felt they couldn't join students for the sit-in but played a large role in the campaign, from bringing food to the students sitting-in, speaking at rallies, and organizing marches. Still, the number of campaigns where workers are involved, let alone in the leadership, is small. Although these solidarity movements can help improve conditions for workers, they can also lead to negative outcomes if those directly affected don't have a voice in the organizing.

Workers' involvement in living wage campaigns is especially important in the struggle for implementation. Living wage coalitions can play
a role in improving implementation, but it is workers who are best posi-
tioned to know if their employer is violating any of the provisions of the
ordinance. Workers are also the ones with the greatest incentive to make
sure the laws are enforced, since they need the living wage. Organizations
in solidarity with workers can fight on behalf of workers to implement
the ordinance, but workers have a material interest in getting employers
to comply with the law.

Changing Ideology about Wages and Work

Beyond economic and employment effects, living wage campaigns are a
vehicle for popular education around issues of inequality and low
wages.[26] Campaigns in Oregon have worked with Just Economics to
develop a popular education curriculum for meetings and workshops, to
raise awareness around the living wage movement. The Pittsburgh living
wage campaign developed a half-hour curriculum that has been used in
churches and union halls. More than two hundred people are trained to
run the workshops, and more than five thousand people have attended
at least one of the sessions. The Center for Popular Economics developed
a full-day workshop for the Harvard Living Wage campaign, helping
activists to counter the arguments against a living wage, which has
also been used with organizations such as United Students Against
Sweatshops.

As the living wage movement spread to the United Kingdom, the
Christian social justice group Church Action on Poverty took on the issue.
In 2002 it sponsored the Lent Minimum Wage Challenge, calling on
members to live off of the national minimum wage for the six weeks of
Lent to raise awareness about working poverty. Seventy people participated in the challenge, and the campaign was adopted again for Lent 2003.
Church Action on Poverty produced a booklet on the topic for potential
participants, which provided information on the minimum wage and
living wage, and guidance on how to take part in the Lent Challenge and
share experiences with others.

At the heart of the living wage movement is an ideological battle about
the role of government in regulating markets. This was highlighted in
Albuquerque, New Mexico, after the nearby city of Santa Fe passed its
citywide living wage ordinance in 2003. Albuquerque city councilors

passed a resolution "endorsing the right of businesses to determine wages based on market considerations; and endorsing the efforts of municipal government to promote free enterprise and partner with the business community to foster a healthy economic environment."[27] According to council member Greg Payne, who introduced the resolution, the intent was to prevent Albuquerque from doing "anything incredibly stupid" like Santa Fe. This example shows how the living wage concept can be antithetical to those who support mainstream economic development policies—policies that call for less government regulation on business and an extension of the free market.

Living wage advocates see the movement in this light as well. In fact, many living wage supporters believe one of their greatest successes has been in getting the concept of "living wages" adopted in other arenas—in their cities and elsewhere. When asked about the original aspirations of the campaign, Tammy Johnson, formerly of Progressive Milwaukee, notes that one goal was "to shape the public debate on the issue." In her opinion, "It has worked. I think the phrase 'living wage job' is in the vocabulary now in a way that it wasn't two or three years ago. When jobs are being created, people will ask, 'Is it a livable wage job?'" Similarly, Van Slambrouck writes in the *Christian Science Monitor*, "[These campaigns] illustrate the breadth of support, growing power, and shifting politics of a movement that, while only five years old, has overthrown traditional notions of how local economics work." These comments and others like them reveal the impact the movement has had on general perceptions about work, wages, economic development, and poverty.

Some activists have noted that the campaigns have made politicians accept and promote the idea of raising wages. According to Christie Nordstrom of the Campaign for a Sustainable Milwaukee, "Politicians are coming out left and right in support of living wage jobs. For example, when Ameritech was cutting 400 jobs, there were city, county and state politicians speaking to preserve family-supporting jobs." When signing the Baltimore ordinance, Mayor Kurt Schmoke stated, "I want to underscore the point that this is an important step, but just the first step. Wages have to be increased in this country."[28] Tammy Johnson also believes that the success of the living wage campaigns and the rhetoric of "living wages" contributed to pressuring national legislators to raise the minimum wage in 1995: "Legislators saw these going on around the country, and saw that people supported the idea, and realized they should pass it or they might not get re-elected in 1996."

It is easy to discredit the comments of living wage supporters as "wishful thinking." Activists are likely to look for positive outcomes from their efforts even when they don't exist. However, even some opponents of the ordinances have made comments supporting the concept of living wage jobs. For example, Duluth, Minnesota, mayor Gary Doty noted, "It's something we can live with. We're not chasing low-paying jobs. Our success in business development has been with high-paying jobs. We still have a quality work force and a quality of life that can't be taken away." Los Angeles mayor Riordan, who originally vetoed the ordinance in his city, later began to state publicly that paying living wages is an employer's "moral responsibility," that it is "ultimately good for business."[29] And in hearings to strengthen coverage of the ordinance in 1998, Los Angeles City Council member Joel Wachs, known as a "taxpayer advocate" and not as a worker advocate, stated, "Not since the rent-stabilization laws of the 1970s has the city created an ordinance of such importance."[30]

Even the *Los Angeles Times*, which had editorialized strongly against the living wage during the campaign, slowly began to change its stance after the law was in place. As the Living Wage Coalition kept the issue alive during its implementation struggles, the *Times* began running stories sympathetic to the law. Columnist Shawn Hubler profiled a Los Angeles International Airport baggage claim worker in a story about the airlines' reluctance to comply with the law. Hubler wondered why the airlines are so resistant, when "a couple more bucks an hour for these workers isn't going to break anyone."

Employers are also acknowledging the merits of a living wage. Since 1999, the business press—including *Business Week*, the *Wall Street Journal*, and *Entrepreneur* magazine—have published articles favorable to the living wage movement. A growing number of employers extol the benefits of paying a living wage: both in better morale and lower turnover of the work force but also in creating a sense of fairness desired by customers and some management.[31] For example, a prominent Florida-based law firm elected to institute its own twelve-dollars-per-hour living wage policy for all employees nationwide in 2000, at a reported cost of $1 million.[32]

This is not to suggest that employers will come to see the value of the movement and voluntarily agree to pay higher wages, or that activists can rely on elected officials to raise wage standards. Rather, it suggests the power of the movement to affect the public discourse and public perceptions of fairness. The idea is also spreading beyond the borders of the

United States. Of course, the living wage struggle has existed in other countries for many years (such as widespread campaigns in South Africa and Australia). But in the past couple of years, labor leaders and community activists in Japan, England, and Canada have worked with U.S. living wage activists to help extend the fight against low wages into their own countries.

Furthermore, some groups are introducing the living wage idea into other arenas. In Los Angeles, clergy members active in the living wage campaign have now introduced living wage resolutions in their churches and religious conferences. The sixteen-denomination Southern California Ecumenical Council adopted a resolution urging congregations, schools, and other religious institutions to pay their own employees a living wage. The Los Angeles Episcopal church contingent took a living wage resolution to its national convention, where it passed without much debate. Linda Lotz formerly of Clergy and Laity United for Economic Justice echoes Tammy Johnson's point about the concept of a "living wage": "The terminology is accepted now, where it wasn't two years ago."

Despite these anecdotes, it is hard to measure the actual impact of the campaigns on ideology about wages, particularly in these specific cities. A Lexis-Nexis search verifies that the term living wage was used more frequently as the movement grew. In 1990, a search of major newspapers finds 139 references to living wage; by 2002, this number had grown tenfold, to 1,460.[33] Gallup polls seem to show a slight increase in the number of people favoring an increase in the national minimum wage over time: 78 percent of U.S. adults favored a national increase of 90 cents in 1995; in 1999, 82 percent favored a $1.30 increase.[34] There is little poll evidence about support for living wage ordinances. However, a 1999 poll in San Francisco found interesting results. Approximately 60 percent of voters said they supported enacting a living wage ordinance of ten dollars or eleven dollars per hour. According to the pollsters, when asked about an ordinance at nine dollars per hour, "support drops off significantly, as liberal voters say they are disinclined to support a weak Living Wage Ordinance."[35]

Building Labor-Community Coalitions

In chapter 2, I reviewed a list of reasons why labor unions have experienced declining political clout in recent decades, which includes their inability to form alliances with other groups in their communities. Have the living wage campaigns helped address this weakness? There appears to be wide agreement among living wage supporters that the campaigns have helped spark a new era of labor-community collaboration. Jen Kern of ACORN says of the growing alliance between different organizations, "It's an active coalition that just never existed before."[36]

The chance to build new alliances is perhaps the most important reason that labor unions have been involved in living wage campaigns. This has been especially important for central labor councils that are trying to increase their visibility in their communities. Southern Arizona Labor Council president Ian Robertson commented on his role in the Tucson campaign, "I'm tired of being called a labor boss, and that we're only interested in collecting dues. Here was an opportunity for labor to be a community partner."[37] Some national unions have also realized the value of the movement for this purpose. In the summer of 2001, the Communication Workers of America's National Committee on Equity recommended that the union leadership and locals promote living wage campaigns, in part to "build and sustain permanent and powerful community, labor and religious coalitions."[38]

On the local level, unions that haven't traditionally worked together are seeing the value of living wage coalitions to advance a broad agenda, including labor rights. In Sonoma County, California, a coalition has developed that includes active participation from SEIU, the International Brotherhood of Electrical Workers (IBEW), and the Carpenters union, as well as the Greens and groups such as the Sonoma County Council on Aging, Sonoma County Peace and Justice Center, and Women in Action. According to Marty Bennett, a lead organizer on the campaign, the coalition worked hard to build a campaign and draft an ordinance that would "develop a common agenda for labor in the region." Bennett suggests that a recent political failure for organized labor may have been the trigger for seeking these new alliances:

> A year ago we lost on a four-three vote at the Santa Rosa City Council for a comprehensive project labor agreement and card check neutrality on a new hotel and conference center constructed with city redevelopment monies. Many in the building trades I think see that the living wage coalition can become a vehicle to build support in the community for "high road/social equity" local economic development projects.

John Walsh of the Sonoma area carpenters' union and Steve Benjamin of the electricians (IBEW) agree. Beyond their fervent belief that fighting for a living wage is simply "the right thing to do," Walsh and Benjamin both see the value in building a broad coalition that "sets a tone of justice in the workplace." Although working with some of these groups can be challenging, due to cultural and ideological differences, Benjamin comments, "Anytime you can establish new relationships like this, it's a good thing."

Los Angeles

Some observers note that the living wage ordinance victory was a major contributing factor to the growing strength of the larger labor movement in Los Angeles. Madeline Janis-Aparicio, of the Living Wage Coalition, argues that the campaign was a key ingredient to the revival of labor in Los Angeles: "The Living Wage Ordinance has been a catalyst to build momentum for issues that improve the standard of living for workers in Los Angeles." It is not only supporters of the law who note its importance. An article in the *Los Angeles Business Journal* examining what they perceived as a decreased voice in the region listed the ordinance as the business community's biggest loss of 1997.

By September 1998, Patrick McGreevey, of the *Daily News* of Los Angeles, wrote of unions gaining power in Los Angeles. He cites a string of recent victories for the unions, starting with the living wage ordinance and including the election of the labor-backed slate for the city charter reform commission; winning "lucrative contracts" in April for hotel workers with 14 major unionized hotels; winning the largest pay raises in many years for city employees; and seeing their allies on the city council become a solid majority. In addition, even Mayor Riordan began to develop a relationship with Los Angeles County Federation of Labor president Miguel Contreras. After negotiating with the labor federation over issues such as the mayor's prized airport expansion project, Riordan appointed Contreras to the airport commission, giving a seat on the board for the first time to a representative of organized labor.

Despite shrinking union membership in southern California, many agreed that the Los Angeles unions seemed to have more power than before. Council member Joel Wachs, who had been in office for twenty-seven years, noted in 1998 that "the city employee unions are stronger than I've ever seen them with respect to influence over the City Council. Most council members will not buck the unions. There are more council members today who will vote 100 percent for what the unions want."[39] In addition, the new leadership of the national AFL-CIO has given special attention to Los Angeles since the ordinance was passed, by, for example, holding a biennial convention there in 1997, scheduling their national con-ference there for 1999, and selecting the Los Angeles airport as one of seven organizing sites in the country targeted for assistance by the national body. In addition, the AFL-CIO hired more than a hundred interns to work for Los Angeles area unions during recent summers through its national "Union Summer" program, designed to train young people for union organizing jobs.

In addition to the continued activities of the coalition itself, member organizations also grew as a result of the living wage campaign. LAANE, the backbone of the coalition, has expanded considerably, nearly tripling its staff. It is now operating out of much larger offices and has a number of projects underway. Besides living wage implementation, LAANE cur-rently is conducting a subsidy accountability research project, organizing hotel workers in the city of Santa Monica, and assisting living wage cam-paigns in California.

Perhaps the most notable outgrowth of the living wage organizing is the group Clergy and Laity United for Economic Justice (CLUE). CLUE formed just as the living wage campaign was getting underway. It con-tinued to grow and work closely with labor unions in Los Angeles to raise awareness about low-wage work and the right of workers to a living wage during the implementation process. CLUE members first began to intro-duce living wage resolutions in their churches and religious conferences but then expanded their activities. For example, CLUE established a "Java for Justice" campaign, involving more than sixty priests, rabbis, and min-isters who eat meals in luxury hotel dining rooms and then stand up and deliver sermons, asking patrons to ask the management to negotiate with the hotel workers union. CLUE now has employed staff persons and has a membership active in welfare reform, union organizing, farm worker rights, and other campaigns related to organizing workers.

Tucson

Although some of the groups that worked together in the Tucson cam-paign had worked together before, many had not. In fact, some of the groups involved had historically been on opposite sides. Ian Robertson, who is a member of the United Steelworkers of America, commented on the way in which the living wage campaign helped build new alliances: "Come on, I work in a mine, and now I'm sitting down with people from Earth First!" According to Rolando Figueroa, the campaign helped solid-ify many existing organizations and coalitions.

The campaign also led to the formation of the Workers Rights Board, in conjunction with Jobs with Justice. The Workers Rights Board is made up of a diverse cross-section of leaders from the community who use "education, moral persuasion, personal contact, community outreach, and public pressure to encourage employers to abandon practices such as discrimination, poor safety practices, and interfering with workers' efforts to exercise their democratic rights to organize."[40] The purpose of the board is to provide a collective, community voice for unorganized and vulnerable workers and to set a community standard for workplace justice.

In their first public activity, not long after the living wage ordinance was passed, the Workers Rights Board took on the issue of environmental racism and workers' rights. The board held a hearing on Brush Wellman, one of the largest manufacturers of beryllium in the world. The company was not only fighting the workers trying to organize with the Machinists Union in several states, it had also been exposing workers and the community to toxic pollutants for more than twenty years. As of 2003, the community has not been able to get Brush Wellman out of their town. However, the coalition had succeeded in getting the county to demand more frequent testing of the Brush Wellman facilities. They have also continued to educate the larger community about the issues, through public meetings, videos, and a mural.

Baltimore

In the preceding section, I discussed the ways in which fighting for implementation of the living wage ordinance has expanded and strengthened the Solidarity Sponsoring Committee in Baltimore. But has the living wage organizing in general helped to create labor-community coalitions? To answer this question in the Baltimore context is difficult, as the church-based community group BUILD formally maintains the Industrial Areas Foundation "no-coalition" policy. Therefore, the campaign was never intended to develop stronger alliances between community groups or between BUILD and Baltimore area labor unions. In fact, several Baltimore activists have negative impressions of BUILD, specifically because of their unwillingness to work collectively. When asked whether BUILD has cooperative relationships with any organization, longtime homeless rights activist Curtis Price responded "Absolutely not. Absolutely not. They don't work with groups unless they are completely in control. They are too big and too powerful, and they can set their own terms—and they do."[41]

However, living wage organizing has cemented relations between BUILD and AFSCME, which joined forces to found the Solidarity Sponsoring Committee. But although SSC is officially a local of AFSCME, there is some debate among SSC members and supporters as to whether or not the organization should follow the path of more traditional unions and fight for a collective bargaining agreement. One of the lead organizers for BUILD, Jonathan Lange, used to work for the Amalgamated Clothing and Textile Workers Union, and "his experience led him to believe that contracts can calcify a struggle."[42] Lange and Miciotto say that collective bargaining agreements require staff to deal with grievances and that they don't want to become a traditional union that is trapped into just servicing members.[43] In addition, Miciotto claims that the SSC model can be superior to typical unionization campaigns: "Justice for Janitors wins 45 cents wage increase only. We don't want that—the living wage is a *43 percent* increase."

So why did SSC affiliate with AFSCME? In part, the union was valuable for its resources, including space in the AFSCME building, but SSC organizers also felt it was important for their workers' organization to be formally affiliated with a union to prevent other unions from trying to raid them. Therefore, the alliance is strategic and not necessarily the preferred mode of organizing for BUILD leaders. Instead, they would prefer to build a new form of organization—or perhaps, return to an older style of union organizing, "a John L. Lewis, new CIO model." According to Janice Fine, an MIT student who has studied BUILD, Lange believes that this alternative model of organizing will "help counteract any negative images or experiences black workers might have had with unions."[44]

Whether BUILD can create a new type of organization is not yet clear. Regardless, BUILD continues to be a major player in Baltimore and Maryland politics, as witnessed by their efforts in the 1998 state elections. The group registered ten thousand new voters and participated in a vigorous get-out-the-vote drive that resulted in a city voter turnout 9 percentage points higher than the previous election.[45] Although BUILD is a nonprofit, and therefore officially nonpartisan, it was widely acknowledged that the group's work would benefit the incumbent Governor Glendenning. Glendenning won by a large margin, and subsequently invited BUILD members to his inauguration. He also made a personal appearance at a BUILD meeting to assure members that he would keep his campaign promises. A few months after the election, Glendenning helped push through a piece of legislation that would contribute to BUILD's

Joseph Fund, a state fund that would help disadvantaged residents in times of economic hardship.

Boston

Monica Halas of Greater Boston Legal Services notes that the Boston living wage campaign was remarkable in its ability to build a new relationship between the labor movement and the community organization ACORN. The two groups had not worked together closely in the past, but when ACORN organizer Lisa Clauson approached Boston Central Labor Council president Tony Romano about the idea, Romano was intrigued. Although the labor council had not been known as an activist group, Romano was eager to get his member unions on board. Through the course of the campaign, relations between ACORN, the labor council, and the State Federation of Labor deepened. Romano and others were impressed when ACORN continued to deliver what they promised: turnout at rallies, visibility for the campaign, and strategic thinking about how to get council and mayoral support.

When the ordinance was held up after passage, the mayor attempted to negotiate only with labor and cut ACORN out of the picture. According to Halas, the last thing the mayor wanted was a formal role for ACORN in the Living Wage Advisory Committee. But labor leaders held firm: the city had to designate a seat for ACORN, and they had to keep the community hiring hall (ACORN's priority) in the ordinance. In the end, both things were preserved.

The Living Wage Advisory Committee opened up a way for the new allies to institutionalize their relationship. According to Halas, the committee "really cemented their relationship, and there have been so many positive spin-offs out of that." These spin-offs include the successful effort to raise the state minimum wage in 1998, pass a statewide and city of Boston Earned Income Tax Credit, and introduce a state corporate accountability law. When Boston Justice for Janitors went on strike in 2002, Tony Romano and ACORN president Maude Hurd were arrested together in an act of civil disobedience supporting the janitors.

The alliance may not seem a natural one. ACORN's base is primarily African American members in Dorchester and Roxbury, while the labor council has stronger ties in the white working class. Yet, the strength of the new relationship is noticeable. After the initial living wage victory, the State Federation of Labor honored Maude Hurd, president of ACORN. Tony Romano presented the award, telling the crowd that of all the things he had done in his labor career, the opportunity to work on the living wage campaign was the most meaningful.

Conclusion

This chapter highlights the importance of using different measures to determine implementation outcomes. In many cities the number of workers actually covered by an ordinance is quite small, and in numerous cities workers who should be receiving higher wages are not because of weak implementation.

However, implementation as measured by other outcomes shows considerable achievements for the organizations involved. The strength of the living wage movement has been acknowledged by journalists, politicians, opponents, and supporters, with the concept adopted by a wide number of organizations. As for the impact of the living wage movement on building the political strength of the groups involved and creating strong labor-community coalitions, the outcomes vary. In Baltimore, BUILD has used the living wage idea to strengthen itself and to contribute to its political agenda. However, the group continues to work primarily on its own and has not used the living wage organizing to build alliances with other community or labor groups in the region.

In contrast, the living wage advocates in cities such as Milwaukee and Los Angeles have used the campaigns as a platform from which to build alliances with groups they had not worked with previously. Episcopal minister Dick Gillett noted that many in the religious community had negative images of unions and that the living wage campaign created an ideal place for dispelling some of these notions:

> The living wage victory in Los Angeles raised the possibility that a real awakening and a willingness to rekindle the fires for a new agenda for justice might be at hand in the form of a promising new partnership of religious faiths with the diverse and progressive sectors of the community, and even with some politicians with a conscience.[46]

In Milwaukee, the executive director of the job training organization Esperanza Unida, remarked that the Campaign for a Sustainable Milwaukee was different from previous coalition attempts: "I've never seen so many people working together to focus on the root cause of our social problems."[47] *The Milwaukee Labor Press* also commented on the degree to which the alliances built in the Campaign for a Sustainable Milwaukee were crucial for the group's success in fighting for community hiring in the convention center project:

> Without the help of community groups labor would not have gotten a project agreement on the Midwest Express Center and Miller Park. Community groups helped turn it around, and labor in turn helped them get language in the agreement that said 25 percent of the workers on the project must be minorities and 5 percent must be female.[48]

Although the Campaign for a Sustainable Milwaukee no longer exists, ties built through the living wage campaign remain.

From the beginning, the living wage movement created a space for workers and activists to talk and educate themselves and the public about the economy and broader social change. In Pittsburgh, the Alliance for Progressive Action noted that actually winning living wage legislation was only one minor goal in a larger organizing plan—which held economic education as its main goal. The coalition developed its own curriculum and trained more than two hundred volunteers. Over several years, more than five thousand people attended living wage educational sessions in churches, union halls, schools and neighborhood centers. In Tucson, more than a thousand volunteers walked through neighborhoods to talk to residents about economic issues. These opportunities create space for an alternative dialogue about the nature of wages and the economy. As Pima County Interfaith Council organizer Jaime Huerta notes, a main goal is to challenge the "market is God" ideology that is so pervasive in the United States.

In the end, living wage campaigns may have their greatest impact in their ability to challenge standard rhetoric about economic development, capital mobility, and the so-called laws of supply and demand. In campaign after campaign, community members are raising questions about their local economy. They are asking why after a long period of economic growth so many workers continue to earn poverty wages. Living wage campaigns help people organize to consider alternatives. In the time of capitalist globalization, they create the hope for people to have a voice in how their local economies are run.

11

THE FUTURE OF THE LIVING
WAGE MOVEMENT AND
LESSONS FOR POLICY
IMPLEMENTATION

The living wage movement is helping spotlight the fundamental responsibility of government to ensure that fairness and justice for all prevail in our communities. It would seem that this simple truth needs no reinforcing; after all, these values are deeply embedded in our national history. But they have been all but forgotten in recent times in the boundless pursuit of economic gain and the concomitant disparagement of government.

> Reverend Canon Richard Gillett, "The Living Wage Movement: It's about More than Just Wages," *The Witness* website, April 22, 2000

We are joining forces with religious groups. With the students. With other unions. With groups throughout the community. We cannot be isolated for the very simple reason that we are not alone.

The things we are fighting for—respect, dignity, a living wage, the chance for our children to have a better future—these are things that all people want. When you are fighting for what is right, you do not—you cannot—stand alone. Other people who believe in these causes stand with us.

We also have justice in our corner. And patience as well.

> Maria Elena Durazo, a leader in the Los Angeles living wage campaign and president, HERE Local 11, quoted in *Chicago Tribune*, June 7, 1998

Contrary to skeptics' claims, the recent recession has not slowed down the living wage movement. Some thirty new ordinances have passed since early 2002, with new campaigns continuing to emerge. Whether or not the recession is behind us, one thing is clear: the demand for living wages will not disappear.

As a result, opponents have dramatically increased the financial and organizational resources they invest fighting living wage laws. In May 2002, Newt Gingrich sent a letter to several top national executives inviting them to an anti–living wage conference cosponsored by the conservative think tank, the Employment Policies Institute. Their call for action emphasized that "in 2001 alone, advocates of a free market have lost one living wage battle every 14 days on average." The conference offered "a promising approach to changing the outcomes," demonstrating that Gingrich and his allies recognize the movement's political potential. Although the numbers of workers affected by living wage campaigns is modest, the indirect effects are substantial. In a number of campaigns, activists have gone beyond basic demands for higher wages to a thorough critique of the market.

In recent years the living wage movement has continued to grow in new directions. While there were fewer ordinances passed in 2002 and 2003 than in previous years, the scope and coverage of the new laws has greatly expanded. It is certainly possible that the effects of the recession are only now being fully felt at the local level, as state budget shortfalls trickle down. As such, it is likely that some of the city council members who supported the living wage movement during the boom times will begin to back away from anything that might suggest higher taxes or business regulations. Similarly, traditional labor leaders may be more reticent to spend their limited political capital pushing their allies in mayoral and council seats in times of tighter budgets. And administrators, looking for new ways to cut costs, may step up the efforts to privatize, hoping to save money by outsourcing services to employers who will pay much lower wages.

But it is unlikely, even in the face of these very real challenges, that activists will abandon their struggle to raise wages at the local level. Since 1994, advocates have expanded the scope of the movement, found new targets, refined their arguments, and developed sophisticated understandings of their local governments. One such example of an expanded living wage agenda is the emergence of community benefits agreements.[1] Building on the success of living wage campaigns, community benefits agreements require municipal leaders to ensure that employers provide living wages, environmental protections, job security, and child care in order to receive economic development assistance from cities. Because they are project-specific, the agreements are not restricted by federal laws such as the National Labor Relations Act. Hence they can require legal measures and protections that generalized living wage ordinances cannot, such as health insurance and card-check or neutrality agreements to assist in labor organizing.

Another means of expansion discussed earlier is the spread of living wage campaigns to college campuses. These campaigns have the same advantage as community benefits agreements because they are essentially new administrative policy. The United Students Against Sweatshops' Living Wage Working Group interprets "living wage campaign" broadly, as "*any* campaigns in solidarity with campus workers, whether [they're] helping to win a better contract with wage increases or health care access, to win an organizing drive, to kick a nasty contractor off campus, etc.— not just campaigns to adjust wages for the cost of living."[2] University campaigns have the potential to extend living wage coverage to a large number of workers, in no small part due to the increasing privatization of food service, janitorial, and security work on campuses. They also have the opportunity of mobilizing hundreds of student activists in a manner that parallels the vibrant anti-sweatshop movement. Activists are also beginning to make the connections between anti-sweatshop and living wage organizing, as evidenced by the December 2002 national living wage day of action, coordinated on over a dozen campuses by United Students Against Sweatshops.

Whether or not the current policy—city-based ordinances covering service contractors and subsidy recipients—continues to motivate activists, it is abundantly clear that the ideological basis of the living wage movement has taken root nationally. This expansion is significant because the ordinances alone will not solve our current problems with rising poverty, growing inequality, and falling real wages. While winning a local piece of legislation can deliver real benefits to workers, living wage ordinances should be understood as constructive tools for further organizing, not solutions in and of themselves.

Lessons for Policy Implementation

Why are policies implemented well in some municipalities and not in others? What explains the variation in living wage enforcement from city to city? The lessons presented in this book have broad implications for implementing local policy. The case studies presented have highlighted several key factors that determine what happens after living wage ordinances are passed. In a few cases "street-level bureaucrats" are managing to successfully enforce the laws. Such an outcome requires at least some dedicated staff, with the authority and resources to do the work. They are held accountable for implementation; have a manageable ratio of staff to contracts and economic development projects; and work within a city administration that is politically neutral, if not supportive of effective enforcement. Success in these cases also relies in part on the personal inclinations of the staff, whether they support the goals of the ordinance or are simply motivated to do their job well, regardless of the content.

But why is this type of successful implementation so rare? One reason is that, in addition to existing capacities to enforce policy, enforcement of the living wage requires effort and competence. In each city, the administrative staff must work with individuals in every municipal department that contracts out for services. The living wage administrator must ensure that the information about the law flows back and forth between the enforcing agency and the contracting agency, as well as between the contracting agency and the vendor. To do the job well, the enforcing agency must maintain a list of covered contracts, solicit compliance reports from contractors, and conduct independent verification. When contractors don't submit reports or don't pay the living wage, the enforcing agency must continue to push the employers to comply and impose penalties when necessary. Because the process can be burdensome and fraught with daily unpleasant interactions, it is unrealistic to expect effective enforcement unless incentives are provided.

More specifically, in order for an initiative to have a chance of success within the city government, the staff involved need to know that it matters to their supervisors that the job is done well and that their standing within the city depends on effective implementation of the law. This was not the case in many of the cities examined in this study. Rather, what was missing in almost every city was a real commitment to enforcing the law by higher levels of the city administration. The living wage law, as perceived by many in the city administration, guarantees wage increases for workers at the expense of private-sector contractors (who experience reduced profits) or the city (which faces increased bid prices).[3] This runs counter to most current approaches to city management, which are based on profit-led urban development strategies and the expectation that city departments reduce costs wherever possible. It is for this reason that city administrators have not provided incentives for staff to enforce the laws. This exemplifies negative power, where city officials, backed by powerful interests, send a clear signal that implementation is not a priority, leading to a lack of enforcement. As a result, city staff have at best contradictory attitudes toward living wage implementation.

Instead of relying on city staff, living wage advocates need to pursue other strategies to improve implementation. This might involve utilizing outside pressure, working formally with the city, or doing some version of both. The narratives in this study have shown that a great deal of variation in implementation can be explained by the activity of nongovernmental organizations. In cities where these organizations participated in monitoring and enforcement, implementation was simply more successful.

Why are outside tactics necessary? In the case of the living wage movement, where ordinances are passing at high rates in cities throughout the country, council members may "go with the flow" and vote for a living wage proposal even if they do not fully support the law. It is even possible that they will vote for the ordinance cynically assuming that it will not be enforced. Even those council members who do support the law may be reluctant to put much effort into ensuring compliance, as the process is generally not in the public eye and yields little in terms of new public support. If anything, these council members may fear pushing large and often powerful employers to comply. It is unlikely that even the most dedicated council members could do much to fight for enforcement since they do not have the time or staff to be in constant contact with beneficiaries.

But outside tactics alone aren't always enough. Contrary to what some activists believe, those campaigns where coalition leaders have ties to elected officials and city staff have a greater likelihood of implementation. When city leaders are educated about the living wage issue and invested in the law prior to enactment, this can strengthen their commitment to enforcement when conflicts arise. Working on the inside can also integrate activists into the municipal political process. Living wage advocates become policy experts, on equal footing with city officials, and they often end up serving on implementation task forces or other formal bodies. Moreover, community organizations cannot expect to ensure compliance solely on their own. Connections through networks with city council members are not only necessary for the passage of the law, they are essential for implementation. In fact, these networks may be more crucial after policy enactment. It is city council members and city staff who have access to much of the information needed for implementation, such as what contracts the city holds. Inevitably, revisions in the law will be necessary, and here the support of council members is required.

Adopting an inside-outside approach can also improve the city's capacity to enforce laws. These tactics give greater legitimacy to city staff to do their job, contribute some of the necessary information and resources, and pressure the city to commit adequate staff and resources to implementation. Second, both methods can help clarify the ordinance. In treating implementation as an ongoing process, there is space for evaluation, assessment, and any modifications needed to ensure that the ordinance is meeting its objectives.

It appears that the involvement of nongovernmental organizations is a prime variable explaining implementation success. However, it is not enough just to bring any community partner into the process. To be effective the community organizations must have the motivation to monitor the ordinance. This is more likely to occur with organizations that directly or indirectly represent or low-wage workers. In addition to providing an obvious incentive to monitor implementation, those seeking to represent low-wage workers also have access to information about noncompliance. For example, in Baltimore, the Solidarity Sponsoring Committee found out that school bus drivers were not getting the living wage they were entitled to during their organizing efforts, and in Los Angeles, the living wage coalition discovered various cases of noncompliance through worker trainings and organizing efforts at the airport. It was this information that spurred the organizations to protest noncompliance in city council hearings and to push for the covered firms to pay the living wage. In many cities, the coalitions or member organizations never know of cases where workers are not receiving living wages because they never establish contact with the low-wage workers covered by the law.

It is clearly difficult to build the skills and organizational strength needed to pursue inside and outside tactics for implementation. The stories from cities with living wage ordinances suggest that when coalitions pursued both tactics during the campaign to pass a living wage, they are more likely to have the capacity to maintain these same tactics after the law is enacted, improving the chances for more meaningful implementation. In other words, the character of the actual campaign affects the likelihood of implementation success.

Similarly, contrary to what common sense and what many political analysts might suggest, the campaigns that are somewhat contentious—that polarize opponents and supporters and generate public awareness around the living wage issue—are those with the greatest chances of enforcement. This is because contentious politics can serve to demonstrate to the city government the power behind the living wage and can give legitimacy to the city when it goes on to enforce an ordinance that employers oppose. Contentious campaigns also help build a coalition's internal capacity, an essential skill once attention turns to the more mundane but crucial enforcement issues.

The inside-outside strategy discussed here can improve the chances of implementation of living wage ordinances. Of course, there are other goals that many activists want to pursue in their campaigns beyond winning higher wages for covered workers. These include building coalitions, organizing workers, raising public awareness about the problems facing the working poor, and influencing larger ideological battles around urban development, income inequality, and the nature of work. Further research is surely needed to determine the best ways to use living wage campaigns to fulfill these larger ambitions, because in these cases, a dual inside-outside strategy may not be as relevant.

It is clear from the research presented in this book that the integration of nonstate actors into the process of policy administration can greatly improve the likelihood of successful implementation. These groups are not equally effective, however, and must have the incentive to represent potential beneficiaries and must have real stakes in the outcomes—stakes beyond a basic support for the concept of the law. Implementation and monitoring take resources and enormous effort. Organizations strapped for time will only pursue these efforts if they perceive direct gains, such as unionizing low-wage workers or winning raises for community residents whom they represent.

Could the implementation problems be solved if organizations pressured the city to put adequate resources into monitoring and to guarantee that persons sympathetic to the law be in charge, such as activists in the municipal unions? This could improve implementation considerably, but it is doubtful that the state will ever be able to efficiently and effectively enforce the law on its own. Employers can submit falsified wage records, as one school bus contractor admitted to doing in Baltimore. Without direct contact with workers on site, it is difficult to obtain reliable information about wages paid. And given that much of the city's contracted work force is seasonal and temporary, the task of gathering wage data directly from them is even more difficult. For this reason, having community organizations participate in the implementation of the ordinance can help the city, as it saves on resources and provides more accurate data. Furthermore, these organizations can continue to monitor city performance and insist that city employees not be pressured by management to neglect their monitoring duties.

Keeping in mind the unique circumstances of each local experience, I write these conclusions in the hopes that they might be of use to organizations planning to run their own living wage campaigns or other local policy initiatives. I argued here that the living wage ordinances are relatively clear in their goals but are conflictual. Left open for future research remains the issue of whether or not implementation would look similar when the policy was more ambiguous or less conflictual. It seems apparent that policies that are more consonant with the dominant ideology of the city administration will be more likely to be enforced by city officials themselves, relying less on the input of NGOs. Nevertheless, I argue throughout that the involvement of nonstate actors will continue to enhance implementation, because of their increased ability to gather information and their incentive to monitor the state.

The findings of this book hold many important lessons for progressive groups searching for new organizing strategies within the current political landscape. Most important, we see that progressive policies can be successful even in times when the left is weak and allies of the left are in precarious positions inside city governments. In addition, these cases show that living wage campaigns can have positive outcomes even when the direct policy mandates are not met. In fact, some activists (and opponents of the laws) argue that the main purpose of the campaigns is not so much about achieving a wage increase for covered workers as it is about creating a foundation for larger organizing efforts.

Civil Society and Policy Implementation

The lessons of living wage implementation also have broader implications for democratic governance. Although participation of civil society does not guarantee expansive enforcement, in the case of the ordinances studied here, involvement of nongovernmental organizations greatly increased the likelihood of successful implementation. This finding gives credence to those who argue that traditional forms of governance are inadequate, and that civil society can enhance the capacity of the state under the right conditions.

What is of note here is that citizens can in fact play a significant role in the monitoring and implementation of policy, even where governments oppose or are reluctant to enforce the laws in question. The conclusions suggest that not only should governments find ways to incorporate civil society into policy implementation but that citizens may have to demand a role for themselves. Furthermore, the inclusion of civil society in policy formation and implementation is not simply a technical matter. It can be politically contentious. Implementation is an extension of the political struggle that occurs when governing bodies initially consider legislation, so there is no reason to expect that conditions will necessarily change. But as with the initial policy campaign, conflict can push supporters to deepen their political alliances and power.

These findings argue against the claim that governments are becoming impotent in the age of globalization. With the living wage movement, local governments across the United States have managed to pass, and in some cases enforce, policies that run counter to the prevailing economic paradigm. In particular, municipal legislators across the country have passed living wage ordinances despite the fact that opponents argue that they are harmful to local business climates. Rather than being constrained to mainstream economic development policies, city and county leaders have passed dozens of progressive ordinances and have not seen the dire predictions of detractors come to fruition.

Confronting Corporate Hegemony

Although I have argued here that community involvement both internally and externally can improve policy implementation, I must also note the limitations of this strategy. In fact, broad systematic enforcement of progressive policies is not likely to happen unless there is a widespread transformation of the normative foundations of governance. As long as a proworker policy is at odds with mainstream values, implementation struggles will pull activists in multiple directions. There are not enough resources or time for vigilance on every front. As Bruce Nissen points out in *Fighting for Jobs*, workers fighting plant closings have had little success persuading their local governments to play an activist role in protecting jobs on their behalf because doing so would violate "deeply embedded ideological beliefs that identified 'community welfare' with private corporate supremacy in all major economic decision making."[4]

A number of scholars have pointed to the need for labor-community coalitions—and larger political movements—that will confront this hegemonic power of neoliberal governance. For example, Nelson Lichtenstein makes a strong case for the power of ideology in shaping our legal and political environment. It was the persistence of the "labor question" that set the stage for the fight over industrial democracy and industrial citizenship in the 1930s and 1940s.[5] The power of the labor movement as a social movement, based on real numbers but also on normative claims for universal rights, helped to enforce the laws that were passed in that period.

Another illustration of this issue comes from historian Eric Fure-Slocum, who shows how Milwaukee's socialist legacy and strong labor movement allowed a serious working-class challenge to capitalist economic growth policies in the 1940s. Amidst intense debate about the future of the city, working-class organizations were able to put forth their own principles for development, which entailed:

> An insistence that the critical decisions a city faced were political issues and not matters of technical engineering or administration; a demand that political and social access take priority over designs to achieve greater political efficiency or increased productivity in the use of urban space; a requirement that cities retain their fiscal autonomy, particularly to respond to the needs of workers in times of economic hardship; and an image of a city defined and interpreted by class.[6]

These principles contrasted sharply with the growth policies that eventually won out in Milwaukee and most other U.S. cities. However, as Fure-Slocum notes, the progrowth position was not always seen as the "common sense" option.

But as Nelson Lichtenstein has also demonstrated, there can be substantial variation in how normative claims are pursued, shaping institutions, ideology, and what is considered "common sense." For example, at some point in the postwar period, the labor movement shifted its focus away from universal, class-based issues toward firm-centered bargaining. This left tens of thousands of workers on their own, unrepresented by unions and marginalized within the industrial relations framework that unions helped to create. The desire to expand citizenship rights was then taken up by the civil rights movement of the 1950s and 1960s, and later the women's movement. Lichtenstein argues, however, that because there was not a strong intertwining of civil rights and the labor movement, the victories of the 1960s ended up emphasizing individual rather than collective rights. As a result, in the current period workers' greatest job security comes from anti-discrimination laws that may protect individuals but not the working class as a whole. Lichtenstein argues that the future of the labor movement lies not only in organizing but in the revival of the ideas of collective rights and industrial democracy. At the same time, it is necessary to incorporate the lessons of the civil rights movement and not to deny the individuality and heterogeneity of workers.

Building a serious normative challenge to the current mainstream economic development policy—which privileges business climate and corporate profit over worker welfare—is a long-term struggle. An emphasis on this larger struggle is no guarantee that living wage laws, or other proworker policies, will be enforced. There are still technical and administrative aspects, as well as resource constraints, that will always be a challenge for effective implementation. However, changing priorities might at least make living wage enforcement more likely. Let's return to the scenarios presented in chapter 1—cases where legislation was passed but where implementation was stalled or weakened due to employer resistance or pressure from corporate lobbyists. Imagine a scenario where the right to join a union was considered a basic human right, where only the most egregious employers would consider attempting to stop unionization drives, and where such employers would be considered social deviants.[7] Might this change the frequency with which corporations violate basic labor and environmental laws?

Filmmaker Michael Moore suggested a similar idea in the documentary *Bowling for Columbine*. Moore asked a television executive why crime shows only focus on the arrests of black men for offenses such as drug dealing and never highlight corporate criminals who are overwhelmingly white men. Moore's film suggests that societal values should perhaps shift so that corporate criminals are seen as dangerous and harmful. In the case of workers' right to join unions: if societal values were shifted so that employers, rather than unions, were seen as greedy and corrupt, it would make it easier for unions to organize. But even more important than the employer's image is the intensity of employer opposition to unions. It isn't just about corporate greed: there is a structural reason why employers try to keep wages down. This must be defined as the "problem." This would mean identifying the capitalist drive for more and more profit as the problem, rather than defining the problem as the ways in which worker organizations infringe on that drive for profit. Again, this kind of normative transformation would not guarantee that workers would choose to join unions, but it would make it more likely, as well as easier for workers to make a real choice.

Of course, there are serious practical limits on such transformation in the context of today's political economic climate. Redefining the problem can only accomplish so much within this system, and any major transformation would have to come with a radical shift in economic and power relations. But returning to the example of Los Angeles, we can see how steady and ongoing organizing by the living wage coalition and its member organizations has had an impact on city politics. Once known as an anti-union and anti-worker town, Los Angeles, as embodied politically in its city council, has made several decisions in recent years that prioritized human need over business profitability or the city budget's bottom-

line. Despite objections and legal threats from the national airline industry and major employers such as McDonald's, the city council decided to
extend the living wage requirement to the Los Angeles International
Airport. They believed they must do what they could to get higher wages
for the workers who screened baggage and swept floors.

What might eventually address the larger inequities would be a social
movement that brought together broad sectors of society. Dan Clawson
argues that the "next upsurge" that makes gains for workers' rights is
likely to happen only when the labor movement fuses with other social
movements, transforming both in the process.[8] As Jen Kern states, living
wage campaigns may offer that opportunity, as they are "uniquely
capable of bringing together labor, religious leaders, and community organizations."[9] If these campaigns can sustain their widespread appeal, they
may, in turn, lead to a larger and more influential movement for social
and economic justice.

Appendix A

ADDITIONAL TABLES

Table A.1. Existing municipal living wage ordinances, through December 2003

City or county	Population (2000)	Year passed	Follow-up
Alexandria, VA	128,283	2000	
Ann Arbor, MI	114,024	2001	
Arlington County, VA	189,453	2003	
Ashland, OR	19,522	2001	
Baltimore, MD	651,154	1994	
Bellingham, WA	67,171	2002	
Berkeley, CA	102,743	2000	Amended 2002 to add marina
Boston, MA	589,141	1997	Amended 1998 & 2002
Bozeman, MT	27,509	2001	
Broward County, FL	1,623,018	2002	
Buffalo, NY	292,648	1999	
Burlington, VT	38,889	2001	
Cambridge, MA	101,355	1999	
Charlottesville, VA	45,049	2001	
Chicago, IL	2,896,016	1998	Expanded 2002
Cincinnati, OH	331,285	2002	
Cleveland, OH	478,403	2000	
Cook County, IL	5,376,741	1998	
Corvallis, OR	49,322	1999	
Cumberland County, NJ	146,438	2001	
Dane County, WI	426,526	1999	
Dayton, OH	166,179	2003	

(Table A.1.—cont.)

City or county	Population (2000)	Year passed	Follow-up
Denver, CO	554,636	2000	
Des Moines, IA	198,682	1996	
Detroit, MI	951,270	1998	
Duluth, MN	86,918	1997	Amended 2000
Durham, NC	187,035	1998	
Eastpointe, MI	34,077	2001	2001 ballot to repeal is defeated
Eau Claire County, WI	93,142	2000	
Fairfax, CA	7,319	2002	
Ferndale, MI	22,105	2001	
Gary, IN	102,746	1989	
Gloucester County, NJ	254,673	2001	
Hartford, CT	121,578	1999	
Hayward, CA	140,030	1999	
Hazel Park, MI	18,963	2002	Repealed 2002
Hempstead, NY	56,554	2001	Repealed 2001
Hudson County, NJ	608,975	1999	
Ingraham County, MI	279,320	2003	
Jersey City, NJ	240,055	1996	
Lakewood, OH	56,646	2003	
Lansing, MI	119,128	2003	
Los Angeles City, CA	3,694,820	1997	Amended 1998
Los Angeles County, CA	9,519,338	1999	
Louisville, KY	256,231	2002	
Lawrence, KS	80,098	2003	
Madison, WI	208,054	1999	
Marin County, CA	247,289	2002	
Meriden, CT	58,244	2000	
Miami Beach, FL	87,933	2001	
Miami-Dade, FL	2,253,362	1999	
Milwaukee City, WI	596,974	1995	
Milwaukee County, WI	940,164	1997	
Minneapolis, MN	382,618	1997	Amended 1998
Missoula, MT	57,053	2001	
Monroe County, MI	145,945	2001	Repealed 2003
Montgomery County, MD	873,341	2002	
Multnomah County, OR	660,486	1996	Amended 1998
New Britain, CT	71,538	2001	
New Haven, CT	123,626	1997	
New Orleans, LA	484,674	2002	Overturned by court 2002
New York City, NY	8,008,278	1996	Expanded 2002
Oakland, CA	399,484	1998	Expanded to cover port 2002
Omaha, NE	390,007	2000	Repealed 2001
Orlando, FL	185,951	2003	
Oxnard, CA	170,358	2002	
Oyster Bay, NY	2,262	2001	
Pasadena, CA	133,936	1998	

(Table A.1.—cont.)

City or county	Population (2000)	Year passed	Follow-up
Pima County, AZ	843,746	2002	
Pittsburgh, PA	334,563	2001	Repealed 2001
Pittsfield Township, MI	30,167	2001	
Port Hueneme, CA	21,845	2003	
Portland, OR	529,121	1996	Amended 1998
Prince Georges County, MD	801,515	2003	
Richmond, CA	99,216	2001	
Rochester, NY	219,773	2001	
Sacramento, CA	407,018	2003	
Salem, OR	136,924	2001	
San Antonio, TX	1,144,646	1998	
San Fernando, CA	23,564	2000	
San Francisco, CA	776,733	2000	Expanded to city 2003
San Jose, CA	894,943	1998	
Santa Clara County, CA	1,682,585	1995	
Santa Cruz County, CA	255,602	2002	
Santa Cruz, CA	54,593	2000	
Santa Fe, NM	62,203	2002	Expanded to city 2003
Santa Monica, CA	84,084	2001	Overturned by ballot 2002
Sebastopol, CA	7,774	2003	
Somerville, MA	77,478	1999	
Southfield, MI	78,296	2002	
St. Louis, MO[a]	348,189	2002	
St. Paul, MN	287,151	1997	
Suffolk County, NY	1,419,369	2001	
Taylor, MI	65,868	2002	
Toledo, OH	313,619	2000	
Tucson, AZ	486,699	1999	
Ventura County, CA	753,197	2001	
Warren, MI	138,247	2000	
Washtenaw County, MI	322,895	2001	
Watsonville, CA	44,265	2002	
West Hollywood, CA	35,716	1997	
Westchester County, NY	923,459	2002	
Ypsilanti Township, MI	49,182	1999	
Ypsilanti, MI	22,362	1999	
	Ordinance passed:	Ordinance in effect:	
Total population with LW:			
In cities	31,162,813	29,793,968	
In counties	30,640,579	30,494,634	

Sources: ACORN National Living Wage Resource Center; United States Census Bureau, population estimates.

[a] An earlier ordinance was approved by voters in 2000. The city refused to implement, and a state supreme court ruled that parts of the initiative had to be repealed because of state law. Advocates launched a campaign for a new ordinance, which the city council approved in 2002.

Table A.2. Living wage ordinances, other jurisdictions

Entity	Year passed
Arlington County School Board, VA	2003
Central Arkansas Library Commission	2001
Harvard University, MA	2001
Johns Hopkins University, MD	2002
Milwaukee School Board, WI	1996
Port of Oakland, CA	2002
Richmond School Board, VA	2001
San Antonio University Health System, TX	2002
San Diego Metropolitan Transit Development Board, CA	2000
Stanford University, CA	2002
Washtenaw County Road Commission, MI	2001
Wesleyan University, CT	2001

Table A.3. Municipalities with direct living wage policies[a]

Municipality	Year passed
Barre City, VT	1999
Bexar County, TX	2000
Burlington, VT	1998
Dayton, OH	1998
Gainesville, FL	2001
Hidalgo County, TX	1999
James City County, VA	2001
Montpelier, VT	1998
Orange County, NC	1998
Tompkins County, NY	2003
Travis County, TX	2000

[a] These municipalities have established "living wage" policies or ordinances that establish living wage levels for all direct city or county employees. They do not cover private sector employers that hold contracts or receive subsidies from the municipality. In some cases, the city or county has subsequently gone on to pass an ordinance covering contractors or subsidy recipients.

APPENDIX B

LIVING WAGE RESOURCES

General Campaign Advice and Technical Support

ACORN Living Wage Resource Center
1486 Dorchester Avenue
Boston, MA 02122
phone: 617-740-9500
fax: 617-436-4878
email: jkern@acorn.org
web: http://www.livingwagecampaign.org

Legal Resources

Brennan Center for Justice at New York University School of Law
161 Avenue of the Americas, 12th Floor
New York, NY 10013
phone: 212-998-6730
fax: 212-995-4550
email: brennan.center@nyu.edu
web: http://www.brennancenter.org/

Guild Law Center for Economic and Social Justice
733 St. Antoine, 3rd Floor

Detroit, MI 48226
phone: 313-962-6540
fax: 313-962-4492
email: mail@sugarlaw.org
web: http://www.sugarlaw.org/

Good Jobs First (particularly for economic development subsidy information)
1311 L Street NW
Washington, DC 20005
phone: 202-737-4315
fax: 202-638-3486
email: info@goodjobsfirst.org
web: http://www.goodjobsfirst.org/

Legal Services
Ellen Wallace, President
NOLSW/UAW Local 2320
113 University Place, 5th floor
New York, NY 10003
phone: 1-800-UAW-2320
fax: 212-228-0097
email: ewallace@att.net
web: http://www.geocities.com/~uaw2320/

Research Resources

Center for Labor Research and Studies
Florida International University
University Park
Miami, FL 33199
phone: 305-348-2616
fax: 305-348-2241
email: Bruce.Nissen@fiu.edu
web: http://www.fiu.edu/~clrs

Economic Policy Institute
1660 L Street NW
Suite 1200
Washington, DC 20036
phone: 202-775-8810

fax: 202-775-0819
email: epi@epinet.org
web: http://www.epinet.org

Political Economy Research Institute
University of Massachusetts-Amherst
Gordon Hall
418 N. Pleasant Street, Suite A
Amherst, MA 01002
phone: 413-545-6355
fax: 413-545-2921
email: peri@peri.umass.edu
web: http://www.umass.edu/peri

University of California-Berkeley Labor Center
2521 Channing Way
Berkeley, CA 94720-5555
phone: 510-643-2621 or 510-643-7079
fax: 510-642-6432
email: kjacobs9@uclink.berkeley.edu or mreich.econ.berkeley.edu
web: http://laborcenter.berkeley.edu

For more information on implementation
see http://fightingforalivingwage.org.

Appendix C

IMPLEMENTATION MEASURES

Assigned value of 1 if:

Administration

Ordinance language in request for proposals for contracts

City inserts living wage language into requests for bids

Employers required to post notices at worksites

City develops and makes available posters, requires them to be posted

Rules and regulations are established to determine coverage and apply ordinance

City develops regulations post-enactment with clear list of covered contracts

City assigns implementation to a particular department and staff person

Department and one or more persons assigned to implementation

Training provided for other city departments that let contracts

City enacts procedures to ensure other contracting departments aware of ordinance and responsibilities

Easy to get information about the ordinance

Makes information about the ordinance easily available on the city website, or easy to reach a knowledgeable staff person by phone

Monitoring

Employers file payroll records on request of city	Employers required to make full payroll records available to city on request of city staff
Employers file payroll records on regular basis	Employers required to submit payroll records on regular basis (e.g., biweekly, monthly, or quarterly)
Contracts regularly reviewed by city staff	City staff have a system to review payroll records at regular intervals, regardless of complaints filed
Worksites regularly monitored	City staff have a system to visit worksites at regular intervals, regardless of complaints filed

Enforcement

Waivers from ordinance difficult to obtain	At least one case where a request for waiver was denied by city officials
City applies penalties to those in noncompliance	At least one case where city applies penalties of some form to a company in noncompliance

Evaluation

City staff writes implementation evaluation reports	City conducts some evaluation of implementation post-enactment
City attempts to close loopholes in ordinance	City staff pursue at least one attempt to improve ordinance to ensure effective implementation

NOTES

Chapter I. The Politics of Implementation

1. *Boston Globe* 1997.
2. Interview with the author, 1998.
3. E.g., Pressman and Wildavsky 1973, Van Meter and Van Horn 1975, Bardach 1977.
4. Bardach 1977.
5. The literature is vast. For good overviews, see, e.g., Nakamura and Smallwood 1980; Palumbo and Calista 1990; Goggin, Lester, Bowman, and O'Toole 1990; and Lester and Goggin 1998.
6. E.g., Van Meter and Van Horn 1975; Mazmanian and Sabatier 1983.
7. E.g., Lipsky 1978; Lipsky 1980.
8. E.g., Merton 1957; Selznick 1957; Michels 1959; Rohr 1988.
9. Maynard-Moody, Musheno, and Palumbo 1990; Wood 1990.
10. Putnam, Leonardi, and Nanetti 1993.
11. Fung and Wright 2003. The term *civil society* is often used loosely. There is, of course, great difference in some respects between the churches and clubs of Italy that Putnam writes about and the small school neighborhood councils constructed to run the public schools in Chicago (see Fung and Wright 2003).
12. See, e.g., Domhoff 1967.
13. There are not clear definitions that distinguish between advocacy groups, interest groups, constituency groups, nongovernmental organizations (NGOs), secondary associations, voluntary associations, and civil society. Often the terms are used interchangeably, or to refer to similar phenomenon. Cohen and Rogers define secondary associations as those organizations which exist between the state and the family but do not include formal political organizations such as parties. Others include political party members in their definition of civil society. The term NGO has been used most commonly in a global context but is gaining currency in the United States.
14. See, e.g., Selznick 1957; Radin 1977; Desai 1989 for implementation research that does examine the role of community groups.

15. Bearak 1996.
16. Associated Press 2002; Browning 2003.
17. *Federal Human Resources Week* 2002.
18. Barstow and Bergman 2003a and 2003b.
19. U.S. Environmental Protection Agency 2000.
20. Clawson, Neustadtl, and Weller 1998.
21. AFL-CIO, http://www.aflcio.org/yourjobeconomy/rights/rightsatwork/. Accessed November 15, 2003. See also Bronfenbrenner 2000.
22. Williams 1997; Lazarovici 2003.
23. See, e.g., Pollin and Luce 1998; Pollin and Brenner et al. 1999; and Pollin, Brenner, and Luce 2002.

Chapter 2. Setting the Stage

1. Clavel and Kleniewski 1990.
2. Glickman 1997, 66.
3. Useful discussions about the ideological debates and differences between the family wage, living wage, fair wage, minimum wage, prevailing wage and union wage can be found in Kessler-Harris 1990; Hart 1994; Glickman 1997; Pollin and Luce 1998; Boris 2002; and Figart, Mutari, and Power 2002. Numerous scholars have written about the role of women in early minimum wage/family wage campaigns, including Humphries 1977; Boris 1994; and Frank 1994. Thanks to Eileen Boris for pointing out to me the need to connect the legacy of women reformers in the early minimum wage campaigns to the current living wage movement.
4. For histories of the minimum wage see, e.g., Nordlund 1997; Waltman 2000; and the U.S. Department of Labor website, http://www.dol.gov/dol/topic/wages/minimumwage.htm. Accessed November 30, 2003.
5. U.S. Department of Labor, Fact Sheet #14: Coverage under the Fair Labor Standards Act.
6. See Waltman 2002, chapter 3.
7. The Economic Policy Institute offers a variety of useful papers and tables on the historic and current minimum wage. See http://www.epinet.org, especially Bernstein and Schmitt 2000. Accessed March 16, 2004.
8. "Working Poor" is defined by the Bureau of Labor Statistics as persons who spent more than twenty-seven weeks per year working or looking for work and lived in families with incomes below the poverty level (Chilman 1991).
9. Other reports were produced in 1989 (Klein and Rones) and 1992 (Gardner and Herz). The Bureau of Labor Statistics now produces "A Profile of the Working Poor," based on the Current Population Survey, on a semiregular basis. These reports are available though the *Monthly Labor Review*.
10. The search showed the use the term *working poor* to increase steadily throughout the period. After 1989, it appears 1,101 times in 1990, 1,139 in 1991, 1,836 in 1992, 2,920 in 1993, and 3,055 by 1994. It may be that the increase is in part due to more sources becoming available for the database for this period. However, searches restricted to particular newspapers with consistent archives show a similar trend.
11. Reich 1997.
12. See, e.g., National Priorities Project 1998; Mishel, Bernstein and Schmitt 2001; as well as various years in late 1990s.
13. Lichtenstein 2002.
14. Eisinger 1988.
15. Lemann 1994. As a number of scholars have shown, loopholes such as these are likely no accident. Business lobbyists probably built them in from the start, with plans to use them just as they did. On the role of business lobbyists and policy loopholes, see, for

example, Domhoff 1971; Domhoff 1978; Dye 1986; and Clawson, Neustadtl, and Weller 1998.

16. As cited in Eisenger 1988.

17. Lemann (1994) writes that the War on Poverty failed because it was unpopular with white voters, who did not support spending public money on the programs, and with legislators, who felt that the bottom-up strategy promoted by the program interfered with the "pork-barrel opportunities embedded in virtually every other Federal program." The Model Cities program let legislators back into the development process, but there was still not enough money allocated to its implementation. The program was originally supposed to serve a handful of cities, but in order to get it passed, the Johnson administration expanded it to 150 sites, which ensured 150 votes in the House. By expanding the coverage, the power of the funds was greatly diluted, and so the program had little impact.

18. Kossy 1996.

19. Pollin and Luce 1998.

20. Kossy 1996.

21. Most southern states created economic development programs in the 1920s and 1930s, and Mississippi legalized the use of municipal bonds to finance plant construction in 1936. However, it can be argued that competition between regions occurred long before then. Southern states were already promoting themselves as a good place to do business after the Civil War, under the "New South" campaigns to industrialize the region (Eisinger 1988; Weinbaum 2004). Also see Loveridge 1996.

22. Peterson 1981, 22.

23. Ibid., 28. Note that Peterson also writes of the need of cities to attract high-skilled workers, as well as capital.

24. Weinbaum 1997, 252–53.

25. Levy 1990.

26. Reese 1993.

27. Eisinger 1988.

28. Thomas 2000.

29. Burstein and Rolnick 1995, 1.

30. Ebbert 2002; Connolly presentation 2003.

31. Peters and Fisher 2002a, 2.

32. Ibid., 3. For more details on these calculations, see Peters and Fisher 2002b.

33. Talanker and Davis 2002.

34. Davis and Brocht 2002.

35. Good Jobs New York, New York City's Biggest Retention Deals database, located at http://www.goodjobsny.org/deals.htm. Accessed March 15, 2004.

36. Fung and Wright 2003, 4.

37. Thomas Foster (1997) points out that despite the strong anti-government and pro-downsizing rhetoric of the 1980s, federal employment actually increased throughout the decade. It wasn't until 1991 that a thirty-year employment trend was reversed. After Clinton signed the "Reinventing Government Act" (Executive Order 12862) in 1993, downsizing was pursued more vigorously. Foster argues that downsizing does not always match party affiliation or rhetoric, and sometimes leaders will claim to be downsizing but in reality will be hiring more in other areas, such as cutting military spending while increasing spending on specialized programs like "Star Wars." As Peter Drucker (1989) notes, "The Reagan Revolution in the United States and the Thatcher Revolution in Great Britain [were] not 'anti-government,' for all their rhetoric. Both President Reagan and Prime Minister Thatcher . . . consistently increased the size and scope of their respective governments." See Sunoo 1998 for more information on the impacts of Clinton's executive order.

38. See, e.g., Bumiller 1983 and Kurtz 1988 for examples on city downsizing.

39. Walters 1998.

40. Bureau of Labor Statistics. Of course, outsourcing is not the only cause of the slow or negative job growth. Factors such as computerization have played a role as well.

41. Sclar 2001.

42. Zachary 1996.

43. Pagano and Shock 2000.

44. Sclar 1997.

45. International City/County Management Association 2003.

46. Rehfuss 1989 and Pollin and Luce 1998 provide more detail on the impact of privatization on earnings and working conditions.

47. Cranford 2001.

48. Goetz 1994.

49. E.g., Krumholz 1991; Dowall 1996; Wasylenko 1997.

50. Clavel and Kleniewski 1990, 209.

51. Goetz 1994.

52. Cohen and Rogers 1995.

53. Some consider public job training to be a mainstream strategy, as it reduces the costs of training to the firm. This may be the case for firm-specific training, or training funds provided directly to firms to establish their own programs. Job training as a progressive strategy refers to more general training, such as vocational schools, where the skills learned are transferable between firms and possibly between different types of jobs. For an excellent discussion of job training as social policy, see Lafer 2002.

54. Peschek 1997.

55. Other legislation covering government purchasing includes "Buy American Acts" of 1850 and 1933; the Davis-Bacon "Prevailing Wage" Act of 1931 (amended in 1935); open procurement acts of 1809 and 1860; the Vinson-Trammel Profits Limitation Act of 1934; and others. See Denison 1941; Ballaine 1943.

56. Denison 1941.

57. Troy 2002.

58. *Pittsburgh Post-Gazette* 2001.

59. Livingston 2000.

60. Grow 1998.

Chapter 3. Overview of the Movement

1. Some people credit Des Moines, Iowa, and Gary, Indiana, as the first campaigns, as they passed living wage ordinances in 1988 and 1991, respectively. However, I call Baltimore the first because the Baltimore campaign was the first to explicitly use the living wage rhetoric. Although the ordinances passed in Des Moines and Gary resemble what has come to be known as a living wage ordinance, the Des Moines ordinance was called a "minimum compensation policy," and the Gary ordinance a "prevailing wage." For information on the historical use of the term *living wage*, and struggles for living wages in the earlier part of the century, see Glickman 1997.

2. A full list of these may be found in appendix A, table A.1. The ACORN Living Wage Resource Center defines only official city ordinances that apply to at least some private sector employers as living wage ordinances. This means that voluntary guidelines, such as the living wage resolution in Northampton, Mass., is not included in their list. It also means that a small handful of ordinances applying only to city or county employees are not included. A list of the latter can be found in appendix A, table A.3.

3. Santa Monica Living Wage Commission of Inquiry 2003.

4. Until 2002, Washington, D.C., was the only city with its own minimum wage. The D.C. minimum wage is set at one dollar above the federal minimum wage.

5. It is difficult to keep track of the many living wage campaigns that start and stop on campuses around the country. One source for updates can be found at:

http://www.campuslivingwage.org/goals_and_victories.html#victories. Accessed March 16, 2004.

6. Jaffe 1999.
7. Peschek 1997.
8. Interview with author, 1997.
9. Tilly 2003, 7.
10. Gillett 2002.
11. Maestri 2002.
12. Peschek 1997.
13. This is not to say that all unions were exclusionary. There are a number of counterexamples of the labor movement and various social movements working together in the 1960s and 1970s, such as the United Farm Workers, District 1199, the United Packinghouse Workers Association, and AFSCME.
14. See, e.g., Yates 1999; Lichtenstein 2002.
15. ACORN 1997.
16. Peschek 1997.
17. Burtman 1997.
18. However, not all workers are covered by existing federal and state minimum wage laws. For example, certain categories of tipped workers are excluded, as are agricultural workers. In addition, certain categories of firms are not covered, such as businesses grossing less than $500,000 per year.
19. There has been a small effort, mostly by the union UNITE, to pass "procurement ordinances" that would attach living wage standards for goods purchases. This has been successful in a few cities but has always been separate from living wage campaigns.
20. Interview with author, 1997.
21. This wage rate is calculated by dividing the U.S. Census Bureau annual poverty threshold for a family of four ($18,390) by 2,080 hours. However, since most low-wage workers work less than 40 hours per week and less than 52 weeks per year, the actual hourly wage necessary to reach the poverty threshold for most low-wage workers is higher.
22. For information on the inadequate federal measure of poverty, see, e.g., Citro and Michael 1995; and Sklar, Mykyta, and Wefald 2001.
23. A number of organizations have attempted to develop more realistic measures of the income necessary to meet a family's basic needs. See, e.g., Boushey, Brocht, Gundersen, and Bernstein 2001; the National Priorities Project 1998; Wider Opportunities for Women, Family Self-Sufficiency Standards reports; and Sklar, Mykyta, and Wefald 2001.
24. For more on the estimated benefits to workers see, e.g., Pollin and Luce 1998; Howes 2001; Brenner 2003; and Reich, Hall, and Jacobs 2003.
25. A number of stories have appeared profiling the impact of the wage increase on Alexandria workers. These include Bradley 2000 and Koeppel 2001.
26. Koeppel 2001.

Chapter 4. A Closer Look at Living Wage Campaigns

1. Jordan 1997a.
2. This section draws in part from Luce 2001b.
3. *Arizona Republic* 2000.
4. The ordinance also required that 60 percent of the employees hired by contractors on city projects be city residents, but this provision was revoked after the first year because of the difficulty tracking employee addresses.
5. Korte and McCain 2002; email communication to author from Dan LaBotz, November 14, 2002.
6. Korte and MacCain 2002; memo from Bob Park, November 19, 2002.

7. The information on Providence comes from interviews and conversations with DARE director Sara Mersha, Rhode Island Jobs with Justice organizer Matthew Jerzyk, DARE members, the DARE website http://www.daretowin.org (accessed August 20, 2003), the Providence Jobs and Living Wage Campaign website http://www.rijwj.org/livingwage.htm (accessed August 20, 2003), and the author's personal observations from meetings, rallies, and hearings.

8. Campaign flyer available at http://www.rijwj.org/LivingWageRally%20Nov.15.pdf. Accessed December 3, 2003.

9. Interview with author, 2002.

10. Some in the coalition initially wanted to require all city jobs to be filled with local residents. The coalition decided that it would be too hard to get support from unions for this clause, as most of the public sector unions opposed local residency requirements for city jobs, so this was adapted to a community run hiring hall for contractor jobs only.

11. Levitz 2000; Gallo and Mersha 2000.

12. *The Providence Journal-Bulletin* 2001.

13. For example, at the May 2, 2001, city council hearing, more than a hundred people turned out to support the ordinance. More than two dozen testified in favor, while only three testified against (Dujardin 2001).

14. See articles by Franklin S. Prosnitz, editor, and Michael Pare, managing editor, as well as numerous unsigned articles in the *Providence Business News* throughout 2001.

15. Arditi 2001.

16. Taricani 2002.

17. Smith 2002.

18. In particular, the coalition focused their efforts on the city elections of November 2002. They held candidate forums on the living wage in key city council wards and with the mayoral candidates. This resulted in the election of two strong living wage supporters in wards where there had previously been no support.

Chapter 5. Living Wage Outcomes

1. Most county governments are run by a County Board of Supervisors and a county executive. Although I will review city and county living wage ordinances, I use the terms city council and mayor throughout the following chapters as shorthand for city and county leadership.

2. See, e.g., O'Neill and Hill 2003 and Mac Donald 2002 for arguments that welfare reform has been a success. For a good overview of welfare reform and various perspectives on its effectiveness, see Blank and Haskins 2002.

3. Fung, O'Rourke, and Sabel 2001.

4. Troy 2002.

5. Memo from Ariana Ghasedi, October 4, 2001.

6. Zubrensky 1995.

7. Moses 1997.

8. Newton 1997.

9. Jackie Goldberg was the initial sponsor of the living wage ordinance.

10. Interview with the author, 1997.

11. LAANE was called TIDC (Tourism Industry Development Council) at the time. It changed its name to LAANE in 1998.

12. Shuster 1998a.

13. Technically, June Gibson was first brought into the BCA to oversee implementation, but Gibson and the work were soon transferred to the CAO office.

14. Sander and Lokey 1998b.

15. Interview with the author, 1998.

16. Rohrlich 1998a.

17. Hill and Weissert 1995.
18. Walker 1998.
19. Norm Coleman had been a vigorous opponent of the living wage in 1995 when it was run as a ballot initiative. When a much watered-down proposal was presented in 1997, he chose not to oppose it. Grow 1998; Duchschere 1997b.
20. The St. Paul Living Wage policy requires firms that receive $100,000 or more in economic development assistance to pay their employees at least 110 percent of the federal poverty level for a family of four.
21. Much of this information on the Target deal relies on material from *Minneapolis Star Tribune* reporter Kevin Duchschere. This includes articles from January 3 and October 23, 1997; October 29, 1998; February 7, 8 and 17, 2001; and October 15, 2002.
22. When Coleman ended up running for governor in 2002, his largest single donor was the Target Corporation, providing him with $55,650 in hard money and $25,000 in soft money. Other large donations, totaling $33,500, came from Minnesota Mutual executives (Gordon 2002).
23. Interview with author, 1998.
24. Clawson, Neustadtl, and Weller 1998.
25. Seltzer 1995a, 376–77.
26. See, e.g., Seltzer 1995b, Lichtenstein 2002.
27. Fung and Wright 2003.

Chapter 6. Implementation

1. Maria Whyte presentation, Cleveland, Ohio, September 8, 2001.
2. McLanahan 1980.
3. Ibid.
4. Palumbo and Calista 1990, 6.
5. Matland 1995.
6. Palumbo and Calista 1990.
7. Giloth 1993.
8. Matland 1995, 156.
9. Grant and Trautner 2002.
10. Interview with the author, 1998.
11. Jackson 1994b.
12. Jackson 1994a.
13. Dempsey 1995.
14. Bruce Nissen (1995) discusses a similar example of local officials identifying community needs as defined by the needs of corporations. When a community group tried to fight a plant closing in Indiana, they called on their local and state government to demand the company stay open, modernize, and retain jobs. Government officials refused to intervene in the company's business. They accepted consultant's reports that said the company should be able to close based on its market position and profitability. Rather than define the problem as finding a way to save jobs, government officials saw the problem as the company's right to make a profit.
15. Jessop 1990. Jessop quotes Poulantzas, "Class struggle is not confined to civil society, but is reproduced within the heart of the state apparatus itself" (30).
16. Wright 1997.
17. Wright's (1997) data analysis of prostatist and anti-capitalist views of various public sector employees in the United States and Sweden broadly supports his hypotheses that such ideological differences exist between workers in different class-by-sector categories. In particular, like the private sector, working-class employees in the public sector are more supportive than middle class employees of working-class struggles and of "an expansive role of the state in society." He also finds that the public sector working class in the United

States is divided ideologically, with employees in the decommodified services holding greater anti-capitalist views than their counterparts in the political superstructure, while the Swedish public sector working class is more ideologically homogenous.

18. International City/County Management Association 1997.

19. Elmore 2001.

20. Ibid.

21. Chouinard, http://www.ci.eugene.or.us/ASD/Finance/Budget_com/FY03/LW_Pres/. Accessed March 16, 2004.

22. Based on Mr. Chouinard's analysis, the living wage subcommittee of the Budget Committee in Eugene, Oregon, determined that they were not able to develop a fiscally responsible solution to the living wage proposal. As of early 2003, the living wage campaign in Eugene, Oregon, had been stalled by this subcommittee.

23. Interview with author, 2002.

24. E.g., Berry, Berry, and Foster, 1998, and Echeverri-Gent, 1995.

25. State-theorists have debated the source and importance of state capacity in policy formation and implementation. Skocpol and other state-centered theorists argue that states generally possess certain infrastructural capacities that can provide them the power to pass and implement policy, such as the ability to police. Skocpol and Amenta (1986) and Finegold and Skocpol (1995) argue that it was the existence of a federal infrastructure that allowed the opportunity for autonomous state action in the passage and implementation of the Agricultural Adjustment Act (AAA) in the 1930s. Specifically, the preexisting system of land-grant colleges created the opportunity for agricultural economists to carry out their own research. The infrastructure of the colleges allowed the economists to the resources necessary to carry out their research plans. In contrast, they argue, the state was not able to autonomously implement industrial policy at that time because the capacity was not there. The National Recovery Act (NRA) failed because the state had never developed the ability to administer it. In particular, there was no mechanism in place to monitor hundreds of new industrial codes in millions of workplaces (Finegold and Skocpol 1995).

26. International City/County Management Association 1997.

27. Gilbert and Howe 1991.

28. Markusen 1984.

29. These include Cleveland; Dane County, Wisconsin; Denver; Duluth; Hartford; Hayward; Los Angeles City and County; Milwaukee County; New Haven; Oakland; Pasadena; San Fernando; San Jose; Santa Cruz; St. Paul; Tucson; West Hollywood; and Ypsilanti. Of these, the cities that have produced reports as required include Duluth, Hartford, Hayward, Los Angeles County, New Haven, and Pasadena. Cities that have produced reports sporadically include Corvallis, Dane County, Los Angeles city, Oakland, and San Jose.

30. Flint 1997.

31. Toledo Area Chamber of Commerce 2000.

Chapter 7. Fighting from the Outside

1. MacLennan 1988.

2. Ibid., 53.

3. Gilbert and Howe 1991.

4. Schumaker 1975.

5. E. E. Schattschneider, as quoted ibid., 489.

6. Ibid., 490.

7. See the classic articulation of this position in Dahl 1961.

8. Gilbert and Howe 1991, 208. Emphasis in the original.

9. Quadagno 1992, 623.

10. O'Rourke 2002.

11. Niedt et al. 1999, 5.

12. Interview with author, 1998.
13. Niedt et al. 1999, 9.
14. Lally 1996.
15. Matthews 1996.
16. Matthews 1997.
17. Ibid.
18. Bowie 1998.
19. The council also voted themselves a $10,000 per year raise, raising their salaries to $85,000 per year (Parsons and Long 1998). When they wanted to give themselves another raise in 2002, the Chicago living wage coalition took the opportunity to fight for an expansion of their ordinance. In November 2002, the council voted 49–0 to raise the living wage from $7.60 to $9.05. They then approved a raise for themselves, going to $98,000 after three years (*Chicago Tribune* 2002).
20. Luce 1999.
21. Gillett, interview with the author, 1998.
22. *Los Angeles Business Journal* 1998.
23. Shuster 1998b.
24. Shuster 1998a.
25. Shuster 1999.
26. Cleeland and Mehta 1999.
27. Coalition for Economic Justice 2001.
28. Williams 2000.
29. Whyte presentation 2001.
30. Habuda 2003.
31. Email from Alliea E. Groupp, May 14, 2002.
32. Guild Law Center press release 2002.
33. E.g., Piven and Cloward 1979.

Chapter 8. Coalitions Playing a Formal Role

1. Secondary associations are defined as "the wide range of nonfamilial organizations intermediate between individuals or firms and the institutions of the state and formal electoral system." (Cohen and Rogers 1995, 7).
2. Ibid., 21.
3. Hemenway 1995.
4. Cohen and Rogers 1995, 88.
5. Hemenway 1995, 86.
6. Weil 1991.
7. Hirsch, Macpherson, and Dumond 1997.
8. Parker 1997, 318.
9. Federal Register 1949. Thanks to Mark Nelson for providing me with this reference.
10. A copy of the paycheck insert, Living Wage Form 11, is available at http://www.ventura.org/gsa/bid/lw-11.pdf, on the useful County of Ventura living wage website. Accessed November 1, 2003.
11. City of Los Angeles Living Wage Ordinance, Ordinance 172336.
12. Bronfenbrenner 2000.
13. The language states that covered employers "shall also be in compliance with federal law proscribing retaliation for union organizing."
14. See, e.g., Solo 1997; Kingsley and Gibson 1997; Kamat 2002.
15. Hirst 1994.
16. Fung and Wright 2003, 16.
17. Free State Project, http://www.elsol.org/f_liblinks.html. Accessed March 16, 2004.
18. Most of the big accounting firms, such as PriceWaterhouse Coopers, KPMG, and Ernst & Young conduct these kinds of audits for a fee. One example of the auditors hired

by corporations for this kind of work is Verite, a not-for-profit firm located in Amherst, Massachusetts.

19. Cole 1975, 762; see also Zimmerman 1972.

20. Cole 1975. Cole found that the programs least successful in improving the delivery of goods and services and increasing citizen trust were those that had either a narrow program scope and little citizen participation, or those that had a broad scope and broad involvement.

21. http://www.policeaccountabilitycampaign.org/pamphlet.html. Accessed March 16, 2004.

22. Human Rights Watch 1998.

23. Shapiro 1997.

24. Human Rights Watch 1998, n.p.

25. Ibid.

26. E.g., Parkins 2002; Kapoor 2001; Harless 2001; Orr 1979; and South 1986.

27. South 1986.

28. Other arenas that have utilized citizen participation include economic development, such as the Community Block Grant Development Program (Rimmerman 1985), Industrial Revolving Funds (Craypo and Paar 1993); job training and youth employment (Levin and Ferman 1985); and foster care (Byrnes 2002; Jennings, McDonald and Henderson 1996). Many cities have also established a range of community or citizen commissions and boards to allow public input into a wide range of local issues.

29. Jen Kern of ACORN usually tells living wage campaigns to be wary of city councilors calling for a task force for more research before they can consider an ordinance, since this is usually just a stall tactic. The possible negative outcomes of task forces have also been noted in the anti-sweatshop movement on college campuses. Activists charge that administrators have created "research task forces" to study an issue as a way to stall passage of a code of conduct. See, for example, United Students Against Sweatshops, "Making your campaign happen on campus—Organize!" available at http://www.people.fas.harvard.edu/~fragola/usas/docs/organizing.doc (accessed November 1, 2003). In this guide, the authors warn students about the tactics used by administrators to deal with student activists: "They [administrators] send the issue to a committee dominated by administrative interests, study the issue to death, and drown it in a complicated bureaucracy."

30. This information comes from interviews with Focareta and a report produced by him in 2002.

31. Tramer 2002.

32. Davis 2002.

33. Gibson email, July 12, 2002.

34. Cheryl Monzon, interview with the author, 2003.

Chapter 9. Factors Needed for Successful Implementation

1. Ken Jacobs points out that the same dynamic may also occur with the enforcement of community hiring hall language in living wage ordinances.

2. Pierson 1994.

3. Interview with the author, 2003.

4. Clawson, Neustadtl, and Scott 1992, 61.

5. Ibid., 101.

6. Email from Murray Rosenbluth to author, November 15, 2002.

7. Interview with the author.

8. In establishing criteria by which to judge nongovernmental regulatory systems in the arena of sweatshop/factory monitoring, O'Rourke (2003) suggests that such systems should be judged by their "legitimacy": "Are key stakeholders involved in all stages of

standard setting, monitoring and enforcement?" (31). This would suggest that having employers (as key stakeholders) on living wage task forces would be desirable, as it would add legitimacy.

9. Turchinetz 2002. Available at http://www.rijwj.org/mimi.pdf. Accessed March 21, 2004.

10. Email communication with the author, November 29, 2002.

11. Whyte presentation 2001.

12. Bronson 2003.

13. Coniff 1999.

14. Western 1997.

15. Human Rights Watch 1998.

16. Perry, http://www.sfbctc.org/lstandards.htm, accessed April 5, 2003.

17. Email to author, March 30, 2003.

18. E.g., Domhoff 1967; Dye 1986.

19. Clawson, Neustadtl, and Scott 1992, 96.

20. Beder 1998; *Campaigns & Elections* 1999.

21. E.g., Hunter 1953; Dahl 1961; Bachrach and Baratz 1970.

22. On city planning see, e.g., Simmons 2001; on antismoking see, e.g., Samuels and Glantz 1991; Traynor, Begay, and Glantz 1993; on wetlands protection see, e.g., Payne 1988; on alcohol excess see, e.g., Gruenewald, Millar, and Roeper 1996; and Wolfson, Wagenaar and Hornseth 1995; on health and safety see, e.g., Fletcher 1996.

23. Richards 1998.

24. Ibid.

25. Esbenshade 2001.

26. Ibid., 115.

27. Email from Tom G. Turner, October 15, 2001.

28. There are a total of 18,632 businesses in the city.

29. Grant and Trautner 2002.

30. O'Rourke 2003.

31. Piven and Cloward 1979.

32. Quadagno 1992.

Chapter 10. Other Outcomes beyond Implementation

1. AFL-CIO website, "The Threat to Workers' Freedom to Choose a Union," http://www.aflcio.org/voiceatwork/threat.htm. Accessed November 1, 2003.

2. For a review of legal restrictions on living wage ordinances, see Sahu 2001.

3. Luce 2001b.

4. For a fuller account of the Wesleyan effort, see Clawson 2003.

5. More information about the Los Angeles, Baltimore, and Milwaukee campaigns and outcomes can be found in Luce 1999.

6. Los Angeles Alliance for a New Economy 2002.

7. City News Service 2002a, 2002b, 2002c; Oldham 2002; Business Wire 2002.

8. Galvin 1995.

9. Interview with author, 1998.

10. Jeter 1997.

11. Ibid.

12. Pierre 1998.

13. Interview with author, 1998.

14. Curry 1999.

15. This section draws from Luce 2002a.

16. Chen 2003.

17. Card and Krueger 1995; Wicks-Lim 2002.

18. Osterman 2000.
19. Interview with author, 1998.
20. Dean, presentation, Washington, D.C., September 2002.
21. Korte and McCain 2002.
22. Korte 2002.
23. Korte and McCain 2002.
24. Seigel 1997.
25. Shields 1999.
26. Part of this section draws from Luce 2002b.
27. Velasco 2003.
28. Seigel 1994.
29. Newton 1998.
30. In their "decade-by-decade look" at the "bottom-up history" of key moments in Los Angeles politics, Gottlieb and Dreier (1998) refer to the 1992 Rodney King riots and the 1997 living wage ordinances as the major events of the decade.
31. See, e.g., Kraut, Klinger and Collins 2000.
32. The policy was later revoked when Bill McBride, the lawyer behind it and eventual Democratic candidate for governor of Florida, left the firm. See Allison 2002.
33. The search does not find a linear increase in the use of the term but a fairly consistent upward trend. As of early 2003, the year with the highest number of references is 2001, with 1,514 articles mentioning "living wage" in major newspapers. This increase includes references to other countries.
34. Roper Center at University of Connecticut 1995 and 1999.
35. Binder 1999.
36. Van Slambrouck 1999.
37. Luce 2001a.
38. Communication Workers of America Civil Rights Department 2001.
39. McGreevey 1998.
40. Communication Workers of America Local 7026 2000.
41. Interview with author, 1999.
42. Interview with author, 1998.
43. Ibid.
44. Both quotes are from Janice Fine, interview with the author, 1998.
45. *Baltimore Sun* 1999.
46. Gillett 1997.
47. Norman 1994.
48. As cited in Eimer 1999.

Chapter 11. The Future of the Living Wage Movement and Lessons for Policy Implementation

1. Gross 2002.
2. Benjamin McKean, National Organizer, USAS. Email to Student Living Wage Campaign list, November 22, 2002.
3. Note that existing research on the economic impact of the laws argues that the ordinances will not necessarily lead to substantial cost increases for firms or the city. For example, Pollin and Luce (1998) show that the cost of the Los Angeles ordinance for the average firm would amount to less than 1 percent of their total costs of production. I argue here that despite this research most city managers still believe that the living wage ordinance will involve substantial costs for employers and/or the city.
4. Nissen 1995, 159.
5. Lichtenstein 2002.
6. Fure-Slocum 2000, 285.

7. Indeed, on December 10, 2003, the AFL-CIO sponsored a national day of action on International Human Rights Day around the message "Worker's Rights are Human Rights."

8. Clawson 2003.

9. As quoted in *The Black Commentator* 2002.

REFERENCES

ACORN. 1997. "Behind Enemy Lines: A Quick Look at Our Opponents." Washington, D.C.

AFL-CIO. "The Threat to Workers' Freedom to Choose a Union." Available at http://www.aflcio.org/voiceatwork/threat.htm. Accessed November 1, 2003.

———. "Your Rights at Work." Available at http://www.aflcio.org/yourjobeconomy/rights/rightsatwork/. Accessed November 15, 2003.

Allison, Wes. 2002. "Candidate's Credo Sketched in Law Firm's Culture." *St. Petersburg Times.* April 7. 1B.

Arditi, Lynn. 2001. "Canvasser's Go Door-to-Door in Providence to Campaign for a 'Living Wage' of $12.30 an Hour." *Providence Journal-Bulletin.* August 5. F1.

Arizona Republic. 2000. "Pay, Benefits Top Issues to Contract Workers." August 1. A1.

Associated Press. 2002. "Wal-Mart Lawsuit." December 19.

Bachrach, Peter, and Morton S. Baratz. 1970. *Power and Poverty: Theory and Practice.* New York: Oxford University Press.

Ballaine, Wesley C. 1943. "How Government Purchasing Procedures Strengthen Monopoly Elements." *The Journal of Political Economy* 51 (6): 538–46.

The Baltimore Sun. 1999. "Party On, Governor." January 21. 1E.

Bardach, Eugene. 1977. *The Implementation Game: What Happens after a Bill Becomes a Law.* Cambridge, Mass.: MIT Press.

Barstow, David, and Lowell Bergman. 2003b. "Deaths on the Job, Slaps on the Wrist." *The New York Times.* January 10. A-1.

———. 2003a. "At a Texas Foundry, An Indifference to Life." *The New York Times.* January 8. A-1.

Bearak, Barry. 1996. "Kathie Lee and the Sweatshop Crusade." *The Los Angeles Times.* June 14. A-1.

Beder, Sharon. 1998. "Public Relations' Role in Manufacturing Artificial Grass Roots Coalitions." *Public Relations Quarterly* 43 (2): 20–23.

Bernstein, Jared, and John Schmitt. 2000. "The Impact of the Minimum Wage: Policy Lifts Wages, Maintains Floor for Low-wage Labor Market." Briefing Paper. Washington, D.C.: Economic Policy Institute.

Berry, Frances Stokes, William D. Berry, and Stephen K. Foster. 1998. "The Determinants of Success in Implementing an Expert System in State Government." *Public Administration Review* 58 (4): 293–306.

Binder, David. 1999. "Preliminary Results: San Francisco Vote Survey on Living Wage Ordinance." August 13 Memorandum. San Francisco: David Binder Research.

The Black Commentator. 2002. "The Living Wage Movement: A New Beginning. Bread, Power, and Civil Rights in 19 Languages" 2 (May 8). Available at http://www.blackcommentator.com/. Accessed November 15, 2003.

Blank, Rebecca M., and Ron Haskins, eds. 2002. *The New World of Welfare.* Washington, D.C.: The Brookings Institution.

Boris, Eileen. 2002. "The Living Wage as a Feminist Issue: A Historic Perspective." Talk at the UCSB Women's Center, November 1.

———. 1994. *Home to Work: Motherhood and the Politics of Industrial Homework in the United States.* New York: Cambridge University Press.

Boston Globe. 1997. "A Flawed Wage Ordinance." August 14. A18.

Boushey, Heather, Chauna Brocht, Bethney Gunderson, and Jared Bernstein. 2001. *Hardships in America: The Real Story of Working Americans.* Washington, D.C.: Economic Policy Institute.

Bowie, Liz. 1998. "2,000 Nonunion School Workers to be Paid $7.70 an Hour in July." *The Baltimore Sun.* February 25. 3B.

Bradley, Paul. 2000. "'Living Wage' Contracts in Effect; Alexandria Law Praised, Criticized." *The Richmond Times Dispatch.* November 26. C1.

Brenner, Mark. 2004. "The Economic Impact of Living Wage Ordinances in New England." University of Massachusetts-Amherst. Political Economy Research Institute Research Report.

Bronfenbrenner, Kate. 2000. "Uneasy Terrain: The Impact of Capital Mobility on Workers, Wages, and Union Organizing." Report Submitted to the U.S. Trade Deficit Review Commission. Ithaca, N.Y.: Cornell University Press.

Bronson, Peter. 2003. "Protect the Unions, Soak the City Taxpayer Again." *Cincinnati Enquirer.* October 22. Available at http://www.enquirer.com/editions/2003/10/22/loc_bronson22.html. Accessed March 20, 2004.

Browning, Ron. 2003. "Wal-Mart Sued for Overtime." *The Indiana Lawyer.* January 29. 1.

Brull, Steven V. 2000. "What's So Bad about a Living Wage?" *Business Week.* September 4. 64.

Bumiller, Elisabeth. 1983. "Two Mayors' Tales of Two Cities; Toledo's DeGood, Phoenix's Hance in Worst of Times." *The Washington Post.* January 28. D1.

Bureau of Labor Statistics. National Industry-Occupational Matrix. http://data.bls.gov/oep/nioem/empiohm.jsp. Accessed June 23, 2001.

Burnett, Erin, and James Mahon Jr. 2001. "Monitoring Compliance with International Labor Standards." *Challenge* 44 (2): 51.

Burstein, Melvin L., and Arthur J. Rolnick. 1995. "Congress Should End the Economic War Among the States." *The Region Magazine.* Federal Reserve Bank of Minneapolis. March.

Burtman, Bob. 1997. "Minimal Theories." *Houston Press.* January 16.

Business Wire. 2002. "McDonald's Corporation Agrees to New Los Angeles Airport Concession Policies, Programs." August 20.

Byrnes, Edward Cahoon. 2002. "Initial Findings on Cross-System Utilization of Citizen Foster Care Review Board Recommendations." *Systems Research and Behavioral Science* 19 (5): 485–98.

California State Auditor. 1995. "Trade and Commerce Agency: The Effectiveness of the Employment and Economic Incentive and Enterprise Zone Programs Cannot Be Determined." Report 93019.

Campaigns & Elections. 1999. "Trends in Grassroots Lobbying Consultant Q&A." 20 (1): 22–26.

Card, David, and Alan B. Krueger. 1995. *Myth and Measurement: The New Economics of the Minimum Wage.* Princeton: Princeton University Press.

Chen, Sue. 2003. "Ad Hoc Committee Seeks Input on Living Wage Policy." *The Phoenix.* February 27. Available at http://www.sccs.swarthmore.edu/org/phoenix/2003/2003-02-27/news/12723.php. Accessed March 20, 2004.

Chicago Sun-Times. 2002. "Pucinski to join Ryan Cabinet." July 11. 17.

Chicago Tribune. 2002. "Aldermen Raise 'Living Wage,' then Treat Themselves." November 7. 6.

Chilman, Catherine S. 1991. "Working Poor Families: Trends, Causes, Effects, and Suggested Policies." *Family Relations* 40 (2): 191–98.

Chouinard, Lauren. City of Eugene, Ore. Power Point presentation. Available at http://www.ci.eugene.or.us/ASD/Finance/Budget_com/LW_Pres/index.htm. Accessed March 16, 2004.

Citro, Constance F., and Robert T. Michael, eds. 1995. *Measuring Poverty: A New Approach.* Washington, D.C.: National Academy Press.

City News Service. 2002a. "LAX McDonald's." July 23.

——. 2002b. "LAX McDonald's." August 20.

——. 2002c. "LAX McDonald's." September 24.

Clavel, Pierre, and Nancy Kleniewski. 1990. "Space for Progressive Local Policy: Examples from the United States and the United Kingdom." In *Beyond the City Limits: Urban Policy and Economic Restructuring in Comparative Perspective,* ed. John R. Logan and Todd Swanstrom. Philadelphia: Temple University Press.

Clawson, Dan. 2003. *The Next Upsurge: Labor and the New Social Movements.* Ithaca, N.Y.: Cornell University Press.

Clawson, Dan, Alan Neustadtl, and Denise Scott. 1992. *Money Talks: Corporate PACs and Political Influence.* New York: Basic Books.

Clawson, Dan, Alan Neustadtl, and Mark Weller. 1998. *Dollars and Votes: How Business Campaign Contributions Subvert Democracy.* Philadelphia: Temple University Press.

Cleeland, Nancy, and Seema Mehta. 1999. "Host Marriott Lifts Pay at LAX." *Los Angeles Times.* January 21. C2.

Coalition for Economic Justice. 2001. "City of Buffalo Sued for Incompetence by Local Advocacy Groups." Press release. July 12.

Cohen, Joshua, and Joel Rogers. 1995. "Secondary Associations and Democratic Governance." In *Associations and Democracy,* ed. Erik Olin Wright. London: Verso.

Cole, Richard L. 1975. "Citizen Participation in Municipal Politics." *American Journal of Political Science* 19 (4): 761–81.

Communication Workers of America Civil. Rights Department. 2001. "Report of the National Committee on Equity to the 63rd Annual Convention." July 24.

——. Local 7026 (Tucson, Ariz.). 2000. Available at http://www.cwa7026.com/. Accessed February 10, 2003.

Coniff, Ruth. 1999. "Interview with Patricia Ireland." *The Progressive* 6 (8): 35.

Connolly, Mary Jo. Presentation to Western Massachusetts Jobs with Justice. Holyoke, Mass. February 3, 2003.

Crandall, Joshua. 2001. "Leadership with a Vision." *AFSC Iowa Program News*. Available at http://www.afsc.org/cro/ia/fao105.htm. Accessed March 30, 2003.

Cranford, Cynthia. 2001. "Contesting Gendered and Racialized 'Flexibility' in the City: Organizing Justice for Janitors in Los Angeles." Paper presented at Two Faces of the New Work Order conference. Toronto, Canada.

Craypo, Charles, and Jerry Paar. 1993. "Employee Buyouts and Loans to Preserve Jobs: The South Bend Experience." In *Comparative Studies in Local Economic Development: Problems in Policy Implementation*, ed. Peter B. Meyer. Westport, Conn.: Greenwood Press.

Curry, Julia. 1999. "Students Work with Community/Labor Groups to Raise Wages at Johns Hopkins." *Labor Notes*. April 10.

Dahl, Robert. 1961. *Who Governs?* New Haven: Yale University Press.

Davis, Karen A. 2002. "Living Wage Ordinance One Step Closer to Reality in Watsonville." *Santa Cruz Sentinel*. September 12.

Davis, Kate, and Chauna Brocht. 2002. *Subsidizing the Low-Road: Economic Development in Baltimore*. Washington, D.C.: Good Jobs First.

Dean, Amy B. "Victories in San Jose from Living Wage, Labor Peace and Retention." Presentation to AFL-CIO Central Labor Council meeting. September 20, 2002.

Dempsey, Bill. 1995. Memo to Living Wage Ordinance Work Group. Milwaukee, Wis.

Denison, Edward F. 1941. "The Influence of the Walsh-Healey Public Contracts Act Upon Labor Conditions." *The Journal of Political Economy* 49 (2): 225–46.

Desai, Uday. 1989. "Public Participation in Environmental Policy Implementation: Case of the Surface Mining Control and Reclamation Act." *American Review of Public Administration* 19 (1): 49–65.

Domhoff, G. William. 1978. *The Powers That Be: Processes of Ruling-Class Domination in America*. New York: Random House.

——. 1971. *The Higher Circles: The Governing Class in America*. New York: Vintage Books.

——. 1967. *Who Rules America?* Englewood Cliffs, N.J.: Prentice-Hall.

Dowall, David E. 1996. "An Evaluation of California's Enterprise Zone Programs." *Economic Development Quarterly* 10 (4): 353–68.

Drucker, Peter F. 1989. *The New Realities*. New York: Harper and Row.

Duchschere, Kevin. 2002. "Can a Spiffy Field's Perk up St. Paul Retail?" *Star Tribune*. October 15. 1A.

——. 2001a. "Council Urged to Support Dayton's Deal." *Star Tribune*. February 17. 3B.

——. 2001b. "St. Paul Delays Dayton's Deal Over Wage Issue." *Star Tribune*. February 8. 3B.

——. 2001c. "Deal Approved to Keep Dayton's in St. Paul." *Star Tribune*. February 8. 2B.

——. 2001d. "Living-Wage Waiver for Dayton's Debated." *Star Tribune*. February 7. 4B.

——. 1998. "Critics Say St. Paul Doesn't Always Stick to Living Wage Policy." *Star Tribune*. October 29. 7B.

——. 1997a. "St. Paul City Council Approves Expansion Deal for Minnesota Mutual." *Star Tribune*. October 23. 7B.

——. 1997b. "St. Paul Council OKs Living-Wage Policy." *Star Tribune*. January 3. 1B.

Dujardin, Richard C. 2001. "Living Wage Measure Weighed before Council." *The Providence Journal-Bulletin*. May 3. 1C.

Dye, Thomas R. 1986. *Who's Running America? The Conservative Years*. Englewood Cliffs, N.J.: Prentice-Hall.

East Bay Alliance for a Sustainable Economy. 2003. "Living Wage Implementation at the Port of Oakland: One Year Status Report." Oakland, Calif.

Ebbert, Stephanie. 2002. "Follow-Up Found Lax after State Tax Break." *The Boston Globe*. December 19. B1.

Echeverri-Gent, John. 1993. *The State and the Poor: Public Policy and Political Development in India and The United States*. Berkeley: University of California Press.

Eimer, Stuart. 1999. "From 'Business Unionism' to 'Social Movement Unionism': The Case of the AFL-CIO Milwaukee County Labor Council." *Labor Studies Journal* 24 (2): 63–81.

Eisinger, Peter. 1988. *The Entrepreneurial City*. Madison: The University of Wisconsin Press.

Elliott, Robert H. 1981. "The Policy Adoption-Implementation Spiral." *International Journal of Public Administration* 3 (1): 113–41.

Elmore, Andrew. 2001. "The Impact of Living Wage Laws on Service Contracts and Local Economic Development Programs." University of California Institute for Labor and Employment, Working Draft.

Employment Policies Institute. 2000. *Living Wage Policy: The Basics*. Washington, D.C.

Esbenshade, Jill. 2001."The Social Accountability Contract: Private Monitoring from Los Angeles to the Global Apparel Industry." *Labor Studies Journal* 26 (1): 98–120.

Federal Human Resources Week. 2002. "OSHA Reports Increase in Workplace Inspections and Fines." 9 (34). December 24.

Federal Register. 1949. 14 (December 16): 7516.

Figart, Deborah, Ellen Mutari, and Marilyn Power. 2002. *Living Wages, Equal Wages: Gender and Labor Market Policies in the United States*. London: Routledge.

Finegold, Kenneth, and Theda Skocpol. 1995. *State and Party in America's New Deal*. Madison: University of Wisconsin Press.

Fletcher, Meg. 1996. "Scaffolding Law on Edge." *Business Insurance*. June 24: 2.

Flint, Anthony. 1997. "Council OK's 'Living Wage' Requirement." *Boston Globe*. July 31. B5

Florida Times-Union. 2001. "A Bad Idea." November 16. B-6.

Focareta, Dave. 2002. "Minimal Enforcement: The Cleveland Living Wage Law's First Year." Cleveland, Ohio: Policy Matters Ohio.

Foster, Thomas. 1997. "The Inevitability of Government." *Challenge* 40 (4): 83–96.

Frank, Dana. 1994. *Purchasing Power: Consumer Organizing, Gender, and the Seattle Labor Movement, 1919–1929*. Cambridge: Cambridge University Press.

Fung, Archon, Dara O'Rourke, and Charles Sabel. 2001. *Can We Put an End to Sweatshops? A New Democracy Forum on Raising Global Labor Standards*. Boston: Beacon Press.

Fung, Archon, and Erik Olin Wright. 2003. *Deepening Democracy: Institutional Innovations in Empowered Participatory Governance*. London: Verso.

Fure-Slocum, Eric. 2000. "Cities with Class? Growth Politics, the Working-Class City, and Debt in Milwaukee during the 1940s." *Social Science History* 24 (1): 257–305.

Gallo, Alisa, and Sara Mersha. 2000. "The IMF, World Bank and Providence Wages." *The Providence Journal-Bulletin*. September 26. 4B.

Galvin, Kevin. 1995. "Baltimore Community Coalition Hones Model for Labor Movement." *The Daily Record*. July 6.: 3.

Gardner, Jennifer M., and Diane E. Herz. 1992. "Working and Poor in 1990." *Monthly Labor Review* 115 (October): 20–28.

Gilbert, Jess, and Carolyn Howe. 1991. "Beyond 'State vs. Society': Theories of the State and New Deal Agricultural Policies." *American Sociological Review* 56: 204–20.

Gillett, Richard. 2002. "The Living Wage Movement: It's about More than Just Wages." Available at http://thewitness.org/agw/gillett.041002.html. Posted to *The Witness* online magazine website April 22.

———. 1997. "Living Wage Ordinance: A Victory for the Working Poor." *Tikkun* 4 (12): 47.

Giloth, Robert P. 1993. "From Cannery Row to Gold Coast in Baltimore: Is this Development?" In *Comparative Studies in Local Economic Development: Problems in Policy Implementation*, ed. Peter B. Meyer. Westport, Conn.: Greenwood Press.

Glickman, Lawrence B. 1997. *A Living Wage: American Workers and the Making of Consumer Society.* Ithaca, N.Y.: Cornell University Press.

Goetz, Edward G. 1994. "Expanding Possibilities in Local Development Policy: An Examination of U.S. Cities." *Political Research Quarterly* 47 (1): 85–109.

Goggin, Malcolm L., James P. Lester, Ann O'M. Bowman, and Lawrence J. O'Toole Jr. 1990. *Implementation Theory and Practice: Toward a Third Generation.* Glenview, Ill.: Scott, Foresman.

Good Jobs New York, New York City's biggest retention deals database. Available at http://www.goodjobsny.org/deals.htm. Accessed March 15, 2004.

Gordon, Greg. 2002. "Beneficiaries of St. Paul Growth Fill Coleman Coffers." *Star Tribune.* November 2. 16A.

Gottlieb, Robert, and Peter Dreier. 1998. "From Liberty Hill to the Living Wage." *LA Weekly.* October 2. 30.

Grant, Don S., and Mary Nell Trautner. 2002. "Employers' Opinions on Living Wage Ordinances." Working Paper. Tucson: University of Arizona.

Greenhouse, Steven. 1999. "Activism Surges at Campuses Nationwide, and Labor is at Issue." *The New York Times.* March 29. A14.

Gross, Julian, with Greg LeRoy and Madeline Janis-Aparicio. 2002. "Community Benefits Agreements: Making Development Projects Accountable." California Public Subsidies Project Working Paper. Washington, D.C.: Good Jobs First and the Los Angeles Alliance for a New Economy.

Grow, Douglas. 1998. "The River City's Mayor Pulls Another Fast One." *Star Tribune.* November 9. 2B.

Gruenewald, Paul J., Alexander B. Millar, and Peter Roeper. 1996. "Access to Alcohol: Geography and Prevention for Local Communities." *Alcohol Health & Research World* 20 (4): 244–31.

Guild Law Center. Press Release. "Four Firms Charged with Cheating on Workers Right to a Living Wage." October 25, 2002.

Habuda, Janice L. 2003. "Group Wants to Help Enforce Living-Wage Law; Compliance a Key Issue." *Buffalo News.* March 5. B3.

Harless, James. 2001. "Local Government Environmental Advisory Boards." *Public Management* 83 (6): 20.

Hart, Vivien. 1994. *Bound by Our Constitution: Women, Workers, and the Minimum Wage.* Princeton: Princeton University Press.

Hemenway, David. 1985. *Monitoring and Compliance: The Political Economy of Inspection.* Greenwich, Conn.: JAI Press.

Hill, Jeffrey S., and Carol S. Weissert. 1995. "Implementation and the Irony of Delegation: The Politics of Low-Level Radioactive Waste Disposal." *The Journal of Politics* 57 (2): 344–69.

Hirsch, Barry T., David A. Macpherson, and J. Michael DuMond. 1997. "Workers' Compensation Recipiency in Union and Nonunion Workplaces." *Industrial and Labor Relations Review* 50 (2): 213–36.

Hirst, Paul. 1994. *Associative Democracy: New Forms of Economic and Social Governance.* Amherst: University of Massachusetts.

Howes, Candace. 2001. "The Impact of a Large Wage Increase on the IHSS Home Care Workers in San Francisco County." Unpublished article.

Human Rights Watch. 1998. *Shielded from Justice: Police Brutality and Accountability in the United States.* New York: Human Rights Watch.

Humphries, Jane. 1977. "Class Struggle and the Persistence of the Working-Class Family." *Cambridge Journal of Economics* 1 (Sept): 241–58.

Hunter, Floyd. 1953. *Community Power Structure: A Study of Decision Makers.* Chapel Hill: University of North Carolina Press.

International City/County Management Association. 2003. "Profile of Local Government Service Delivery Choices, 2002–2003." Summary of results.

———. 1997. "Reinventing Government: Implementation at the Local Level 1997." Summary of results.

Jackson, Harold. 1994a. "Wage Policy Feared, Cheered. Council OKs Measure to Raise Contract Service Workers' Pay." *The Baltimore Sun.* December 10. 1b, 2b.

———. 1994b. "Schmoke Threatens to Veto Minimum-Wage Bill." *The Baltimore Sun.* November 1. 3b.

Jaffe, Ina. 1999. "Living-Wage Law about to Be Passed in Los Angeles County." National Public Radio, Morning Edition, June 11.

Jennings, Mary Ann, Tom McDonald, and R. Ann Henderson. 1996. "Early Citizen Review: Does it Make a Difference?" *Social Work* 41 (2): 224–31.

Jessop, Bob. 1990. *State Theory: Putting Capitalist States in Their Place.* University Park, Pa.: The Pennsylvania State University Press.

Jeter, John. 1997. "Md. Shields Jobs from Welfare Law." *The Washington Post.* May 4. A1, A11.

Jordan, Robert A. 1997a. "Roache Kept 'Living Wage' Alive." *Boston Globe.* August 7. D4.

———. 1997b. "Boston Needs a 'Living Wage.'" *Boston Globe.* May 13. C4.

Kamat, Sangeeta. 2002. *Development Hegemony.* London: Oxford University Press.

Kapoor, Ilan. 2001. "Towards Participatory Environmental Management?" *Journal of Environmental Management* 63 (3): 269–80.

Kern, Jen. 2001. "Working for a Living Wage." *Multinational Monitor* 22 (1–2): 14–16.

Kessler-Harris, Alice. 1990. *A Woman's Wage: Historical Meanings and Social Consequences.* Lexington: University Press of Kentucky.

Kingsley, G. Thomas, and James O. Gibson. 1997. "Civil Society, the Public Sector, and Poor Communities." Washington, D.C.: The Urban Institute.

Klein, Bruce W., and Philip L. Rones. 1989. "A Profile of the Working Poor." *Monthly Labor Review* 112 (October): 3–11.

Knaff, Devorah. 1998. "Harvesting Justice: Stoop Laborers' Daughter Earns Union Respect from L.A.'S Powers." *Chicago Tribune.* June 7. 3.

Koeppel, David. 2001. "Minimum Wage Can Be Bumped above Minimal." *The New York Times.* July 18. G1.

Korte, Gregory. 2002. "'Living Wage' Law Approved." *The Cincinnati Enquirer.* November 28. 1C.

Korte, Gregory, and Marie McCain. 2002. "'Living Wage' Law Sought for Cincinnati." *The Cincinnati Enquirer.* November 14. 1B.

Kossy, Judith A. 1996. "Economic Restructuring and the Restructuring of Economic Development Practice: A New York Perspective, 1985–1995." *Economic Development Quarterly* 10 (4): 300–14.

Kraut, Karen, Scott Klinger, and Chuck Collins. 2000. "Choosing the High Road: Businesses that Pay a Living Wage and Prosper." Boston: Responsible Wealth.

Krumholz, Norman. 1991. "Equity and Local Economic Development." *Economic Development Quarterly* 5 (4): 291–300.

Kurtz, Howard. 1988. "Learning to Live with Less; Budget Cuts Have Limited Impact in Newark." *Washington Post*. June 1. A1.

Kuttner, Robert. 1997. "The 'Living Wage' Movement." *Washington Post*. August 20. A25.

Lafer, Gordon. 2002. *The Job Training Charade*. Ithaca, N.Y.: Cornell University Press.

Lally, Kathy. 1996. "City's Future Hinges on 'Living Wage.'" *The Baltimore Sun*. October 27. 6F.

Lazarovici, Laureen. 2003. "This is America, Where we Have Freedom..." *America@Work*. Washington, D.C.: AFL–CIO.

Lemann, Nicholas. 1994. "The Myth of Community Development." *The New York Times*. January 9. 27.

LeRoy, Greg. 1994. "No More Candy Store: States and Cities Making Job Subsidies Accountable." Washington, D.C.: Good Jobs First.

Lester, James P., and Malcolm L. Goggin. 1998. "Back to the Future: The Rediscovery of Implementation Studies." *Policy Currents* 8 (3): 1–9.

Levin, Martin A., and Barbara Ferman. 1985. *The Political Hand: Policy Implementation and Youth Employment Programs*. New York: Pergamon Press.

Levitz, Jennifer. 2000. "Demonstrators Demand Union Pledge from Paolino." *The Providence Journal-Bulletin*. September 27. 1B.

Levy, John M. 1990. *Economic Development Programs for Cities, Counties, and Towns*. 2d ed. New York: Praeger.

Lichtenstein, Nelson. 2002. *The State of the Union: A Century of American Labor*. Princeton: Princeton University Press.

Lipsky, Michael. 1980. *Street-Level Bureaucracy: Dilemmas of the Individual in Public Services*. New York: Russell Sage Foundation.

———. 1978. "Standing the Study of Implementation on its Head." In *American Politics and Public Policy*, ed. Walter D. Burnham and Martha Weinberg. Cambridge, Mass: MIT Press.

Livingston, Sandra. 2000. "A Living Wage: City Considers Linking Contracts, Aid, to Higher Minimum Pay." *Cleveland Plain Dealer*. January 16. 1H.

Los Angeles Alliance for a New Economy. 2002. *A Study in Corporate Irresponsibility: McDonald's Corporations' Operations at LAX*. Los Angeles, Calif.

Los Angeles Business Journal. 1998. "Will the Party Last?" August 3. 42.

Loveridge, Scott. 1996. "On the Continuing Popularity of Industrial Recruitment." *Economic Development Quarterly* 10 (2): 151–58.

Luce, Stephanie. 2002b. "'The Full Fruits of Our Labor': The Rebirth of the Living Wage Movement." *Labor History* 43 (4): 401–9.

———. 2002a. "Life Support: Coalition Building, and the Living Wage Movement." *New Labor Forum* 10 (spring/summer): 81–92.

———. 2001a. "Building Political Power and Community Coalitions: The Role of Central Labor Councils in the Living Wage Movement." In *Central Labor Councils and the Revival of American Unionism: Organizing for Justice in Our Communities*, ed. Immanuel Ness and Stuart Eimer. New York: M. E. Sharpe.

———. 2001b. "The Fight for Living Wages." In *From ACT UP to the WTO: Urban Protest and Community Building in the Era of Globalization*, ed. Benjamin Shepard and Ronald Hayduk. London: Verso.

———. 1999. "The Role of Secondary Associations in Local Policy Implementation: An Assessment of Living Wage Ordinances." Ph.D. diss., University of Wisconsin-Madison.

Mac Donald, Heather. 2002. "Don't Mess with Welfare Reform's Success." *City Journal* 12 (1): 34–45.

MacLennan, Carol. 1988. "The Democratic Administration of Government." In *The State and Democracy: Revitalizing America's Government*. Institute for Policy Studies. New York: Routledge.

Maestri, Father William. 2002. "Wage Hike Vote Important to Catholic Families." *Clarion Herald* 41 (2). January 16. Available at http://clarionherald.org/20020116/maestri.htm. Accessed March 21, 2004.

Markusen, Ann R. 1984. "A Marxist Theory of Metropolitan Government." In *Marxism and the Metropolis: New Perspectives in Urban Political Economy*, ed. William K. Tabb and Larry Sawers. New York: Oxford University Press.

Matland, Richard E. 1995. "Synthesizing the Implementation Literature: The Ambiguity-Conflict Model of Policy Implementation." *Journal of Public Administration Research and Theory* 5 (2) (1995): 145–74.

Matthews, Robert Guy. 1997. "School Bus Contactors Overcharged City by Some $133,000, Audit Says." *The Baltimore Sun*. August 2. 2B.

———. 1996. "Bus Aides Miss Out on July Pay Raise." *The Baltimore Sun*. December 12. 1C, 4C.

Maynard-Moody, Steven, Michael Musheno, and Dennis Palumbo. 1990. "Street-Wise Social Policy: Resolving the Dilemma of Street Level Influence and Successful Implementation." *The Western Political Quarterly* 43 (4): 833–48.

Mazmanian, Daniel A., and Paul A. Sabatier. 1983. *Implementation and Public Policy*. Glenview, Ill.: Scott, Foresman.

McGreevey, Patrick. 1998. "Unions Gaining Power in L.A." *Daily News of Los Angeles*. September 7. N1.

McKuen, Pamela Dittmer. 2002. "The Cost of Safety; High-Rise Facade Work is Expensive and Inconvenient, but Ordinance May Offer Relief." *Chicago Tribune*. October 6. 1.

McLanahan, Sara S. 1980. "Organizational Issues in U.S. Health Policy Implementation: Participation, Discretion, and Accountability." *Journal of Applied Behavioral Science* 16 (3): 354–69.

Merton, Robert K. 1957. *Social Theory and Social Structure*. Glencoe, Ill.: Free Press.

Michels, Robert. 1959. *Political Parties: A Sociological Study of the Oligarchical Tendencies of Modern Democracy*. Translated by Eden & Cedar Paul. New York: Dover.

Mishel, Lawrence, Jared Bernstein, and John Schmitt. 2001. *The State of Working America 2000/2001*. Washington, D.C.: Economic Policy Institute.

Moses, Eric. 1997. "Regulations Governing the City's 4-month-old Living Wage Ordinance Went into Effect Today." City News Service. September 10.

Nakamura, Robert T., and Frank Smallwood. 1980. *The Politics of Policy Implementation*. New York: St. Martin's Press.

National Priorities Project. 1998. "Working Harder, Earning Less." Report. Northampton, Mass.

Neumark, David. 2001. "Living Wages: Protection for or Protection from Low-Wage Workers?" National Bureau of Economic Research, Working Paper 8393.

Newton, Jim. 1998. "Agency Says 'Living Wage' Law Covers Airport Guards, Janitors." *Los Angeles Times*. June 11. 3.

———. 1997. "Mayor Trying to Keep LAX Exempt from New Pay Law." *Los Angeles Times*. October 2. A1.

Niedt, Christopher, Greg Ruiters, Dana Wise, and Erica Schoenberger. 1999. "The Effects of the Living Wage in Baltimore." Washington, D.C.: Economic Policy Institute Working Paper No. 119.

Nissen, Bruce. 1995. *Fighting for Jobs: Case Studies of Labor-Community Coalitions Confronting Plant Closings.* Albany: State University of New York Press.

Nordlund, Willis J. 1997. *The Quest for a Living Wage.* Westport, Conn.: Greenwood Press.

Norman, Jack. 1994. "Activists Work on Economic Plan with Jobs in Mind." *The Milwaukee Journal.* September 23. B1, B6.

Oldham, Jennifer. 2002. "McDonald's OKs Higher Pay at LAX." *Los Angeles Times.* July 24. 4.

O'Neill, June, and M. Anne Hill. 2003. *Gaining Ground, Moving Up: The Change in the Economic Status of Single Mothers under Welfare Reform.* Center for Civic Innovation, Manhattan Institute. Civic Report No. 35.

O'Rourke, Dara. 2003. "Outsourcing Regulation: Analyzing Non-Governmental Systems of Labor Standards and Monitoring." *Policy Studies Journal.* Forthcoming.

———. 2002. "Motivating a Conflicted Environmental State: Community Driven Regulation in Vietnam." In *The Environmental State under Pressure, Social Problems and Public Policies Series,* ed. A. P. J. Mol and F. H. Buttel. Amsterdam: Elsevier.

Orr, David W. 1979. "U.S. Energy Policy and the Political Economy of Participation." *The Journal of Politics* 41 (4): 1027–56.

Osterman, Paul. 2000. "Report on the Impact of the Valley Interfaith Living Wage Campaign." Cambridge, Mass.: MIT Sloan School of Management.

Pagano, Michael A., and David R. Shock. 2000. "City Fiscal Conditions in 2000." Washington, D.C.: National League of Cities.

Palumbo, Dennis J., and Donald J. Calista. 1990. "Opening up the Black Box: Implementation and the Policy Process." In *Implementation and the Policy Process: Opening Up the Black Box,* ed. Dennis J. Palumbo and Donald J. Calista. Westport, Conn: Greenwood Press.

Parker, Eric. 1997. "Youth Apprenticeship in a Laboratory of Democracy." *Industrial Relations* 36 (3): 302–23.

Parkins, John. 2002. "Forest Management and Advisory Groups in Alberta: An Empirical Critique of an Emergent Public Sphere." *Canadian Journal of Sociology* 27 (2): 163–85.

Parsons, Christi, and Ray Long. 1998. "Early-Retirement Plans Fizzle." *Chicago Tribune.* December 2. 1.

Payne, Cymie. 1998. "Local Regulation of Natural Resources: Efficiency, Effectiveness, and Fairness of Wetlands Permitting in Massachusetts." *Environmental Law* 28 (3): 519.

Perry, Doug. No date. "San Francisco Supervisors Approve Labor Standards Enforcement Ordinance." *Organized Labor.* Available at http://www.sfbctc.org/lstandards.htm. Accessed April 5, 2003.

Peschek, Joe. 1997. "A Living Wage? Campaigns Attach Strings To Public Contracts." *Dollars and Sense* 210 (March/April): 28–29.

Peters, Alan H., and Peter S. Fisher. 2002a. "The Effectiveness of State Enterprise Zones." *Employment Research* (W. E. Upjohn Institute) 9 (4): 1–3.

———. 2002b. "State Enterprise Zones: Have They Worked?" Kalamazoo, Mich.: W.E. Upjohn Institute.

Peterson, Paul E. 1981. *City Limits.* Chicago: University of Chicago Press.

Pierre, Robert E. 1998. "It's Official; School Is Work." *Washington Post.* June 8. C8.

Pierson, Paul. 1994. *Dismantling the Welfare State.* Cambridge: Cambridge University Press.

Pittsburgh Post-Gazette. 2001. "City News." June 3. B-6.

Piven, Frances Fox, and Richard Cloward. 1979. *Poor People's Movements: Why They Succeed, How They Fail.* New York: Vintage Books.

Pollin, Robert, Mark Brenner et al. 2000. "Economic Analysis of Santa Monica Living Wage Proposal." 2000, Political Economy Research Institute, Research Report Number 2.

Pollin, Robert, Mark Brenner, and Stephanie Luce. 2002. "Intended vs. Unintended Consequences: Evaluating the New Orleans Living Wage Proposal." *Journal of Economic Issues* 36 (4): 843–76.

Pollin, Robert, and Stephanie Luce. 1998. *The Living Wage: Building a Fair Economy.* New York: The New Press.

Pressman, Jeffrey L., and Aaron Wildavsky. 1973. *Implementation: A Look At The Failed Attempt of The Federal Economic Development Administration to Create Jobs in the City of Oakland, California.* Berkeley: The University of California Press.

The Providence Journal-Bulletin. 2001. "Deadly to the Economy." April 24. 4B.

Putnam, Robert D., with Robert Leonardi and Raffaella Y. Nanetti. 1993. *Making Democracy Work: Civic Traditions in Modern Italy.* Princeton: Princeton University Press.

Quadagno, Jill. 1992. "Social Movements and State Transformation: Labor Unions and Racial Conflict in The War On Poverty." *American Sociological Review* 57: 616–34.

Radin, Beryl A. 1977. *Implementation, Change, and the Federal Bureaucracy.* New York: Teachers College Press. Columbia University.

Reese, Laura A. 1993. "Categories of Local Economic Development Techniques: An Empirical Analysis." *Policy Studies Journal* 21: 492–506.

Rehfuss, John A. 1989. *Contracting Out in Government.* San Francisco: Jossey-Bass.

Reich, Michael, Peter Hall, and Ken Jacobs. 2003. "Living Wages and Economic Performance: The San Francisco Airport Model." Unpublished manuscript. University of California, Berkeley: Institute of Industrial Relations.

Reich, Robert. 1997. *Locked in the Cabinet.* New York: Knopf.

Richards, Cindy. 1998. "Beastly Price of City's Beauty." *Chicago Tribune.* October 29. 1.

Rimmerman, Craig. 1985. "Citizen Participation and Policy Implementation in the Columbus, Ohio CDBG Program." *Public Administration Quarterly* 9 (3): 328–341.

Rohr, J. 1988. "Bureaucratic Morality in the United States." *International Political Science Review* 9 (3): 167–179.

Rohrlich, Ted. 1998a. "Special Report: Study of 'Living Wage' Ordinance Finds That Only 750 of about 5,000 Covered Workers Have Gotten Raises in 15 Months. It Offers a Lesson in How Bureaucratic Loops Can Leave a Law in Knots." *Los Angeles Times.* September 13. B1.

Roper Center at University of Connecticut. 1999. "Public Opinion Online." November 11.

——. 1995. "Public Opinion Online." February 5.

Sahu, Saura James. 2001. "Living Up to the Living Wage: A Primer on the Legal Issues Surrounding the Enactment and Enforcement of Living Wage Laws." Detroit, Mich.: Guild Law Center.

Samuels, Bruce, and Stanton A. Glantz. 1991. "The Politics of Local Tobacco Control." *The Journal of the American Medical Association* 266 (15): 2110–17.

Sander, Richard, and Sean Lokey. 1998. "The Los Angeles Living Wage in Operation: A Preliminary Evaluation." Report Presented to Los Angeles City Council, August 20.

Santa Monica Living Wage Commission of Inquiry. 2003. "Democracy Distorted: A Report on Electoral Deception and Manipulation by Opponents of the Santa Monica Living Wage." Executive Summary.

Schumaker, Paul D. 1975. "Policy Responsiveness to Protest-Group Demands." *The Journal of Politics* 37 (2): 488–521.

Sclar, Elliott D. 2001. *You Don't Always Get What You Pay for: The Economics of Privatization.* Ithaca, N.Y.: Cornell University Press.

——. 1997. *The Privatization of Public Service: Lessons From Case Studies.* Washington, D.C.: Economic Policy Institute.

Seltzer, Andrew. 1995a. "Causes and Consequences of American Minimum Wage Legislation, 1911–1947." *The Journal of Economic History* 55 (2): 376–78.

——. 1995b. "The Political Economy of the Fair Labor Standards Act of 1938." *Journal of Political Economy* 103 (6): 1302–44.

Selznick, Philip. 1957. *Leadership in Administration: A Sociological Interpretation.* Evanston, Ill.: Row, Peterson Press.

Senate Post Audit and Oversight Bureau, State of Massachusetts. 2002. "Return on Investment?" Policy Brief. December.

Shapiro, Bruce. 1997. "When Justice Kills: After Years of Decline Police Brutality Is on the Rise, Sparking a Reform Movement." *The Nation* 264 (22): 21–24.

Shields, Gerald. 1999. "Board Votes to Study Privatizing City Services; Union Leader Describes Idea as Death Threat." *The Baltimore Sun.* January 7. 3B.

Shuster, Beth. 1999. "Airline Ends Wage Impasse." *Los Angeles Times.* January 12. NB-3.

——. 1998a. "Tighter Rules Proposed For Living Wage Law." *Los Angeles Times.* August 21. B1.

——. 1998b. "Few Found Obeying 'Living Wage' Law." *Los Angeles Times.* May 20. B1.

Siegel, Eric. 1997. "City Board Orders Bus Company to Give Back Pay to 17 Workers; Employees Lacked Raises Under 'Living Wage' Law." *The Baltimore Sun.* June 26. 2B.

——. 1994. "Commission Urges New Wage Rates." *The Baltimore Sun.* December 14. 4B.

Simmons, James. 2001. "Whither Local Government Reform? The Case of Wisconsin." *National Civic Review* 90 (1): 45.

Sklar, Holy, Laryssa Mykyta, and Susan Wefald. 2001. *Raise the Floor: Wages and Policies that Work for All of Us.* New York: Ms. Foundation for Women.

Skocpol, Theda, and Edward Amenta. 1986. "States and Social Policies." *Annual Review of Sociology* 12: 131–57.

Smith, Gregory. 2002. "Living Wage Proposal Meets Council Opposition." *The Providence Journal-Bulletin.* April 15. B1.

Solo, Pam. 1997. "Beyond Theory: Civil Society in Action." *Brookings Review* 15 (4): 8.

South, Robert B. 1986. "Environmental Legislation and the Locational Process." *Geographical Review* 76 (1): 20–34.

Sunoo, Brenda Paik. 1998. "Reinventing Government." *Workforce* 77 (2): 60–63.

Talanker, Alyssa, and Kate Davis. 2002. "Economic Development in Washington, D.C." Washington, D.C.: Good Jobs First.

Taricani, Jim. 2001. "Bad to Worse." *The Providence Phoenix.* November 23–29. Available at http://www.providencephoenix.com/archive/features/01/11/22/TARICANI.html. Accessed March 21, 2004.

Thomas, Kenneth. 2000. *Competing for Capital: Europe and North America in a Global Era.* Washington, D.C.: Georgetown University Press.

Tilly, Chris. 2003. "Living Wage Laws in the United States: The Dynamics of a Growing Movement." Department of Regional Economic and Social Development, University of Massachusetts-Lowell.

Toledo Area Chamber of Commerce. 2000. "Toledo City Council Passes Living Wage Ordinance." *The Insider.* July. 1.

Tramer, Harriet. 2002. "City Ready to Enforce its Living Wage Law." *Crain's Cleveland Business.* September 23. 26.

Traynor, Michael P., Michael E. Begay, and Stanton A. Glantz. 1993. "New Tobacco Industry Strategy to Prevent Local Tobacco Control." *The Journal of the American Medical Association* 270 (4): 479–88.

Troy, Tom. 2002. "'Living-wage' Questions Draw Blank at City Hall." *Toledo Blade.* April 4.

Turchinetz, Mimi. 2002. "Testimony of Mimi Turchinetz to Providence City Council." Available at http://www.rijwj.org/mimi.pdf. Accessed March 21, 2004.

U.S. Department of Labor, Fact Sheet #14: Coverage under the Fair Labor Standards Act.

——. Minimum Wage. Available at http://www.dol.gov/dol/topic/wages/minimumwage.htm. Accessed November 30, 2003.

——. North Aurora IL Area Office. 2001. "Aurora OSHA Construction News." 2 (1): 4.

U.S. Environmental Protection Agency. 2000. *Annual Report on Enforcement and Compliance Assurance Accomplishments in 1999.* EPA 300-R-00–005. July 2000.

Van Meter, Donald S., and Carl E. Van Horn. 1975. "The Policy Implementation Process: A Conceptual Framework." *Administration and Society* 6: 445–88.

Van Slambrouck, Paul. 1999. "San Francisco's Fight over Highest 'Living Wage': Cities around the US Consider New Ways to Raise Workers' Pay at Businesses with Local Contracts." *Christian Science Monitor* April 19. 2.

Velasco, Diane. 2003. "Business Wants No Santa Fe Wage Law." *Albuquerque Journal.* April 21. 1.

Walker, Thaai. 1998. "Oakland OKs New 146-Room Downtown Hotel; Union Protests Decision." *The San Francisco Chronicle.* November 11. A17.http://www.frbsf.org/publications/index.html

Walters, Jonathan. 1998. "Did Somebody Say Downsizing?" *Governing Magazine.* February. 17.

Waltman, Jerold. 2000. *The Politics of the Minimum Wage.* Urbana: University of Illinois Press.

Wasylenko, Michael. 1997. "Taxation and Economic Development: The State of the Economic Literature." *New England Economic Review.* March-April. 36–52.

Weil, David. 1991. "Enforcing OSHA: The Role of Labor Unions." *Industrial Relations.* 30 (1): 20–36.

Weinbaum, Eve S. 2004. *To Move a Mountain: Fighting the Global Economy in Appalachia.* New York: The New Press.

——. 1997. "Successful Failures: Local Democracy in a Global Economy." Ph.D. diss., Yale University.

Western, Bruce. 1997. *Between Class and Market: Postwar Unionization in the Capitalist Democracies.* Princeton: Princeton University Press.

Whyte, Maria. Presentation, Cleveland, Ohio. Jobs with Justice Conference. September 8, 2001.

Wicks-Lim, Jeannette. 2002. "How Big Are Ripple Effects from Minimum Wage and Living Wage Increases?" Paper presented at the Meetings of the Allied Social Science Associations, Atlanta, Georgia. January 5, 2002.

Wider Opportunities for Women. Family self-sufficiency reports available at http://www.sixstrategies.org/. Accessed March 21, 2004.

Williams, Bob. 1997. "UFCW to Protest Election, Continue Effort at Bladen Slaughterhouse. Union Rejected at Hog Facility." *Raleigh News and Observer.* August 23. A3.

Williams, Fred O. 2000. "City's 'Living Wage' Law Languishes Year after Passage." *The Buffalo News*. July 21. 6B.

Wolfson, Mark, Alexander C. Wagenaar, and Gary W. Hornseth. 1995. "Law Officers' Views on Enforcement of the Minimum Drinking Age: A Four-state Study." *Public Health Reports* 110 (4): 428–28.

Wood, B. Dan. 1990. "Does Politics Make A Difference At The EEOC?" *American Journal of Political Science* 34 (2): 503–30.

Wright, Erik Olin. 1997. *Class Counts: Comparative Studies in Class Analysis*. Cambridge, U.K.: Cambridge University Press.

Yates, Michael D. 1999. *Why Unions Matter*. New York: Monthly Review Press.

Zachary, G. Pascal. 1996. "Beyond the Minimum Wage." *In These Times*. August 5. 27–29.

Zimmerman, Joseph. 1972. *The Federated City*. New York: St. Martin's Press.

Zubrensky, Ruth. 1995. Letter to Bill Dempsey, Sustainable Milwaukee. September 14, Milwaukee, Wis.

INDEX

STEPHANIE LUCE is an assistant professor at the Labor Center, University of Massachusetts-Amherst. She received her Ph.D. in sociology from the University of Wisconsin-Madison. She has worked as an economist at the U.S. Department of Labor and a research assistant at the Center on Wisconsin Strategy and the Political Economy Research Institute. She is coauthor, with Robert Pollin, of *The Living Wage: Building a Fair Economy* and has written numerous articles on the political and economic impacts of living wage campaigns and ordinances.